THE CAGE

DANCING FOR JEROME ROBBINS AND GEORGE BALANCHINE

1949 –1954

by Barbara Bocher with Adam Darius

Bravos for The Cage

"All fairy tales have a dark side…a riveting story that will take you from the heights of the New York City Ballet to the depths of despair at the fate of such a gifted, vulnerable child. For those who have seen the recent film *Black Swan*, this story proves that sometimes the truth is stranger and a lot more disturbing than fiction"

- Coryne Hall, author of *Imperial Dancer, Mathilde Kschessinska and the Romanovs*

"Superb…Ms. Bocher's years of dancing for Balanchine and Robbins were no fairy tale, unless it be *Beauty and the Beast… The Cage* may well initiate regulations controlling those crimes… has all the reader could want; suspense and adventure, victory and victimization, and a host of challenging concepts which Barbara Bocher and Adam Darius fearlessly throw like gauntlets."

- Hal de Becker, critic for *Dance Magazine*, New York and contributor to *Dance Europe*, London

"Her extraordinary story will transfix you with its accounts of dancing for the world's most famous choreographers, designers, composers and musicians…but *The Cage* is no cosy account of a ballerina's life in front of the footlights. It is unique among ballet books and should be read by every balletomane who has ever sat and applauded the magic on stage. For the truth can be quite different."

- Kay Hunter, co-author of Sir Anton Dolin's *Last Words* and John Gilpin's *A Dance with Life*

Published by Barbara Bocher with Adam Darius, 2012

ISBN-13: 978-1478246589
ISBN-10: 1478246588
LCCN: 2012913469

Front cover: Barbara Bocher in *Symphonie Concertante* and *Swan Lake* (inset)
Back cover: Backstage at City Center in New York, before dancing the leading role
in the ballet *Jinx*, 1951
Cover photos by Walter E. Owen

Front cover design by Kazimir Kolesnik
Book design by Thomas Freundlich

THE CAGE

To my loving parents, Leonard and Virginia Bocher, who, at considerable personal sacrifice, made it possible for me to live my dream – and to my sons, Bob and David, for their unswerving loyalty.

Contents

The authors and publisher wish to thank all relevant parties for the permission to reproduce the photographs in this book. If, however, there are omitted acknowledgments, they will be rectified in any future edition.

ACKNOWLEDGMENTS

For her invaluable legal counsel, my gratitude to Professor Ray Madoff of Boston College Law School. Author of Immortality and the Law, Professor Madoff 's advice has been my guideline throughout this book.

I thank, as well, Shabtay Sammy Henig, New York City attorney-at-law, for his expert reflections.

I have also adhered to the First Amendment of the U.S. Constitution in the statute proposed on June 8th, 1789 by President James Madison.

'The people shall not be deprived or abridged of their right to speak, to write, or to publish their sentiments; and the freedom of the press, as one of the great bulwarks of liberty, shall be inviolable."

To move to the year 2011, without Adam Darius's indefatigable efforts and ceaseless encouragement, never would I have begun these memoirs, let alone gone through the emotional upheaval of completing them. His unswerving belief that my life in the New York City Ballet was a narrative that had to be told, lest those years, now mid-20th century cultural history, evaporate without a trace.

Adam has been a constant cascade of encouragement. My dearest friend, I express my deep appreciation, love, and heartfelt thanks to him. Taking the time from his own hectic schedule as a still globe-spanning dancer and mime artist, his additional long experience as an author has helped me to express my own innermost thoughts with far more emotional accuracy than I could ever have managed on my own.

Further thanks to the internationally acclaimed dancer, actor and mime artist, Kazimir Kolesnik, for his immeasurable help with the many details involved in the completion of this autobiography. His valued opinions, born of his wide experience in circus, dance and physical theatre, are hugely appreciated, as is his striking cover design.

To the applauded Finnish dancer, choreographer and Himalayan trekker, Thomas Freundlich, a man of multiple abilities, my indebtedness for helping to prepare this book for publication.

Still with the Nordic connection, a nod of sincere thanks to deep sea diver Roope Waris for regularly sending Adam's each completed chapter to me as an attachment.

And to Hal de Becker, foremost dance critic of Las Vegas, my many thanks for his ironing out the stray infelicities of the manuscript.

To Leena Vuorjoki, long a mainstay of the Belgian Embassy in Helsinki, a révérence for overseeing the exactitude of French, Italian and German spelling.

To move on to Italy, I also acknowledge Andrea Vitalini, Director General at the historic Teatro della Scala in Milan for his most considerate assistance with archival research.

And last, but not at all least, I thank two of my dearest friends, Anne Stratford and Marjorie Boyle, both of whom have listened with activated interest as each chapter of *The Cage* further unfolded.

Foreword
by Adam Darius

Barbara Bocher, the youngest dancer in the New York City Ballet, was only 14 years old in 1950 when, as stated by British ballet historian Arnold Haskell, she was the youngest dancer ever to appear as a soloist at the Royal Opera House, Covent Garden.

Then, within four years, she vanished. Like a shooting star, she hurtled across the evening heavens, only to disappear seconds later. Why?

Blonde and delicately translucent as a piece of porcelain china, Barbara's dancing was the finest I ever saw in one of such tender years, so polished artistically that, in subsequent decades throughout six continents, I have yet to see her equal. I am referring to the harmony of her movement, her sculptural line and expressiveness and, of course, at the foundation, a virtuoso ballet technique that always served her faithfully, never the reverse. She was, even when I first saw her in 1949, possessor of an arched straight back in high arabesque, until then seen only in Soviet stars such as Marina Semyonova and Maya Plissetskaya.

And yet this baby ballerina stopped dancing at the improbable age of only 18, never in this lifetime to ever grace another stage. There she was, scarcely into her teens and already dancing under the distinguished batons of Igor Stravinsky, Leonard Bernstein, Sir Benjamin Britten and Aaron Copland, alongside the clarinet of Benny Goodman, a choreographic instrument of the two greatest choreographers of the time, George Balanchine and Sir Frederic Ashton, her face painted personally by Sir Cecil Beaton, having tea with the last Viceroy of India, Lord Mountbatten, attending the garden party of playwright and Ambassador Clare Boothe Luce, and being counseled by the Very Reverend James A. Pike, Dean of the Cathedral of St. John the Divine.

In the course of her meteoric career, Barbara was partnered by the ranking premier danseur André Eglevsky, and danced on the stages of the Paris Opera House, Milan's La Scala Opera, and many others.

Then the fairy tale ground to a halt. In this spellbinding and revelatory memoir, Barbara, now 77 and a great-grandmother three times over, excavates her early life, until today kept so secret that not even her four children knew anything of her illustrious background.

What happened? Why was the sleeping beauty left to slumber in the tangled foliage, never to be awakened? What were the contributing factors that ended the career of this remarkable young dancer? Such are the inevitable questions that every reader is justified in asking.

As for myself, beyond my appreciation of Barbara's dancing, there is, above all, my ongoing respect for her sterling character, qualities that shine through in every single page of this book. She was a devoted daughter to her beloved parents, a solid family life that began in the Oklahoma of the mid-1930s, replete with bucking bronco cowboys and beaded and feathered Indians, now called Native Americans.

Moving to New York with her mother to further her training, she was awarded a full scholarship at the School of American Ballet, a favorite of her great pedagogues, all soloists of either the Maryinsky in St. Petersburg, Diaghilev Ballets Russes or the Anna Pavlova Ballet.

It has been said that a virtue in excess becomes a fault. So it was with Barbara, too pure and too young to cope with the runaway forces of bullying and cruelty in which she had been thrust. For here was a girl, barely into her teens, yet contending with persecution that nowadays would be categorized as child abuse. Her chief tormentor, if truth be finally told, was Broadway's celebrated choreographer, the man who was to choreograph *West Side Story* and *Fiddler on the Roof*, Jerome Robbins. As for George Balanchine, the world's ranking choreographer, despite her pleas for help, and evident distress, he repeatedly turned a deaf ear towards her ongoing plight.

Now, in *The Cage*, Barbara Bocher tells her long suppressed story. For ballet lovers far and wide, these startling memoirs are fanned by the very breath of history. Insofar as the author is concerned, 60 years after the events she came to realize that the insulated ballet world breeds a chilling atmosphere of idol worship.

Barbara Bocher, to her credit, has found the strength to confront the hovering ghosts of her trailing past. For the sake of unquenchable truth, this courageous autobiography had to be written, a staggering morality tale for today's equally obsessive dancing youth.

In closing this Foreword, as I gaze out of the window into the autumnal Finnish skies, I venture to say that readers of this book may well wish to join me in my fervent and heartfelt hope:

"Fare thee well, dear Barbara! May the aurora borealis cast its lovely glow upon you!"

CHAPTER ONE

DANCING FOR JEROME ROBBINS

The perpetual California summer of 2011 diffuses its intense oceanic light as I stroll along the beach with its toppling remnants of a child's sand castle. Looking out into the water, beyond the foam, I am fascinated by a group of whales moving towards the cooler waters of Alaska. Listening, I imagine I detect a faint melody from deep beneath the sea, the mysterious song of the whales.

After they are gone, I look across at the gleaming rocks of the Pacific, lashed by the oncoming waves. As swirling patterns, the memories of my dancing days keep returning, one recollection in particular, as an audacious gatecrasher who adamantly refuses to leave.

At first, I try to resist the oppressive image, but it has a mind of its own and persists. Then my private time capsule begins to dissolve, though until now hermetically sealed from the awareness of all my family members, both past and present.

Reversing the almanac to 1951, I had joined the New York City Ballet two years before, in November, 1949, at the age of 14, then the youngest dancer in the company. Never could I have foreseen that I would be persecuted to such a degree that I would choose to retire, after international success, at an age when most people are just beginning to audition.

The tormentor? It was choreographer Jerome Robbins before he became the king of Broadway musicals, though he was already crown prince of the Great White Way, and second only to our beloved George Balanchine in choreographic importance in America.

Throughout these memoirs, I will refer to the master, our Artistic Director, George Balanchine, as Mr B. This is the loving abbreviation used by all members of the company.

The pain-filled recollection I refer to began in a studio at the School of American Ballet on 59th and Madison Avenue in New York City. There could have been no form of instruction that could have prepared me to dance for the likes of a man whose tangled psyche could not have been unknotted even if Freud had resurrected from the grave to help him.

Robbins was to choreograph a new ballet for The New York City Ballet called *The Cage*. It would have music by Igor Stravinsky, arguably the greatest Russian ballet composer since Tchaikovsky. The costumes were to be designed by Ruth Sobotka, a charming Austrian dancer in the company who would, in the future, marry then divorce top film director Stanley Kubrick.

The Cage was scheduled to be premiered during our spring season in June 1951 in our home theatre, The City Center of Music and Drama on 55th Street in New York. Still only 15 years old, I was thrilled to be among the eight dancers chosen to dance in the corps de ballet of this new work. It was always considered a feather in your cap if you were part of the original cast. Little did I realize what was coming! The dancers were all curious and excited about participating in a world premiere, even though the title was a bit ominous.

The costumes, I discovered to my dismay, and not until opening night, under the glaring lights on stage made us look completely naked! We were on display seemingly au naturel. Made of flesh-colored, thin net, the costumes fit like a second skin with coiled snakes appliquéd in a few strategic places. Nevertheless, modest, innocent adolescent that I was, I thought it exposing in the extreme.

The lighting was by the wonderfully creative and award-winning director Jean Rosenthal. There was more than one heated argument about the questionable piercing lights in the opening section. Jean Rosenthal vehemently disapproved, considering such lighting to be dizzying and headache-inducing for the audience. But it was Robbins' ballet, so he got his way, punishing the audience at the very beginning of the work.

Robbins wanted us to fix our hair to "look like wild animals", spiking the ends with gel. Our make up was designed to be threatening, again like savage beasts. It was to later strike me that the most dangerous animal of all was the human variety. Animals kill for survival, for food, not to inflict torture, not to gang rape, not to plant terrorist bombs and not to abuse defenseless youngsters.

I will now recall a rehearsal that, finally, I have been able to exhume from the graveyard of my most shattering memories. The rehearsal shook me to the core and severely tested my ability to maintain my emotional equilibrium. Nowadays what I endured would be called victimization at the workplace, or, far worse, child abuse. Then it had no such label and was conveniently swept under the carpet, for the abuser, Jerome Robbins, invariably had the Midas touch. No one was to question a man who, despite his steamrolling methods, invariably turned even theatrical brass to gold.

As young as I was, I already was artistically experienced, having danced in most of the Balanchine ballets in the repertoire and as well, at the Royal Opera House in London's Covent Garden. I was beginning to perform some demi-soloist parts and was so happy to be among the superb dancers in the company. My enthusiasm to be among them had not abated one iota since George Balanchine personally invited me to join the company.

I had every confidence that under his protective wings, I would be safe, nurtured, and would, one day, reach my full potential. That was my dream and there was not a waking hour that I didn't utilize to make that vision come to fruition.

My parents had taught me to believe that I could climb every rung of ambition's ladder if I worked ceaselessly, cultivated whatever inborn talent I had at birth, and trained without respite from ballet's Hall of Fame teachers.

The fearless confidence of youth was mine. My goal was not for stardom, fame or fortune, but to be able to dance as a true ballerina on the major stages of the world. I was, I thought, well on my way, having already danced in New York, Chicago, London and Paris at the Théâtre des Champs-Élysées where Nijinsky's *Sacre du Printemps* had had its scandalous premiere almost forty years earlier.

A true ballerina, which I yearned to be, awake or asleep, embodied the spiritual heritage of her forebears, the tradition of such 19th-century dancers as the two Carlottas – Grisi, the first Giselle, and Brianza, the first Aurora. With my training from the finest dancers of the Maryinsky, the soul transfusion was direct. I was touched by and felt its gossamer magic.

When Mr. B chose me to dance in the premiere of his new ballet, *Capriccio Brilliante*, which was to have its first performance just a few days before *The Cage*, I was elated.

But the honeymoon of anticipation was abruptly curtailed when the first rehearsal of *The Cage* arrived. Robbins, once settled and seated, told us the narrative of the new work and to my sheltered eyes and ears, it was a very far cry from any ballet I had ever seen or even read about. But I was there to interpret, not to judge. It was, I must point out, not at all the macabre scenario which could be faulted, for the 19th century writer, Edgar Allen Poe, was far more frightening, to cite just one example. What was contentious was Robbins' emotionally violent method of conducting rehearsals.

"The Amazon Queen," he explained, "Yvonne Mounsey, after copulating with the first Intruder, Michael Maule, clamps his head between her thighs and then, with a twist of her legs, snaps his neck. We, the crazed Amazons, then drag his corpse off stage in a veritable feeding frenzy, pecking at his skin before devouring his entrails. Then, A Novice, danced by Nora Kaye, was graphically pulled from between the legs of the Amazon Queen who had just given birth to her. As the second Intruder, Nicholas Magallanes was subjected to some further sexual debasement.

Nicholas Kopeikine, our treasured pianist, who sometimes transposed an orchestral score straight to the piano without missing a note, he, too, was not exempt from Robbins' rage.

"I said start at the top! Can't you hear? Are you deaf or something? Too fast! I said slow down! God damn it! God damn it! Can't you keep a tempo?"

Nicolas, or Kolya as he was affectionately called, was a man of impeccably good manners, so he did not answer Robbins, but became understandably flustered. Collecting himself, he again began, the complex Igor Stravinsky rhythms permeating the strained silence of the rehearsal studio. Mr. B never had Mr. Stravinsky attend a *Cage* rehearsal, fearing, with justification, that the maestro would be unable to tolerate such emotionally aberrant behavior.

Robbins again reminded us that we were to look as monstrous and grotesque as possible. He began to demonstrate what he wanted us to do, telling us that he had experienced a "vision" while under an anesthetic in the hospital for his recent emergency appendectomy. Watching his concepts unfold, I believe that what he experienced was not at all a vision, but a nightmare.

In those days when the word "abortion" couldn't even be mentioned in a movie, what we were doing on stage was, in my estimation, pornography on pointe. Back then, I didn't even know what the word pornography meant, but the gaps in my sexual knowledge were quickly being filled in.

During that rehearsal we could not look ugly or ferocious enough to please Robbins. I think, looking back, that what he wanted was to project his own psychiatric swampland, but no matter how we tried to desperately follow his orders, he could not succeed in expunging the demons in his own conflicted brain. All he could do was rant and rave at his own inability to cathart himself. In the meanwhile, he demanded that we rehearse on pointe with every new version, all of which he would junk for the next tantrum-filled concept.

A bona fide director, such as Elia Kazan, would have been capable of extracting the result he had in mind by leading the dancers through a labyrinth of recalled emotions, observation and fantasy, any one of them or the combination, but Robbins was impotent in that area. He was no director, though he often usurped such a credit. Rather, he was a hysteric, indulging in the most ruthless behavior, upon which he placed no restraints whatsoever. The boiling water of his acute frustration scalded us all, none more so than I, because youngest dancer that I was, who better to bully in his public playground?

The movements he required us to do were clearly destructive to our feet, with repeated stabbing of our toes into the floor, harder and harder, it was never forceful enough. If his aim was to cripple us, in that area he was en route to arrival, for he was turning our feet into pounding hammers. With each successive attempt to do his frenzied bidding, flashes of pain began to shoot up through my feet into my very teeth. I hoped I would faint to escape the by now intolerable pain.

All of us, by now panic-ridden, tried our utmost to bring to life his horror show concepts, but his blatant inability as a dramatic coach only force fed his frustrations. He kept yelling, "People, you are too pretty!" then repeating it until the decibel level escalated into a crescendo of ear-splitting rage.

Most dancers in the company possessed the ability to learn very quickly, to memorize steps as well as the musical score with accuracy after being shown only once. That was thanks to our working for Mr B. It annoyed Robbins no end that we were so quick to learn. He would run out of ideas and be void of material half way through the generous and expensive rehearsal time allotted him. When he would suffer his "writer's block", that was the moment when he would give vent to his violent bursts of ill temper. He would become, not the Robbins who had entered the rehearsal room smiling and friendly, but a tyrant of fearsome proportions.

Out-of-sequence memories jostle each other for precedence in the hall of shame corridors. To temporarily fast-forward to a later rehearsal of Robbins' ballet *Fanfare*, a nasty incident took place on a Sunday afternoon between the matinee and an evening performance at the New York City Center. The British composer Benjamin Britten was coming the following week to conduct his score for the ballet. Robbins was getting more and more nervous about his imminent arrival. As for the dancers, tired after a matinee of four ballets, most of us needed to rest and have a light snack to eat before the evening performance. Not this day!

Robbins scheduled a full cast rehearsal, on stage, and for over an hour he drilled us repeatedly, and we were to remain in our pointe shoes. His demands were insatiable. Shouting at all of us, he made especially cutting remarks to dear Yvonne Mounsey, the Amazon Queen in *The Cage*, who in *Fanfare* was dancing the soloist part of the Harp so beautifully. Yvonne, one of the principal dancers of the New York City Ballet, had previously worked with Léonide Massine's Ballet Russe de Monte Carlo and Col. de Basil's Original Ballet Russe.

Despite her maturity and experience, Robbins couldn't stop verbally assaulting her. She became so disoriented that she, in consequence, went blank and couldn't remember her variation. That lapse made Robbins go ballistic!

He grabbed the New York Times newspaper that was on the side of the stage, vindictively tore it up and threw all the pieces into the orchestra pit, stomping the stage in those familiar tennis shoes! The temper tantrum of a small child, it produced nothing but acute alarm in all of us who were in that tension-bursting rehearsal, robbing us of a much needed rest before dancing the evening, four-ballet performance.

Poor Yvonne, a gracious and gentle woman from South Africa, coming all the way to New York for this! How could we ever have any respect for Jerome Robbins after being subjected to such a needlessly cruel exhibition?

To return to *The Cage* rehearsals, at this point, after having experienced his combativeness, I was very much afraid of him. When a dancer puts herself in the hands of a choreographer, a trust must exist between them. That trust must then be nurtured so that together they can create something wonderful. The dancer willingly allows herself to be the clay and the choreographer becomes the sculptor. She, or he, as the case may be, becomes the medium for the choreographer's creativity. When that trust is broken and fear replaces it, chaos results.

I began to dread Jerome Robbins' rehearsals, for he terrified me with his thunderbolt changes of mood. Trying to avoid him, I started hiding from him. If I spied him in the hallway, I went the other way, quickly getting out of sight. If he was waiting for the elevator, I would duck down the stairs so I didn't have to ride with him. But, evasive as I tried to be, I couldn't escape him for I was chosen to dance in nearly all of his ballets. In order to remain and dance for Mr. B, I had to try to find a way to handle my fear of Robbins.

It was obvious to all of us who were accustomed to the enthusiasm and thoughtful consideration with which Mr. B choreographed, that Robbins demonstrated the exact opposite. Mr. B was always striving to make women beautiful. He loved women! He never raised his voice and always received the utmost respect and admiration from all his dancers.

I was not alone in my adoration of Mr. B. Every dancer in the company felt the same. I still wonder how Mr. B could have entrusted his adoring and adored dancers to the likes of a man like Robbins. Was he too absorbed in the cascading overflow of his own creativity? The difference between the two choreographers was, with a nod to Dostoevsky, the difference between God and the Devil. I dreaded every Robbins rehearsal with stomach-churning fear, while anticipating every Balanchine rehearsal with pure and undiluted joy. Often on the same day, I rehearsed for both Mr B and Robbins, the agony and ecstasy hand wrestling within the course of the same working period.

Robbins often changed the choreography with sometimes five or six versions. We were to retain all versions with equal clarity and then do as his whim demanded. "Let me see version two, no, I like version six better, let me see that, no, that stinks, go back to version three, that was shit!" His coarse language and grappling for creative straws were there for all to witness.

To preface what happened to me on this particular day I have to confess that, unfortunately, I had gained five pounds over a vacation period. There are, of course, greater crimes in this world than gaining a few pounds, but for Robbins, it provided him with yet another convenient peg on which to erupt. Many dancers did succumb to the yo-yo kind of weight management, gaining pounds over a vacation period and then losing the weight quickly when the intense training and rehearsals began for a new season. Sometimes one would be given a reminder and a wink from Mr. B to give up ice cream for a time! We did not need anything more. It was clear that we had to keep our weight under control without being put on the scales like jockeys before a race.

But it was unnecessary to use soul-destroying insults and public humiliation as incentives to encourage dancers to stay sylph-like. I was already concentrating on ridding myself of the extra weight. At that particular rehearsal, I weighed 115 pounds; my usual dancing weight being 110.

The rehearsal was at a point when Jerome Robbins had gone blank, par for the course, and could not come up with any new *Cage* choreography. It was then that he started to scream at me, hissing like a cobra that I looked like "a big fat pig" and made me do a particularly strenuous passage over and over and over again, telling me I was trying to look too pretty when he wanted me to be deadly and disgusting.

Where was even a shadow of the artistry of Hitchcock, Billy Wilder or the later and great Polanski? Couldn't he even have made the effort to try and direct, to shape, contour and withdraw the emotions that he was so pathologically seeking?

I didn't reply verbally, one was never to do that! I tried to show no reaction and continued through the rehearsal with all the professionalism I could muster. How I tried to appear more vicious, which was even more difficult because I now felt in every way disabled.

I was choking back tears but would not give him the satisfaction of caving in! By this time he was screeching at me that I had to learn everyone's part, to understudy every role and be prepared to dance in any part he told me if he wished to switch me around. I knew what his game was; not only to crush me emotionally, but also physically. No survival course of the U.S. Marines could have been more grueling. One reads today of the high incidence of suicide among very young Russian conscripts, a brutal barometer of how power can turn men in charge to dispensers of life-threatening brutality.

In his book, *Dance with Demons*, dealing with the life of Jerome Robbins, author Greg Lawrence describes these malevolent *Cage* rehearsals and how Nora Kaye came to my defense "You know, Jerry, sometimes you're a shit!" But nothing changed. As in *Sacre du Printemps*, I was the Chosen Maiden.

Jerome Robbins was a man always at war with himself, a civil war in which there could be no winner. When he gave testimony before the McCarthy Senate Hearings for the House of Un-American Activities Committee in the 1950s, many people had their careers permanently ruined by his sworn words of betrayal. This cowardly act was perpetrated in order to escape prosecution himself for having been a fully participating card-carrying member of the Communist Party, and to avoid being outed as gay by the powerful television host Ed Sullivan.

A whirlpool of hatred, he also had an ongoing and bitter battle with his father, with his Judaism, with his homosexuality and then, later, with the guilt of having demolished lives in the wake of his infamous Washington, D.C. testimony. The only way he could deal with such utter self-loathing was to let it spill over onto his defenseless victims, the young dancers who were at his mercy, or lack of it.

After that fearful rehearsal thankfully ended, I dragged myself into the big empty ballet studio where I had always been so happy. That day, I felt at the bottom of a murky pit with no means to scale the slimy walls.

I took most of my ballet classes in that wonderful studio. There was a grand piano and large windows along one wall that reached almost from the floor to the ceiling. Outside, a steady stream of rain was splattering the windows. I was relieved there were no lights on in the studio, for in the semi-darkness I could try to hide my acute distress. With some effort, I put my foot on the high barre next to the window to stretch, thinking it might somewhat alleviate the physical pain.

Only then did I notice five spots of dark red blood where each of my toes had bled through the pink satin pointe slippers. I put my head on the knee of my extended leg and started to cry without respite, by then feeling the sharp stabs of pain from my lacerated toes.

As I looked down at the street below through the open window, the thought of jumping out onto the asphalt pavement terrified me even more.

I thought of my mother's words, that I was from "pioneer stock" and that I was to be able to endure anything because such was my early American ancestry. In my deep despair, my thinking and logic told me that jumping out of the window would not be practical because it probably wouldn't kill me, and I wanted to die!

The army camp behavior that had just taken place in the *Cage* rehearsal was a clear breach of children's human rights and certainly had no place in a civilized society, then or now.

I remained at the barre, girding myself for the jabs of pain shooting through my body. Fortunately for me, Francisco Moncion, one of the company's principal dancers, had been looking for me and, when he found me, my swollen feet bleeding at the barre, offered me his strength, solace and belief. As in Mr. B's mythic ballet, *Orpheus*, Frank was indeed a gift from the gods, my welcome and rescuing Dark Angel.

"You're a fantastic dancer," he said to me comfortingly. "Don't let Jerry crush your spirit." Through the tears, I managed to smile at him in sheer gratitude.

To have begun exorcising this period of my early life has not been an easy task, but since every generation breeds new despots, like moths to flame, there are always innocents waiting to be scorched. As the floodgates of memory are unlocked, what I had been subjected to was beyond the boundaries of abuse; it had skirted the borders of torture.

As such, it would have been a dereliction of duty for me to further ignore it. And that, at the other end of the time capsule, age 77, I cannot and will not do!

Staring at the now calmer California sea, still bathed under the dimming light of the late afternoon, my thoughts return to my childhood days in Oklahoma, where Native Americans, then called Indians, could still be seen hawking their silvered and turquoise beaded bracelets. From that earlier Americana, I was reminded of my female forebears whose dreadful suffering made my own nothing by comparison.

CHAPTER TWO

Cowboys, Indians and Shirley Temple

My parents, Leonard S. Bocher (pronounced Bo-shay) and Virginia Ayres Moore were married in 1923. After a dozen years of deliberately delayed pregnancy, on August 26th, 1935 I was born in Anadarko, Oklahoma. My Mom and Dad didn't want to bring a child into this world until they were sure they'd be able to provide advantages for their offspring.

Anadarko, in the late 1930s, was a sparsely inhabited city located in the sprawling Washita River Valley. With a predominantly Native American population, there were still tomahawk echoes of the once Wild West; turquoise and coral beaded necklaces dangling from sun-bronzed throats, dyed eagle-feathered headdresses crowning the majestic heads of tribal chieftains, and cowboys and Indians on galloping horses stirring up spirals of reddened, dusty earth.

As I was growing up in this last frontier milieu, I learned that my ancestors had fled the Roman Catholic persecution of Protestants in both Scotland and France. Fleeing to the New World in the hope of savoring religious freedom, they found themselves subjected to new life-threatening trials.

In the state of Virginia, rampaging Shawnee Indians descended on them with murderous attacks that involved scalping, scorching and abduction. One of them, Mary Moore, my mother's early forebear, lived through the massacre of her family to eventually die peacefully of old age, lovingly surrounded by her own descendants.

Years later, when I had crushing hurdles to overcome, my mother would reinforce my will by reminding me that I had risen from the ashes of durable colonial stock.

As I delved into my family background to the present, I discovered that I had a celebrity relative who was adored by some of the world's most recognizable women. He was the acclaimed couturier Mainbocher, originally Main Rousseau Bocher. Uncle Main, as I affectionately called him, was actually my father's first cousin. A confirmed bachelor, as it was described in those more discreet days, he was doted upon by a scented trail of glamorous ladies.

Mainbocher's roster of clients was a who's who of famous women. One of his most notable, and notorious, clients was Wallis Simpson, the twice-divorced American lady for whom Edward VIII abdicated the throne of England. Mainbocher created Wallis Simpson's entire trousseau as well as planning her wedding on June 3rd, 1937 in France.

His New York salon was at the heart of fashionable Manhattan, next door to exclusive Tiffany's at 57th Street and 5th Avenue. Mainbocher's patrons were devoted to him and included some of the most distinguished women of society, Broadway and Hollywood. Mary Martin *(South Pacific)*, Ethel Merman *(Call Me Madam)*, Greta Garbo *(Camille)*, Helen Hayes *(A Farewell to Arms)* Tallulah Bankhead *(Lifeboat)* and Rosalind Russell *(Auntie Mame)* were among his star-dusted clientele.

Fast-forwarding a decade when I had joined the New York City Ballet, he unfailingly gave me encouragement, sending flowers every time I danced a soloist role in New York. He would sit in the same seat in the first row on the aisle at the City Center, and when escorting Greta Garbo, would enter through a side entrance just after the house lights dimmed. The great Garbo, who like Mainbocher, was a devotee of ballet, had an acute aversion to being recognized in public. While on stage, I used to try, but never quite succeeded, to get a glimpse of the woman who had been Mata Hari and Ninotchka. But the bright spotlights in my eyes had other ideas, thwarting that stargazing wish.

Rewinding to the years before I was born, in 1929 Dad was completely ruined financially by the stock market crash. Times were difficult for them as they were for everyone in the nation. Dad, with his innate resilience, did make a new start and by the time I was born, had recovered enough to have us live in a rented duplex in Oklahoma City.

It was summer and Mom was determined to make me look like the little golden girl, Shirley Temple. Every little girl's mother wanted her small daughter to look like Shirley Temple, and why not? She was adorable and talented, a good little actress and she could sing and dance. She was every one's little darling in the movies, not only in America, but all over the world.

Mom would come at me with the dreaded curling iron! My hair was the same golden color as dimpled Shirley's, but completely straight. Mom would have me sit still so I would not be burned by the sizzling hot iron. The smell of burning hair stays with me, still, and my memory goes back to those awful curling sessions! But I don't hold it against little Miss Temple. It wasn't her fault she was so adorable!

This particular day it was worth it to sit still for the curling session because it was the day for us to use the free coupon the salesman had left at our house the week before. He was going from door to door, talking to the mothers of children in the neighborhood, persuading them to "See if Your Child has Talent" with a coupon from Bernice Hawley's School of Dance in downtown Oklahoma City. This was certainly a clever and winning marketing strategy and my Mom fell for it hook, line and sinker!

Mom dressed me in a pair of shorts, a white blouse with ruffles and my brand new wooden clogs from Holland. Wanting to see if I had any talent, this was a perfect, cost-free opportunity to find out.

All of the kids, girls and boys of all ages, were led to the dance studio where Miss Hawley greeted us with "Hi kids", then directed us to take a place at the lower ballet barre designed for tiny children.

"Okay, kids," she said, "the first one to kick the back of their head gets a nickel." Though I had never before tried such an acrobatic stunt, I thought I had better do what I was told. And so I gave a tremendous kick and whacked the back of my head so hard it made a loud pop heard all the way to the receptionist area outside the practice studio. My little wooden clogs and very strong kick had made it possible for me to win! Right away, Miss Hawley presented me with the coveted nickel, my very first salary! And, I must add, my first dance injury, for I quickly felt a swelling lump on the back of my curling-ironed ringlets!

The lessons in acrobatics, Hawaiian hula, tap, Spanish dancing with castanets, ballet and diction took place every Saturday morning. Each class lasted about a quarter of an hour and it was bliss! I loved going to those lessons, for we got to wear sparkling costumes and perform for appreciative audiences all over town, groups such as schools, women¹s clubs and USO venues for servicemen about to be shipped overseas.

World War II was in full deadly swing with Pearl Harbor shattering the myth of American untouchability.

The owner of the dancing school, Miss Hawley, was a retired vaudevillian, a hoofer who had toured the country doing one-night stands. Then, as vaudeville inexorably faded, facing the reality of paying the endless avalanche of bills, she opened her dancing school.

There was a particular performance in one of her recitals that remains sorely engraved in my memory. I wore a glittering spangled costume, popping out of a box and doing my little acrobatic dance, consisting of walkovers, cartwheels, and, to top it all, walking in a backbend on hands and feet across the stage.

Then, with my body literally folded in half, my feet flopped over my head touching the stage in front of me, I kept smiling at the audience! Everyone clapped! I then, completely forgot what was next! I decided to just stay in the convoluted stretch until I remembered the next steps. My father was in the audience and as the music played on and I didn't budge from my contortionist position, he panicked, thinking I was hopelessly stuck and couldn't disentangle myself from that position. He raced on to the stage and carried me off with the entire audience laughing at his rescuing antics! After that I made a promise to myself that before I ever went on stage again, I would know what I was doing and remember it! I must have kept that promise for, to this day, I still recall some of the choreographic masterpieces that the world's most lauded choreographer, George Balanchine, was to create, and in which I was to dance.

By the time the Second World War began, we were living in Wichita, Kansas. There I took weekly ballet lessons from a Ms. Edler, who put me on pointe when, at age eight, no legitimate teacher would ever have done that since the bones in the feet are not yet fully formed. Thankfully, I never suffered any of the dire consequences of that grave error of judgment.

And what were the two most influential choreographers of my life doing in the late 1930s and early 1940s while I was high-kicking my way to applause as a child? George Balanchine, whose creative genius would set him apart from all others, was choreographing such hit Broadway musicals as *On Your Toes, Cabin in the Sky* and *Louisiana Purchase*. As for Jerome Robbins, he was dancing in the choruses of such Broadway musicals as *Great Lady*, *The Straw Hat Review* and *Keep off the Grass*. Who, seeing the young Jerry then in the blur of those forgettable chorus lines, could ever have foreseen that he would one day be crowned the undisputed dancing king of Broadway? Or that he would so attach himself to me, leech-like, and when he was at his most frustrated, blood-sucking. Where the inept teacher, Ms. Edler, failed to ruin my feet, Jerome Robbins was to almost succeed.

When we later moved to Oklahoma City there were ballet lessons from Fronie Asher whose advice was to alter my own provincial world. For it was Miss Asher who told my parents that she had taken me as far as she could and I now needed to go either to New York or California for more advanced studies. She believed that I had a future career in ballet, though she didn't give any recommendations for ballet schools. My parents were at a loss about which way to turn. Where do we send her and how do we pay for this were the questions uppermost on their minds.

When faced with the decision of where to go to study ballet seriously, I remembered the first ballet our family attended when I was six years old.

That was the performance that mesmerized me then and, consequently, changed the course of my life. To this day it throbs with aliveness in my memory. The company was the Ballet Russe de Monte Carlo and they were in Oklahoma City for one night only.

The great ballerina, Mme Alexandra Danilova, danced the Glove Seller in *Gaîté Parisienne*, with Frederic Franklin as the romantic Baron and Léonide Massine as the ebullient Peruvian. It was lively, vivid and flirtatious with Massine's choreography executed, not as steps, but as an outburst of joie de vivre. And the music by Jacques Offenbach! I sat there spellbound at the sight and sound of magic.

The second ballet was *Schéhérazade* by Michel Fokine, also danced by Mme Danilova as the libidinous Zobeide and Frederic Franklin as the lustful Golden Slave. The lush and exotic score by Rimsky-Korsakov had me floating on some mystical Middle Eastern carpet. After that unforgettable evening, I made up my mind to become a ballerina just like Mme Danilova! She was my inspiration to dance.

Time passed and my small town lessons continued, but like a fly in translucent amber, I began to feel hopelessly trapped. At twelve years

of age, and sensing that I was getting older, I plucked up the cou
to write a letter to the illustrious ballerina, addressing it to the Ballet
Russe de Monte Carlo in New York, In that letter, I wrote of how her
performances had ignited me to dance. With the urgency of youthful
desperation, I asked her what a young girl my age from Oklahoma
needed to do in order to pursue a career in ballet.

Lo and behold, Alexandra Danilova answered my letter in her asser-
tive and individual handwriting, informing me that she would be at
the School of American Ballet in June and that I should come to New
York and audition for enrollment in that prestigious school. There she
would assess me and see if I had any talent!

If Mme Danilova had not answered my letter (which I safeguarded
no less than the Constitution), my life would have moved in a totally
different direction. Fortunately for me, she was diligent about answering her fan mail and almost never turned down an autograph request.

On the basis of that letter alone, Mom and I went to New York
arriving on Memorial Day weekend in 1949. I was thirteen years old.
We trudged across glittering Broadway at 42nd Street with our travel-
worn suitcases in hand after a lengthy ride, three long days and nights
from Oklahoma City on the Greyhound bus. Upon arrival, we had
no reservations for a hotel and, of course, we had no idea whether
I would be accepted for the June ballet classes. What we did know,
with certainty, was that whatever the outcome, even if we were to be
rejected, it would not be for want of trying.

Hungry, dirty and tired, where were we going to sleep? Mom
remembered that my grandmother had once stayed at the Martha
Washington Hotel for Women when she had visited New York. And
so we hailed a taxi driver who took us there through the congested and
honking evening traffic. Luckily for us, the hotel had space and we
found a Horn & Hardart Automat near the hotel for our first dinner
in New York. Famished for a real meal after nibbling on sandwiches,
crackers and greasy spoon take-aways in the bus, we dug in to the
simple food fare set out invitingly on the table.

Monday, the next day, was the big day itself when we would go to the
School of American Ballet on Madison Avenue and 59th Street. What
anticipation, excitement and apprehension I felt, for I knew everything depended on how I looked and how I responded to the steps I

would be asked to do. Would I be accepted and enter the precincts of seventh heaven, or would I, accompanied by my mother, unceremoniously be put on the first Greyhound bus back to Oklahoma?

Unknown to me until my father's death, years later, did I learn that Dad had borrowed on his life insurance in order to finance the trip. And so, on that fateful Monday, on a fragile wing and potent prayer, leaving very early we made our way to George Balanchine's School of American Ballet. Mom and I were both on tenterhooks, communing with whatever mysterious forces determine our elusive joy in life. Entering the rickety elevator of the building, we fervently and silently prayed.

CHAPTER THREE

The Audition

Nervously changing from my street clothes to practice clothes in the dressing room, looking at the other girls I could see that I was dressed inappropriately. With almost worn out ballet slippers secured by an elastic across the instep instead of ribbons, no tights, just bare legs, and a maroon-colored practice outfit my mother had made from the pattern of an ice skating costume, I stood out like a sore thumb next to the other students. I felt and looked like what I was, a country bumpkin, a pretender from the sticks.

That turning point day in the summer of 1949, that day of awkward self-appraisal, I was 13 years old, and suddenly able to see my gauche self in comparison with the sleek girls in my age group. The atmosphere of dedication, devotion and exclusivity of purpose permeated the very walls, unlike the relaxed mood of once-a-week rhythmic relaxation in the dance studios back home.

Also milling about in the waiting area were small groups of early middle-aged women who, though outwardly projecting a pleasant and composed demeanor, were invariably concealing a go-for-broke, horse with blinkers, killer instinct drive for their precious daughters. They were the ballet mamas of whom caricatures have been drawn, and pages of dance books have described.

Though, as I was to realize, they proliferate in the ballet world, there are no ballet mothers, as such, in the world of opera, since opera students are grown up by the time they put their nose to the musical grindstone. Little ballet girls, on the other hand, are led by their one-tracked mothers, some of whom have crossed oceans, trekked across Siberian mountain ranges, and counted pennies to help their daughters become ballerinas. One has only to think of the unswerving mindset of the mothers of Margot Fonteyn, Irina Baronova and Tamara Toumanova, to name some spectacular examples.

Generally speaking, ballet mothers did not strike up friendships with each other, for to do so, in their ambitious eyes, was to give a boost to the competition. And it was fierce, ferocious and hell-bent, for the mothers knew that though there would always be a surfeit of ballet aspirants, the available places would be crushingly few. To be friendly with the mother on either side of you on the bench was to feed the menacing opposition. And so, the ballet mamas sat there, watching everything, missing nothing, willing their daughters to pirouette more, extend higher and balance longer than their class-mates. Sending out their silently voiced instructions to excel, they mentally egged their daughters on, all the while maintaining the most pleasant and agreeable mask-like smiles.

Did my mother, the reader may well ask, become one of this singular breed? Well, I suppose she must have, for her home away from home was to become the School of American Ballet, but I never remember her ever speaking disparagingly of other girls, or even their doting mothers with their serrated-edged and caustic tongues.

As we sat in the waiting area, I also noticed young men in tights and T-shirts, no more than in their early 20s, coming from class, drenched in sweat from what must have been their extreme exertions just completed. At quick glance, they all seemed very personable, conversing with each other very familiarly, and relating to each other with a mutual attentiveness I hadn't seen before among men. A few smiled at me, somehow sensing that I was about to audition. I smiled tentatively in return, for it seemed as if they were trying to reassure me. I liked them immediately for their silent good wishes. They seemed a far cry from the young men I had seen and grown up with in Oklahoma, most of the local young males there being roughhewn, beer-guzzling types, more at home in a saloon than a salon as befitted these sensitive-looking young men.

Suddenly a woman majestically swept into that waiting area, that crowded space vibrating with dreams and determination. There in front of me was faculty member Muriel Stuart, an English-Jewish woman of seasoned years who had been one of the few protégées of the early 20th century's most legendary ballerina, Anna Pavlova, herself half-Jewish. Miss Stuart then became a soloist in Pavlova's company, touring the civilized world with her for eleven years, travelling with her in trains and ships, for planes didn't transport ballet companies in those far-off days.

So expressively beautiful was Miss Stuart's dancing that in Pavlova's only ballet, the elegiac *Autumn Leaves*, Miss Stuart was often mistaken upon her entrance for Pavlova herself, a rapturous response of applause that Miss Stuart knew was reserved only for Pavlova.

Her figure still beautiful, her lovely legs still in evidence, and her pronounced insteps still arching at her instant command, Miss Stuart greeted me warmly and told me to enter the studio and take a place at the barre. I became even more nervous since I had no idea that I would have a private audition, thinking I would be one of many simultaneously being appraised.

My reflection in the mirrored wall across the studio revealed the fresh pink carnation my mother had lovingly pinned in my hair that morning. Miss Stuart, gliding across the floor, proceeded to give me a barre before the center floor exercises. When Miss Stuart had seen enough, she gave me a welcoming hug and told me that I had been accepted as a student for the summer session! She then spoke to mother privately, giving her a no-nonsense evaluation of what she had seen.

"Barbara has the desire and willingness to work hard, the musical sensitivity, the proper build for a dancer and strong arches so important in order to dance on pointe; she has good flexibility, the ability to follow directions and a delightful way about her. That is the combination for success!" Then she disappeared into the teachers' dressing room.

Mother wrote these exact words to my father in Oklahoma and since I have kept all of their correspondence to each other and their letters to me during the years 1949–1954, I am able to quote verbatim.

With Miss Stuart's words ringing in our ears, Mother was overjoyed and I was ecstatic! We rushed to Capezio's, the leading ballet shop some ten blocks away, to purchase pink tights, ballet slippers and a black leotard. I believe my parents had reservations about investing in practice clothes and shoes until they knew whether I would be accepted or not in the summer school. Now they knew.

The following day, I was correctly attired for class, thanks to one of the girls in the dressing room who had volunteered to teach me to sew the ribbons and elastic on my pointe shoes, as well as to darn the toes of my pointe slippers so that the sound would be muffled on landing from jumps. Darning the toes also helped absorb rosin, the sticky powder that was used freely to prevent slipping.

Bless Muriel Stuart. None of us could ever forget that she had been entirely trained by The Swan herself, and had subsequently been her leading female dancer. Miss Stuart, in addressing others, frequently used the word "darling" pronouncing it, "Dahling!" I remember being asked by her to execute a very difficult series of turns in a diagonal line across the studio. To delay the inevitable, I kept going to the back of the line of students and then to the rosin box to obtain a firmer grip on the floor. The rosin box served not only to make us slip-proof, but also as a nervous outlet moments before entering the lion's den, or less threatening, but equally fearful, the performing arena.

"Dahling," she called across to me, "all the rosin in the world won't save you now." The intimidating series of turns were completed with a sigh of relief and surprise that I really managed them. In addition to her vast reservoir of knowledge about classical ballet (she was to write one of the defining treatises on the subject), she helped her students accrue the necessary confidence, and to push themselves beyond their confining limitations.

She gave complex combinations of rapid-fire quick jumps interspersed with *batterie*, demonstrating those beats with an almost Grand Prix speed and facile elevation. Even though her hair was totally silvered and she had celebrated many birthdays, when she danced she was sprayed by some rediscovered fountain of youth, for she became ageless when she demonstrated.

Only if I had been a seer could I have foreseen that one day I, too, would parallel the close of her performing career in the mid-1920s, when she made the heart-wrenching decision to leave the very lodestar of her life, the greatest ballerina in the world, Anna Pavlova, in order to get married.

I too, one day in the mid-1950s, would make such a soul-jarring decision when I would leave the very axis of my own existence, the greatest choreographer in the world, George Balanchine, ostensibly in order to get married. But marriage, in my case, was the escape route from what had turned into a Devil's Island of entrapment.

For the cloudless present, I was placed in "B" class, an intermediate category for the summer session. There was a florist shop just a few doors from the entrance of the ballet school where my mother bought me a fresh carnation to wear in my hair for class every day. To walk into that shop with its aroma of flowered fragrances was to be further fortified for the demanding day ahead.

Every student at the school was better than I when I started there. It was such an uphill battle to learn new steps and endure the length of the classes, each lasting one and a half grueling hours without a moment's respite. I had read that Marie Taglioni, the early 19th century's most illustrious Romantic ballerina, used to lie down in a faint after private lessons with her dancing master father, Filippo. Now I understood such exhaustion. In the beginning, I questioned my survival ability, but by the end of the summer, the heat notwithstanding, I had begun to feel less of a division between my mind's command and body's obedience.

Despite the daily struggle, I was in seventh heaven and nothing could dislodge me, not yet, that is. I did not see Alexandra Danilova, the prima ballerina who had answered my letter and advised me to go to New York. She didn't teach that summer but, most importantly, she had answered my letter and gave me advice that I obeyed as if they had been the Ten Commandments. Many years later, I did meet her and personally thanked her for being the cataclysmic influence at that very early crossroads. She was such an inspiration to generations of dancers, performing, teaching and coaching well into her 80s.

Occasionally, she would take an Oboukhov class and I remember the day quite well when Vera Zorina, Mme Danilova, Maria Tallchief, and Tanaquil LeClercq were all in class together; all of those women had been or were to marry Mr. B, though not Mme Danilova who had lived with him as his common-law wife in the early 1930s, as it was referred to then. The only wife missing was Tamara Geva, his first, the original star of Mr. B's Broadway show, *On Your Toes*. All had been his muses, inspiring him for successive outpourings of choreography for either Hollywood films, Broadway musicals or primarily for the ballet stage. The women in his past, and future, remained on excellent terms with him and, more surprisingly, with each other. Long after his death, his muses still spoke reverently of him, such was his power even beyond the grave.

Toward the end of the summer session, Mr. B came in to watch a pointe class taught by Elise Reiman, one of the faculty members assigned to beginners. That was the first time I had seen him in person. I stared at him, hardly believing that he was actually there in front of me. We were doing *bourrées* across the floor – and what a test that was for my concentration – for I was aware that he seemed to be watching me with a laser-beam focus. After the class, I heard him ask Miss Reiman which one was Barbara Bocher, wishing confirmation of my identity. When I was pointed out to him, he asked why I was in "B" class, his subtext being that I belonged in a higher category. She replied that I had been placed there because I was only 13. My extreme youth didn't seem to faze him, for he told her to arrange for me to go straight into "C" class, which was the next and higher division.

He then turned to my mother, who was tensely observing the conversation in progress, though always with her disarming smile, and told her that he was inviting me to continue to study at The School of American Ballet in the fall with a full scholarship! It was one of the happiest moments in my life! I at once gave vent to my grateful impulse and threw my arms around Mr. B's neck, hugging him in joyful response. Such a spontaneous demonstration of affection seemed to embarrass him no end, for the maestro bowed, blushed and backed away from the flailing arms of the uncontainable 13-year-old.

He was essentially shy by temperament, and a man of few words, but when he did speak in his Russian-accented English, his comments were usually artistic nuggets of gold.

"Your muscles must marry," I recall. "Quick like lightning, you are the music, you must be the music," he would say. "If you are not interested in your foot, nobody else will be," he advised when describing how to present your foot in a *posé arabesque*, and not just to lift it off the ground.

I adored him from the moment I saw him. It was always apparent that George Balanchine was led by higher forces that were not of this pedestrian world. He was, undeniably, a genius, a channel for higher creative currents that funneled through him to his acolyte dancers. What a privilege to have known him and to have danced for him! He is the person whom I regard as the one who has most influenced me in living my life during those years between 1949 and 1954, and then long after in the succeeding decades when my last pair of faded pink satin pointe shoes was dangling from a hook in the dark and airless storage closet.

But that time was part of a future that could then not even be contemplated. New York, New York, it's a wonderful town, as the song went and so it was for us. On the practical side of living in Manhattan, Mom and I continued to stay at the Martha Washington Hotel for Women on 23rd Street. Was it a coincidence that we remained at a hotel named after the wife of the first American President, George Washington? For mother's ancestor, Captain James Moore, had ridden alongside General Washington in the American Revolutionary War.

Coincidence or cosmic design, we settled in quickly, often eating at the Horn and Hardart Automat, a chain of restaurants where they offered healthy food at reasonable prices. With only a handful of nickels one could have any food displayed within the little cubicles lined along the walls. By putting nickels into a little slot next to your choice, you could then open a glass door to remove your food. The baked ham sandwich on a Kaiser roll was four nickels, and that is what I had for lunch every day after class. They also made a delicious Spanish omelet which was often chosen as dinner.

The more upmarket Schrafft's was a few doors down the street and once a week, as an indulgence, Mom and I would stop in for one of those scrumptious chocolate marshmallow sundaes topped with pecan nuts. Mouth-watering just to recall it! Everything was a new experience for me, including pizza which I had never heard of before, since such Italian cuisine had not yet reached the hinterlands of Oklahoma. Now, of course, ethnic food is part and parcel of the national American diet.

When we returned to Oklahoma for a brief time before the fall opening of school, I practiced every day for two hours doing everything I could remember from the School of American Ballet classes. I used the local ballet studio and with my collection of recorded ballet music, *Swan Lake, Sleeping Beauty, Giselle, Les Sylphides* and *Raymonda*, I was inspired and danced until ready to drop! I needed no prodding or pushing to work that hard, the choice being entirely my own. I was insatiable. When I read books, they were ballet books, and when I dreamed, I was Princess Aurora. Asleep or awake, I was nothing less than obsessed and possessed!

After August turned into September, Mother returned to New York with me while my father, of necessity, stayed behind in Oklahoma City to maintain the family business. Someone had to pay the bills! A surge of sadness still envelops me when I remember leaving my father waving goodbye to Mom and me at the bus station. What is more poignant than saying goodbye at any extended departure, that pain felt by both those who leave and those who are left behind?

I would miss Dad terribly. Now 14, I knew it would be the end of my life in Oklahoma as I had known it, of time spent with my aged grandparents, would I ever see them again, for the specter of mortality had now made its presence felt? Gone would be the carefree times with friends my own age who now would be relegated to the pages of early photo albums.

On a seesaw of regret and anticipation, I looked out of the bus window, waving at my father until I could see him no longer. What belief he had in me, and what generosity of spirit to willingly relinquish, not just his daughter, but his wife, leaving himself to cope with his own ongoing aloneness. As the bus drove on along America's vast and faceless highways, those indefinite stretches of asphalt that connect one unfamiliar city with another, I watched the whizzing and billboarded landscapes, vowing to turn my vision into splendor-filled reality.

CHAPTER FOUR

A Passion to Dance

Mother and I, now that we were going to stay in New York for longer than a month, needed more than a claustrophobic hotel room, so we found a larger apartment on 92nd Street. I also enrolled in the School for Young Professionals for my academic studies to cover the next two years. Mom, sharpening her already honed skills of persuasion, convinced the principal that I should go into the ninth grade rather than the eighth where I was supposed to enter. Since my goal was to dispense with all the academic studies as soon as possible, thereby permitting me exclusive focus on dancing, I was pleased to jump a grade. So every Friday I collected my assignments, learned what I had to, then took tests on all the subjects. Without so much as a breather, I would collect the next week's assignments to be completed a week later. In this compressed pattern did I complete five years of school in two years, to graduate from high school with straight A's. When graduation time came around, I wasn't so much proud as relieved, for academia, thankfully, would be relegated to water under the bridge.

At the School of American Ballet there were nine classes a week. The director of the school , as well as of the company, the New York City Ballet, was the Russian Imperial trained and ex-Diaghilev choreographer, George Balanchine. The company was the vision of multi-millionaire and ardent ballet lover Lincoln Kirstein, who had brought Mr. B to America for the express purpose of realizing the dream he had long harbored.

Taking a modern dance class was mandatory, ostensibly on the syllabus to expand our movement vocabulary. It was taught by Merce Cunningham, who had been a soloist with the reigning queen of modern dance Martha Graham. The piano was played by Merce Cunningham's life partner, the avant-garde composer John Cage, who had once subjected an audience to a solo of four complete minutes of absolute silence! We, luckily, were provided with sound, if not music, the plink-plank-plonk school of keyboard hammering, the aural equivalent of children splattering paint on a wall.

We had to dance barefoot and since the floor of the largest studio was made of old, wide wooden planks, I don't recall ever taking a class where, at the end, I didn't have to remove a stray splinter or two. Merce, as was the fashion to address modern dancers by their first names, even teachers, was to head his own company that he kept going throughout his extended life. Such was his determination to keep on dancing that it didn't seem to disturb him one whit to shuffle onto the stage when time and arthritis had replaced his once deep *plié* and soft jump. The fact that he was subjecting his audience to a vision of their own incapacitated future, if they lived that long, mattered not at all to him. He had to be at the center of his choreography, come hell, high water or decrepitude. Martha Graham, his mentor, to her credit, at least stopped at 75, saying that she could "no longer acquit herself with honor."

As for Merce's choreography, it evolved into chance composition, almost like shuffling a bag of numbers then following whichever sequence of numbers one had picked. I found it to be sterile, meaningless and sleep-inducing. Nevertheless, my non-response must have been in the minority, for Merce survived long enough to enter the realm, even while still alive, of dance history.

Insofar as Merce's classes were concerned, I found the movement ungainly and aesthetically indigestible. Later on, the very charming and lovely Janet Collins, the first black American woman to be principal dancer of the Metropolitan Opera Ballet, taught the class. Janet's lessons were much more harmonious and even helpful in expanding my vocabulary of movement, but to paraphrase the musical comedy star Mary Martin, "My heart belonged to ballet."

On the other side of the coin, the character classes with Yurek Lazowski were always an exhilarating tonic. Mr. Lazowski was Polish and had been a principal dancer with the Original Ballet Russe in the days when the decor was by Goncharova, Bakst and Benois, magical designs of vivid folkloristic color. In his classes, we would learn authentic dances from his native Poland, as well as those of Russia and Hungary. He would choose students to partner for the demonstration, and to be selected by him, as I was, proved to be very special. His partnering, as to be expected, was sure, strong and exciting. With him, I felt an extra abandon, especially in the czardas, my favorite, with its speedy footwork and turns. All the steps he taught were colored by a choreographic coquetry, tempered by innocence, woven into those patterns of peasant courtship.

What did it feel like for Yurek Lazowski who had once been a pivotal dancer in such a colorful company, to no longer perform, but to see others, all youngsters, elicit the applause that once he had known, now diminished to a receding echo? This question often came to mind as I observed the dancing stars of yesterday. No one, without exception, can hold back the dawn!

Mme Felia Dubrovska, married to Pierre Vladimirov, was when she graduated from the Vaganova School in St. Petersburg, along with Olga Spessivtzeva, one of the two top graduates. A soloist at the Maryinsky, she later became a principal with the Diaghilev Ballet, creating the role of the Siren in Mr. B's *Prodigal Son*. In her mid-50s, she still demonstrated with impeccable precision, her long slender legs tapering to exceptional insteps.

When she taught variations from the great 19th-century classics, the benches were invariably full of observers, for to watch her just walk across the studio, let alone demonstrate, was to see an imperial grandeur that had long vanished in the River Neva wind. From the land of the ruling Romanovs, she reflected a bygone and courtly presence.

We finished every Dubrovska pointe class with *32 fouettés* before the *révérence*, a deep curtsey for the girls, and then we applauded, thus thanking the teachers for transmitting their treasure chest of knowledge.

There was an adagio class on Thursdays, alternatively taught by Pierre Vladimirov and Anatole Oboukhov, both offering pas de deux from the 19th-century ballets including *Paquita, Don Quixote* and *Giselle*.

Mr. Vladimirov had been possessor of a virtuoso technique, a rousing favorite of the St. Petersburg ballet audiences, and cavalier to a galaxy of ballerinas not equaled then or now. Partner to Mathilde Kschessinska, former mistress to Czar Nicholas II when he was still Czarevitch, he continued to protect her even when he had to marry within his royal circle. So was she a continuing force to be reckoned with at the Maryinsky. It was from Kschessinska's mansion balcony that Lenin announced the Revolution to the massed and frenzied crowds below.

For the Diaghilev Ballet, Mr. Vladimirov was the prince in attendance to Lubov Egorova, Olga Spessivtzeva and Vera Trefilova, but the most celebrated ballerina with whom he danced was Anna Pavlova in whose company he remained until her death, becoming her favorite partner. Every time I hear the music of Chopin, I am taken back to his classes, for Chopin was the composer whose melancholic music invariably accompanied his nostalgically tinged lessons.

Anatole Oboukhov, so generally overlooked in the history books of the dance, yet so unforgettable for anyone who ever studied with him, was considered one of the finest Petrouchkas and Albrechts, succeeding Nijinsky in those roles at the Maryinsky. A true ballet star in old Russia, he had a fan base no less intense than Vassiliev or Ruzimatov were to have in the future.

In his dancing retirement, Oboukhov still had a most powerful personality and when he taught, every nook and cranny of the studio resonated. His classes were exhausting, but always inspirational. You didn't have to try and do your best, you just naturally, unavoidably, inevitably surpassed yourself. As for his adagio class, well that was a direct link back to the Russia of the two-headed eagle. He would sometimes choose me to demonstrate whichever pas de deux he was teaching that day; "Bar-ba-ra." he would call out, rolling all the r's, and when I instantly stood in front of him *sur les pointes* in fifth position, I was the awakened Aurora, the spectral Giselle, or the bewitched Odette, queen of the spellbound swans.

Aside from the inimitable maestro himself, my favorite partner at the school was a Fordham University freshman named Brendan Fitzgerald. With a passion for ballet that put many other devotees in the shade, Brendan was tall, strong and reliable. However, he had the unfortunate compulsion to offend those who could possibly open locked doors for him. Built in to his personality was an unerring ability, no, disability, to ruffle feathers and generally offend indiscriminately. For whatever reason, I was exempted from this blatant shortcoming.

Years later, he became the ballet critic for the *Rome Daily American* newspaper in Italy. There his predilection for sniping and griping found its logical home. Despite these shortcomings, I was very fond of Brendan and was saddened to learn of his later brain cancer death.

Robert Joffrey also took the adagio classes and was, in the future, to found his own company, The Joffrey Ballet, which he directed with his lifelong partner, the dancer and choreographer Gerald Arpino. Robert was brilliant intellectually, having earned a Ph.D from Harvard, but was no great shakes as a dancer. Short of stature, he seemed to be aware of his limitations, because very early he focused on becoming a choreographer.

He liked to dance with me in the pas de deux classes, perhaps because I, too, was small, and therefore made him look taller. I would sometimes hide from him just before the class was to begin, for I much preferred to dance with Brendan, who usually arrived the last second from university.

But the pas de deux class to end all pas de deux classes took place at the rival ballet school, Ballet Arts, situated among the studios of Carnegie Hall. The class was taught by Danish Paul Petroff, a major ballet star of Col. de Basil's Original Ballet Russe, and his wife, the Texan-born Nana Gollner, prima ballerina of the same company throughout Europe in the mid-1930s. Not since the dancer Augusta Maywood, born in 1825, had any American achieved the rank of prima ballerina abroad. that is until the emergence of Nana Gollner in the next century.

Ballet Arts was the feeder school for Ballet Theatre. Since the two schools were rivals, we had to be secretive about attending any of their classes. Virginia Lee, the director of the school, had been choreographer for one of Rudolph Valentino's early silent films. She dismissively referred to the SAB as "the factory on 59th Street". Nevertheless, she would generously permit us to take the pas de deux class free of charge, always observing the lesson herself.

Mr. Petroff had just finished teaching the students the *Black Swan* pas de deux. As Brendan and I began to invest our all into the Petipa choreography, one by one, the other couples stopped dancing, moving to the side of the studio to watch us. At the finish, I held an *arabesque* on pointe for an indefinite time span, the pianist sensing the prolonged balance and waiting for me to come off pointe for the final pirouettes into the emphatic *penché arabesque*. Applause burst forth from everyone in the studio including Paul Petroff and Nana Gollner, and the Broadway and ballet choreographer Agnes de Mille, niece of Cecil B., who had been watching from the crowded doorway.

The response, so unexpected, caused me to burst into joyful tears. That reaction to my 13-year-old Odile was a one-off, a rare high point never to be duplicated on stage. Though I was to dance the Balanchine *Swan Lake* in the corps de ballet, and as a demi-soloist, I always thought I could do justice to the Petipa/Ivanov Odette and Odile. Even the obligatory 32 *fouettés* at the end of the *Black Swan* variation would not have presented any problem for me. But as circumstances and choices decreed, it was not to be. My *Swan Lake* success remained in that Ballet Arts classroom, never to be seen on any stage.

Not long afterwards, Agnes de Mille, choreographer of such Broadway smash hits as *Oklahoma!* and *Carousel,* and ballets *Rodeo* and *Fall River Legend*, was to give me her first autobiographical book, *Dance to the Piper*, inscribed:

To Barbara Bocher
With high hopes!
Agnes de Mille

Back at the School of American Ballet, there were many dancing stars to be seen, a veritable who's who of the Broadway, Hollywood and ballet world; Marc Platt, ex-Ballet Russe and occasional movie star, major film stars Vera Ellen and Cyd Charisse, both partners of Fred Astaire and Gene Kelly, the delightful Ray Bolger of *Wizard of Oz* fame who had just appeared in the Broadway hit, *Where's Charlie?*, a show Mr. B had choreographed, Russ Tamblyn, before *Seven Brides for Seven Brothers*, and virtuoso Tommy Rall, ex-Ballet Theatre and to become known on Broadway and films, and Marge and Gower Champion, later top Broadway musical directors.

I especially remember the majestic young ballerina, the serenely beautiful Svetlana Beriosova, whose life was to become a blueprint for self-destructive tragedy. Was I to stand in the wings alongside her, to become her lady in waiting for the fall of the too early curtain? Who knows what lies in wait for any of us, even the most seemingly blessed at the outset?

Among the promising young students were two who became, indisputably, the greatest of American male dancers. The first was Jacques d'Amboise who, despite his French- sounding name, had a personality as American as apple pie and ice cream. His pleasure in dancing was authentic, his very smile an invitation to join him as he spun through the multiplicity of his pirouettes, or left the ground in defiant elevation, seeming to freeze there for a moment as did basketball stars Michael Jordan and Kobe Bryant.

Jacques's impact on audiences, both in America and abroad, was inevitable, for who could resist such throwaway technique coupled with his joie de vivre? He made a few Hollywood films and was in demand for more, but was put off by the indefinite waits on movie sets and the awareness that being unable to practice was to see the diminution of his hard-earned technique.

Upon his retirement from the stage, he became the founder of the National Dance Institute in New York. Now its Director Emeritus, he continues to transmit his own love of the art to people of all ages. Jacques, a year older than I, shared with me those years between 1949 and 1954. Though we live a continent apart from each other, he in New York and I in California, I continue to have deep and lasting affection for him.

The other outstanding boy was a slightly younger student, Edward Villella, addressed as Eddie by everyone. Starting at an extremely young age for an American boy, aged eight, he was entirely trained at the School of American Ballet. Developing a formidable technique, he became so strong, sharp and swift that his fan base grew with his every performance. His impact, it should be made clear, went far beyond his quicksilver technique, for as a dancing actor, he had simplicity and honesty in all his interpretations. To watch him dance was akin to listening to a haiku poem, pure, spare, and without a syllable in excess.

Now directing his own company, the Miami City Ballet in Florida, with fervent belief he carries on the Balanchine tradition, transmitting the living philosophy of his maestro, Mr. B.

As the 1940s was overtaken by the year 1950, I, as all the other ballet students, had only loose change in my pockets, certainly not enough to pay for nightly tickets to see all the ballet performances I hungered to watch.

The Ballet Russe de Monte Carlo was having a season at the old Metropolitan Opera House on Broadway and 39th Street. Their Family Circle was the highest tier with tickets costing $1.25. When walking down to your seat at that vertigo-inducing height, you had to lean back to offset the extremely steep incline. Always there was the fear of pitching forward over the low railing into the orchestra section five tiers below.

At first, Mom and I would purchase tickets and go every night to see the exciting performances, braving those nosebleed heights of the Family Circle and the endless steps to climb up there from the side street entrance. You really felt a peasant among the nobility, cut off as you were from mingling during the intermission with the elegantly dressed orchestra patrons.

One day after adagio class, Brendan decided we should go to a performance together, without my mother, advising me to dress up in evening clothes. I was full of anticipation, not quite sure what he had in mind. When I met him in front of the opera house, he told me he didn't have tickets but that we were going to sneak in after the first ballet and, when the intermission was ending, drift in with the returning crowd. My heart started to race and I was petrified of being caught, but somehow his bravado was contagious so I went along with him. Every night, we either found empty seats in the back of the orchestra, or stood in the standing room section.

Then the most frightening occurrence took place! The Met employed Pinkerton men for security and one night a tall and stern- looking uniformed Pinkerton guard came straight up to me! I nearly fainted with fright, imagining being taken away in handcuffs and thrown into jail! The guard then surprised us by saying, "I'm not looking, and the stairs to my left lead to the press box. The press box is empty after the first intermission and you can sit there unnoticed every night after the first ballet." I could have hugged him, but refrained, not wanting to cause him discomfort as I did the hapless Mr B.

What a thoughtful gesture on his part. He knew we were ballet students and must have guessed that our funds were nearly non-existent. He then told us that he had watched us every night the entire time we had been sneaking in until finally he could turn a blind eye no longer.

So with our Pinkerton guard in tow, we ascended the spiral stairs of white marble with solid brass handrails, leading to the box with the dark red velvet-covered gold chairs. The view of the stage was perfect and so we enjoyed just about every performance given by all visiting ballet companies that year, missing only the first ballet.

The incredibly thoughtful guard gave us a wink every night, then looked away so that he didn't see us ascending the staircase. Could he ever have known how much his exceptional kindness meant to us both? Perhaps he did. I do hope so.

Not everyone was so sensitive to others as our guard. The first time I was to witness a display of ugly ethnic temper was at a rehearsal for a benefit at Radio City Music Hall, the "showplace of the nation" as it was described, famous for its high-kicking militaristically precise Rockettes. The purpose of the benefit was to raise funds for the newly established state of Israel.

I, with my long family tree of Presbyterian ministers, was chosen to be among those to appear in a Jewish folk dance. It was going to be a star-studded event including Metropolitan Opera baritone Robert Merrill, all accompanied by a full symphony orchestra conducted by the world-renowned maestro Bruno Walter.

During the single rehearsal, Maestro Walter, unable to elicit from the musicians the sound he was seeking, in frustration started to raise his voice at them. With his accelerating displeasure, the musicians played worse rather than better. Leon Leonidoff, the producer of the event and director of the Radio City Music Hall, seated at the back of the theatre, anxiously watched the proceedings and then, red-faced, stormed down the aisle screaming at the conductor to "get going".

"Who do you think you are?" retorted an offended Bruno Walter, "I am not ready! It is not right yet!"

After a further shouting match that made me cringe in my seat, Leonidoff yelled at him, "You second-rate, Third Avenue kike!" after which he stormed off back down the long aisle muttering to himself.

This was the first time I had ever heard that ugly word and though I didn't then know what it meant, it was clear by its thunderbolt sharpness and venom that it was a verbal attack of the ugliest order. To his credit, Maestro Walter did not walk off in a huff and, in a patient voice asked the musicians to begin again, after which everything went off without a hitch. The performance went smoothly and raised a considerable sum of money. If Leon Leonidoff ever apologized to Bruno Walter for his indefensible verbal attack, well, that is a secret that both men took to their graves.

How some people can behave so negatively, instigated as they are by frayed nerves, frustration, jealousy, insecurity or just bursting neuroses. I think of the performing arena, its juxtaposition of beauty, talent and ambition, a triptych of attributes extracting both the best and the worst in the human breast.

Among controversial public figures, there is that supreme film director, Roman Polanski, forced into permanent American exile for having had sexual relations with a girl two weeks away from her 14th birthday. In marked contrast, Jerome Robbins, in choosing me as his 14-year-old victim, though not sexually, scaled pinnacle after pinnacle.

But surely forced sexual entry is not the only form of reprehensible crime in which to inflict suffering on a juvenile. What about the indiscriminate trampling, the demolition of a young girl's perishable dream?

CHAPTER FIVE

Dancing for Balanchine and Stravinsky

O ur very deaths are often the consequence of where we are at any given time. Flying in the wrong plane, driving in the wrong car, turning the wrong corner, keeping an appointment or missing one, so have the lengths of lives of numberless people been determined. This cosmic lottery includes presidents, prime ministers, archdukes and princesses; Anwar Sadat, John and Robert Kennedy, Indira Gandhi, John Lennon, Martin Luther King, Princess Grace and Princess Diana among them.

But it is not just our deaths that are often due to happenstance, it is also our lives. Léonide Massine was a brilliant and prolific choreographer of some of the most popular ballets of the 1930s and 40s, among them the bubbly *Le Beau Danube, Gaîté Parisienne* and *La Boutique Fantasque*, as well as the more profound symphonic ballets such as *Choreartium, Les Présages* and *Rouge et Noir*. Where, one may well ask, are any of those ballets today? Why have they all but disappeared onto the dusty shelves of civic libraries?

Could it be because Massine, one of Diaghilev's favorites, refused Kirstein's American offer as did Serge Lifar, leaving the third choice, George Balanchine, to reap the extraordinary harvest to be?

Lincoln Kirstein was a ballet-obsessed and possessed multi-millionaire, a complex, driven man who envisioned himself as the American equivalent of Serge Diaghilev, the catalytic marriage broker of diversified artistic genius.

I do believe that though Léonide Massine moved in the same rarified circles as the composer Manuel de Falla, the painter Pablo Picasso and the playwright Federico García Lorca (even naming his own son after the to-be-murdered gay Spanish writer), he never totally tapped into his own human oil well. Such was not the case with George Balanchine, who said yes to the right man at the right time, in consequence fulfilling his own strategies. Concurrently, Balanchine became the instrument of Kirstein's personal Napoleonic ambitions.

So with Lincoln Kirstein's moral and monetary support, the New York City Ballet eventually became a reality, opening January 18, 1949 at The New York City Center of Music and Drama, located at 131 West 55th Street. The dream was no longer in semi-hibernation. That first season was made possible because of a masterful deal, negotiated by Mr. Kirstein, to rent the City Center of Music and Drama from the city of New York. The theatre had formerly been used by the Fraternal Order of Free Masons, and was earlier named the Mecca Temple.

Having been hit by hard times, it was in foreclosure due to default in taxes. Then and now owned by the city of New York, it was considered a white elephant by Mayor Fiorello LaGuardia. This was the mayor who, when all of New York City's newspapers went on strike, read the comics on the radio to the children of the city. The world could grind to a halt, but the children had to know what was happening to their favorites, Dick Tracy and Little Orphan Annie!

The City Center held 2,750 people with comfortable orchestra and balcony seating. There was a sufficiently ample stage and a full and very deep orchestra pit with room for more then 50 musicians. Before the poetic, there must be the practical, so we were fortunate to be provided with enough dressing rooms, wardrobe rooms for our costumes and rehearsal rooms.

In this home away from home, there was room to hang scenery above the stage, a boon for the technicians. There were also lots of secret staircases that we were told were off limits to us. Naturally, our curiosity was piqued by such instructions. And so, when we felt we weren't being spied upon, we explored. But it was easy to get lost in the labyrinth of passageways when investigating the forbidden stairs. In one of the windowless rooms we managed to enter, we, the younger dancers, looked up to see mysterious symbols all over the ceiling. The concealed rooms somehow had vibrations and if the walls could talk, we felt they'd have some stories to tell, religious, political or even paranormal.

At the close of the first short season of the New York City Ballet at that theatre, their deficit was $47,000. Lincoln Kirstein paid the amount, in full, from his private funds, although no written agreement existed compelling him to do so. He was a man of honor, his word his bond.

His love for ballet and unfailing determination to bring classical ballet to the American public knew no limits. The following season, the city agreed to rent the theatre to the company for one dollar a year. That symbolic pittance guaranteed the New York City Ballet a home, and George Balanchine the opportunity to flourish.

At the School of American Ballet, Mr. Balanchine occasionally visited classes to see the progress of his students. Sometimes he invited the most promising to join his new ballet company. There were no auditions in those days, but one was invited simply by being observed by Mr. B while taking their usual ballet class. The school was created to be a supplier of dancers, some of whom later became members of the company. It was cutthroat competition and those who weren't accepted, the vast majority, shed bitter tears, some of them too young to overcome such early disappointment. So then and there they stopped dancing.

I was in Pierre Vladimirov's class in mid-October of 1949 and it was during the *adage* section of the class when Mr. B entered the large ballet studio. As soon as I saw him I felt weak and full of apprehension. Would I be able to keep my balance? Was he looking for a new member of the company? Could he possibly choose me? Thankfully, I didn't wobble during the excruciatingly slow combination. Out of the corner of my eye I could see Mr. B talking to Mr. Vladimirov while looking directly at me.

The goal was to look classical, elegant, and ethereal and fuse with the sublimely beautiful strains of our Chopin piano accompaniment. I was in something of a panic thinking of what would happen if I lost my balance or tottered. Despite my frightened thoughts, I managed to smoothly execute the *adage*, a test for coordination, control, fluidity, line, balance and musicality.

All the time, I could feel Mr. B's all-seeing eyes on me and in spite of wanting to note his expression as a telltale sign of my future, I ordered myself to avert his gaze. Don't look at him, I commanded myself. Just dance! He could scrutinize me, but under no circumstances could I scrutinize him back. Float, soar, elevate, even levitate, just surrender to the out-of-this-world music and to the eyes of Mr B, whose on the spot choices could determine one's life course.

Mr. B had another conversation in whispers with Mr. Vladimirov, who, I saw at quick glance, was nodding his head! Mr. B left the classroom. The rest of the class went by in a blur. I could think of nothing but the remote possibility that I might, God willing, be the chosen one! It is no simple task to pirouette while praying to the Almighty!

When the class concluded and the usual applause in appreciation for the revered teacher subsided, I started to leave for the dressing room and there was Mr. B blocking the narrow doorway! He reached out to me, took my hand, looked penetratingly into my eyes and said, "Barbara, do you want to dance for me?" Beaming, no, radiant, no, incandescent, I replied, "Yes", and he responded in his Russian/American English, "Good, you will be member of company," and walked away.

At that moment, my mother came out of the classroom after Mr. B had already disappeared. I told her what had happened and she began to cry, streaming tears that signified the vindication of her decision to leave, albeit not permanently, her Oklahoma home and devoted husband. Hers were tears of relief, joy and gratitude.

I was the only girl chosen from the school to become a member of the company for that fall season and Jacques d'Amboise was the only boy. I was 14 years old and he was 15.

That same afternoon, two of the older corps de ballet girls were assigned to take me into the smallest studio where they started to teach me the beginning of Mozart's *Symphonie Concertante*, to be performed in the coming fall season at the City Center. As the date was November 23, 1949, the opening was just a few weeks away. The two girls sang the Mozart score and demonstrated the steps without benefit of a piano, teaching me almost the entire ballet that same afternoon. They were under pressure, too, for Mr. B had entrusted them with breaking me in, so to speak. They daren't disappoint him!

Painstakingly helpful as they were that day, within a very short time, as my dancing moved from strength to strength, jealousy reared its dangerous head. Soon, in America and then in Europe, those same two ambitious corps de ballet girls, pretending friendship, but masking hostility, waited for or invented opportunities to derail me.

The opening date had arrived and I kept my fingers crossed that I was ready for my public trial by fire. Mr. B had put me at the front of a line of eight corps de ballet dancers on the right side of the stage, to be in place when the curtains opened. I had to be letter perfect and confident from within, because it would not be possible to rely on watching another dancer to give a clue about what steps were next. Stay afloat or go under!

It had been impressed upon me how important it was for every dancer to memorize the score of each of the ballets we were to dance. I was also humbled by Mr. B's trust in me and my ability to learn quickly. There is, with the maestro's choreography, almost a move for every note in the score, so when you learn the music concurrently you learn the steps. Resultantly, the music tells you what to do. There were lots and lots of *battements tendus* with variations of arm movements. Mr. B stuck his head in the studio, took a quick peek and smiled saying, "This is good", then vanished as quickly as he had appeared.

I was struck by the masterful choreography for the corps de ballet. During a short break, when I inquired as to how I would find out when rehearsals took place, I was informed that the daily schedules and the names of the people who were to participate were posted on the school bulletin board at the close of each day.

It then came as a wonderful surprise to find out that we would be paid. I did not even think about those details when Mr. B's invitation came. In actual fact, I was so happy to be a member of the company, I would eagerly have paid *them!* It was also necessary for me to sign a contract and because I was only fourteen years old, I needed a work permit from the city of New York and written permission from both parents in order to accept Mr. B's invitation. After a stressful few days, I was able to sign the contract!

Betty Cage, the business manager of the company, took care of so many of those mundane, prosaic yet all-important details, and in such a collected way. Olive- skinned, with black hair and a slight lisp, she was, I would venture to guess, in her mid-forties. Always dressed very conservatively, she diverted attention from herself to the task at hand. At her fingertips, she seemed always to have an alternative plan B in case plan A fell through.

Through her office door, the inner sanctum of decisions, one could sometimes hear the shrill shouting demands of Melissa Hayden, the raucous responses of Nora Kaye, or the latest rage of Jerry Robbins, the impositional threesome who were laws unto themselves. Despite such endless pressures thrust upon her, Betty remained unflappable, though heaven only knows what went on in that put-upon woman's mind. It was an unenviable job facilitating the smooth running of the company, a hotbed of tension, temperament, talent and, as I was to discover before long, intrigue.

Now in 2011, as I have passed the milestone birthday of 75, looking back through the decades and reflecting on all of the many high points in my life, that invitation of so few words from Mr B stands out as the happiest moment of my early life! A bright future lay before me, so did I wholeheartedly believe, and why not, when barely into my teens, I was chosen by the very heir to Marius Petipa, Lev Ivanov and Michel Fokine, George Balanchine himself, to be the youngest dancer in his New York City Ballet.

Rehearsals were held at all hours to prepare for the fall season. Mr B was creative, energetic and enthusiastic about everything. The repertoire was growing with two new ballets scheduled to be given; *Bourrée Fantasque*, by Mr. B with delightful Chabrier music and costumes by Karinska was a soaring hit; the other, *Ondine*, by William Dollar to Vivaldi music, a deadweight flop.

The impact of George Balanchine inevitably spawned a small battalion of imitators, or to be more diplomatic, followers, choreographers such as William Dollar, John Taras, Todd Bolender and Lew Christensen. But hard as they tried, they paled into comparison next to the original. Looking back in history, the reverse sometimes took place. For example, the Irish composer John Field preceded Chopin, but the Polish composer having already heard John Field, took the quality of his music further and far beyond. As did Shakespeare, possibly the most successful plagiarist in history, who took now unknown plays that had preceded him to an unheard-of and stratospheric level. The American contingent of Balanchine-influenced choreographers, though of varying degrees of attainment, never did put Mr. B out of business. They remained minor planets orbiting around his all-powerful sun.

Now, what was on everyone's mind was the history about to be made, for soon there would be the much-anticipated *Firebird* with choreography by Mr. B. and music by Igor Stravinsky. As if that collaboration wasn't sufficient reason for excitement, the scenery aı costumes would be by the celebrated Marc Chagall. Decades later, Mr. Chagall would design the ceiling of the Paris Opera House.

Poor Michel Fokine. His original production with Tamara Karsavina as the captured and captive firebird was about to take a back seat to his successor's presentation. Ballet is not written in stone. There have been so many subsequent versions of *Firebird*, several retaining only the title.

The other scheduled works were *Symphonie Concertante*, choreographed by Mr. B to Mozart's *Symphonie Concertante in E Flat*; *Symphony in C*, one of Mr B's masterworks, with music by Georges Bizet; *Mother Goose Suite*, choreographed by Todd Bolender with music by Maurice Ravel; *Orpheus*, another Balanchine/Stravinsky collaboration with scenery and costumes by the noted sculptor Isamu Noguchi; and Lew Christensen's *Jinx* with music by one of England's most eminent composers, Sir Benjamin Britten.

Mr. Balanchine's sea of creativity was at high tide with his revival of his *Serenade* to music by Tchaikovsky. I danced in nine of the ten ballets presented that season, with rehearsal time to learn all of them in less than a month!

My mother was allowed to watch every rehearsal and ballet class. She was my best friend and constant companion. There was no time for social events or anything except ballet, ballet and more ballet, an overdose to be sure, and though addictive, not lethal. That is, unless oft-broken hearts could be considered fatal.

That life suited me just fine. School work was sandwiched in as quickly as possible between rehearsals and late at night, then to be delivered to the School for Young Professionals every Friday.

Dance was the sole focus in my life and was all-consuming. I lived in the rehearsal studio, the ballet classroom, and on the stage. That was a normal pattern for me and I, and many of the young talented dancers, committed ourselves, exclusively, to that life.

Just as the maidens whose hearts were ripped out in sacrifices on the top of the Pyramid of the Sun, we also were sacrificial, but self-sacrificial, giving our hearts, not to appease the path of the sun in ancient Mexico, but to please George Balanchine. We also bled, if not from the heart as in Teotihuacán, then from the feet, and we willingly, no, joyfully, underwent that ritual for as long as we could do justice to the master's vision.

To ensure our improvement, we related to each Balanchine class with a sense of marked occasion. To do justice to his combinations, it was very important to be ready and in high gear for his lessons, so I was always warmed up before he entered the studio. The barre work he gave was brief and insufficient to give me a real preparation for the very challenging, innovative and frankly odd combinations we would be asked to do for the center work.

Everyone is different but I felt I required more barre work than he gave us in order to be warmed up. Looking back, I believe giving a barre was a bore for Mr. B., as it was for Michel Fokine who let his dancers do their own barre, then joined them for the center. Impatient, Mr. B dispensed with barre work in a hurry. Though, with hindsight, looking at the roll call of the New York City Ballet wounded, his barre was too brief for protecting overworked joints and tendons.

The center first consisted of an *adage* section, and even though it was a ballet class, he insisted that the girls wear *pointe* slippers. This command was issued in order to enhance our ability to balance in extra slow movements while wearing them, and also to be able to land softly from jumps despite the clunky toe shoes.

I have seen many a performance ruined by the thundering sound of *pointe* slippers pounding the floor, more like a herd of elephants than a pride of lions. One must learn to land silently while wearing those blocked pink-satined torture chambers, no easy task since the toes of *pointe* slippers are very hard and the shank is narrow with stiffened leather.

Instead of *développé* in all positions he would have us do a *promenade* in *à la seconde* while leaning away from the leg, just enough divergence from the pure classical to be risky. Without wearing ballet slippers, I was unable to grip the floor as easily as I could if I had been. Still, we strove to overcome the body's limitations, for he wanted us to expand the capabilities of the fragile human frame.

Our jumping combinations were fast with quick *jetés, brisé volé, entrechat-quatre* and *entrechat-six* interspersed and repeated at least 32 times, then to test your stamina to the limit, once again. The turns were almost always a complicated combination, not just *piqué* turns across the floor, but perhaps one single *saut de basque*, one double *saut de basque* and then *chaîné* turns, repeating the combination at top speed traveling across the floor in a diagonal line. For good measure, he might add four *emboîté* turns and a triple pirouette traveling across the room, always to the right and to the left!

The big jumps, the *grand allégro*, were often given for us to explore our facility to land in unorthodox positions, or to take off in a non-academic way. Always these *enchaînements* were varied. In fact, I do not remember any consistency, for he used the class to experiment with new ideas for something he was choreographing at the moment.

He never commented except to say "Again", so it was hard to deduce what he was thinking. No appreciation was ever in evidence, just a demonstration of what he wanted and then we were asked to repeat each combination twice.

Those classes were exhausting, very difficult and thrilling all at the same time! I did really enjoy them. The classes were innovative, never boring and with wonderful music to lift you. Often he would lean over looking at your feet and clap his hands as fast as he could, meaning to go faster and faster! He would say things like, "Like light-ning" or "You must grow" when in an adagio, and of course when we were jumping he kept urging us to jump "Higher, higher" and never to make a sound when landing. We were all willing to work until we dropped. He commanded our respect, moreover our love, for his genius shone forth even while teaching class.

Those extraordinary lessons, as taught by George Balanchine, with the near symphonic accompaniment of the lone pianist, remain a yardstick for me in uplifting ballet class music. Never once did I, in my dancing years, participate in a class accompanied by canned music, as is often the case nowadays, nor did I ever have to plod through a ballet class with a lifeless pianist providing prosaic, nonde-script sounds. Without music from the spheres, where, otherwise, is that vital and most elusive ingredient – inspiration?

I must have been improving, for Mr. B gave me a demi-soloist part in the second movement of *Symphony in C.* My partner was to be Robert Barnett, now the Artistic Director Emeritus of the Atlanta Civic Ballet which he co-founded with his wife, Virginia Rich, also a former dancer with the company.

Mr. B wanted the many *bourrées* to be "as if not touching ground" and I did my best to seem to levitate to the serene Bizet music. To think that Bizet wrote that music at the age of only 17!

When coaching us, Mr. B would say, "Try hard as you can, then try little bit more". That message has come home to me again and again as I have lived my life. It seems that sometimes you are required to give your all, and then just a little bit more, to survive the treacherous slopes that sooner or later most of us will encounter.

Following that first performance, I received a charming little nosegay of pink sweetheart roses from my teacher, Muriel Stuart, who had joined Anna Pavlova's company at the age of 13, as I had joined Balanchine's company just fractionally older. I kept the faded and withered petals with me at my dressing table for all of the years I danced with the company. They were a reminder of Miss Stuart, the person who believed in me sufficiently to have me accepted into the School of American Ballet. She was later to present me with her defining book, *The Classic Ballet*, with the inscription:

Darling Barbara,
A lovely person and a most gifted dancer.
My love and interest always,
Muriel Stuart, 1952

There was great anticipation over the new Balanchine-Stravinsky *Firebird* to be premiered that season. In love with America and all things American, Mr B had married the most American dancer of them all, Maria Tallchief, great-granddaughter of Chief Peter Bigheart, a full-blooded Osage Indian chief. It was, in fact, Chief Bigheart who had been sent to Washington to successfully negotiate the tax-free oil and mineral rights of the over 2,000 members of the Osage tribe. The bonanza in full force, over 600 acres of Oklahoma land were also allocated to each and every member.

Maria's mother, of early covered wagon, pioneer Irish and Scottish heritage, determinedly moved the family to California in order to further the ballet training of her talented daughters, Maria and Marjorie. Along the route, Maria, to minimize and deflect the inevitable ethnic bullying in high school, connected Tall to Chief, thus becoming Tallchief.

Maria was now Balanchine's newest muse. She surely had to be aware that their marriage was not to be for life, but only, as with Picasso and his muses, for an intense period of creativity. Yet such was the magnitude of Balanchine's particular magnetism, that almost all of his ex-wives and mistresses stayed faithful to his memory, even after his death.

On June 29th, 1953, in a highly publicized ceremony to mark the event, Maria had become Osage Indian royalty, her newly acquired title, Princess Wa Xthe-Thonba, bestowed upon her by virtue of her regal ancestral roots and her elevated status in the international ballet world. Her father, Alexander Joseph Tall Chief, aptly named, was a towering figure, well over six feet tall. When I saw him backstage, I was struck at once by his uncanny resemblance to the Indian on the buffalo nickel. My dad, who had also seen Maria's father, was equally taken by the striking similarity of Maria's father to the iconic face on the coin. Mr. Tall Chief, not only sired two famous ballerinas, he also distinguished himself politically, for he served several terms as Mayor of Fairfax.

Mr. B was very proud, when in Oklahoma to visit Maria's family, he was made an honorary member of the Osage tribe. To commemorate that special occasion, Maria's cousin, Helene, had presented Mr. B with an Osage Indian bracelet. Made of heavy Indian silver, that is, with nickel added to give the bracelet more strength, it was highlighted by a large turquoise stone in the center.

Long after his union with Maria had gone the way of all flesh, Mr. B wore this piece of jewelry, resonating with pre-colonial American history. Even as he was breathing his last on the hospital deathbed, as visitors will attest, he still wore that Osage tribal gift. Much to Maria's regret, that bracelet that she had wanted to retrieve for sentimental value, somehow mysteriously disappeared in the hospital and was never recovered.

Well, if some patients can be molested and even raped, robbing the dead or dying takes only the light fingers of some passing nighttime orderly. No corpse, no matter how distinguished when alive, can file a posthumous complaint with officialdom.

But in 1949, Mr. B was in fine health. Dance for him was life, and life, for him, was the dance. I was fortunate enough to watch him coaching Maria for her solo variation in *Firebird*, and he was saying over and over again, "Like diamond, like diamond!" And did she ever shimmer, glimmer and dazzle! On the opening night, Maria executed an astonishingly swift series of *chaîné* turns interspersed with *saut de basque*, spraying gold dust as she flew in a whirling blur before stopping suspended in *arabesque*. As Maria held her incredible balance, Frank Moncion, as Prince Ivan, ran from the opposite side of the stage to capture her. Then followed the rhapsodic pas deux of the hunter and mystical bird of fire, certainly one of the most mesmeric duets in all the world of ballet.

I think, though it is impossible to quantify, that Maria's Native American origins facilitated her intuitive assimilation of the role, for fire and birds are interwoven in the sacred rituals of her ancestry. With Maria's blazing interpretation, we were transported into the distant land of Russian myth and fairy tales.

Mr. B had located the owner of the original scenery and costumes from a Paris production done years before. Hand-painted by Marc Chagall himself, they belonged to Sol Hurok, the all-powerful impresario, who had managed Fedor Chaliapin, Anna Pavlova, Isadora Duncan, Carmen Amaya, Vicente Escudero and a subsequent galaxy of the finest ballet and opera stars right up unto the one and only Maria Callas.

The scenery and costumes Mr. B wanted had been in storage in the moldy basement of the Champs Elysée Theatre in Paris for years. Mr. Balanchine went to see Sol Hurok and asked if the New York City Ballet could buy them. When asked how much they could pay, Balanchine was uncertain as how much to offer, so asked Morton Baum to call Mr. Hurok the following day.

Mr Hurok had paid artist Marc Chagall $25,000 for them. Mr. Baum, ever conscious of the company's restricted budget, offered a relatively paltry $4,000. Mr. Hurok, known for driving a hard bargain, for whatever his reasons, chose to let Mr. Baum off lightly. So the purchase was completed for $4,250 and the way was now clear for Mr. B to present his new version of *Firebird*.

I was on stage when the delivery of the precious works of art were unfurled. The smell of mildew permeated the entire theatre and the backdrop was damp with signs of mold. The stagehands, conscious of handling ballet history, carefully hung the enormous paintings. One was to be hung in front of the main curtain during the overture, the second was to be seen as a backdrop for the wedding scene at the close of the ballet.

My part in the ballet was as one of the monsters. In fact, I was the first monster to leap on stage and harass the Prince. One of the only verbal compliments I remember receiving from Mr. B, besides a smile and an occasional comment, "Better", was at the dress rehearsal of *Firebird*. In front of the full cast of dancers and orchestra, Mr. B pointed directly at me and exclaimed, "Barbara is best monster!"

Mr. B rarely ever offered any encouragement; one had to rely only on looks of approval and try to tune in to his thoughts so as to guess if he might be pleased. That I had been singled out as his "best monster" was praise, indeed! So did I perceive it as I continued to move as grotesquely as possible.

I had the privilege of wearing the famous hand-painted Chagall horse head over my own head. Yes, I thought of it as a privilege as it topped my baggy, gray cotton body suit. Thus outfitted, instead of complaining that I could hardly see or breathe in that stifling equine costume, I thought of the horse head as a kind of weighted halo painted by the superb artist that Marc Chagall undisputedly was. Flanked by greatness, I threw myself into the weird and wonderful moves with all my heart, hell-bent on scaring Prince Ivan out of his wits!

The legendary composer of *The Firebird*, Igor Stravinsky, was a lifelong friend of Mr. B and, in 1949, came to many of the rehearsals, both for his *Orpheus* and *Firebird*. A shy and introverted little man, the maestro and Mr. B would arrive in the studio together, both smoking incessantly and speaking in animated Russian. If only I could have understood that language!

Mr. Stravinsky wore thick, dark-rimmed round glasses perched halfway down his beaked nose, made more prominent by a slightly receding chin. He was always hunched over, a sign of future osteoporosis, and that made him look shorter than he actually was. At the *Orpheus* rehearsal, I was one of ten furies, writhing in agony in the lower depths of Hades. In *Firebird*, I was one of the menacing monsters. At both of the rehearsals, Mr. Stravinsky hovered over Kolya at the piano, whom he also knew from their shared Diaghilev Ballets Russes period. Intense and radiating energy, he would, at times, move Kolya over on the piano bench and play a passage of his own music, demonstrating the rhythm and emphasis he wanted.

One of the few times I heard the maestro speak English was after one of the long and arduous rehearsals. The maestro said to Mr. B, "Let's go out and get drunk." A little shared tipple would be a momentary refuge from the sounds and movements that endlessly poured forth from their collective brains.

All of us were thrilled when at the first *Orpheus* rehearsal, and again at the first *Firebird* rehearsal, Maestro Stravinsky shook hands with every dancer in the studio, even insignificant furies and monsters such as myself. While cordially shaking hands, he made a courtly bow. This greeting ritual included my mom, who was always on the bench watching in rapt attentiveness.

There she was, a long way from her suburban life in Oklahoma with its still audible echoes of gun-toting cowboys and peace-pipe smoking Indians. Now she was shaking the hand of the composer of such masterpieces as *Petrouchka, Sacre du Printemps, Apollo, Orpheus, Agon* and, of course, *Firebird*.

And there I was, dancing feet away from Igor Stravinsky as he played his own frisson-filled music at the piano, then shaking the hand of the very man who had penned that music, the composer who had been the creative soul mate of impresario Serge Diaghilev, among whose patrons was Misia Sert, who as a child had played the piano for Franz Liszt. How could I be unaware that I was hobnobbing with immortality?

That evening, my mother had very exciting news to relay to my father on the phone in Oklahoma, who, out on a limb financially due to his unswerving belief in me, and deprived of the proximity of his family, experienced vicariously the spine-tingling milieu in which his distant wife and daughter were now immersed.

The rehearsal period ending, our season had begun. Each time Maestro Stravinsky conducted the orchestra, there was a special sense of occasion, for it was an artistic event of major importance. The theatre was always sold out, since Stravinsky was long a monumental and historical figure. When he conducted, he cast a spell on one and all, the musicians, the dancers and the audience themselves.

I was privileged to dance so many times under his baton, including the lead in his ballet *Card Game*. Today, in 2011, it is exactly one hundred years since Igor Stravinsky conducted his ballet *Petrouchka* with his friend and colleague Vaslav Nijinsky in the title role! To think that I had been spiritually and musically linked with such an artist whose career goes back a full century, ten tumultuous decades of life and art, that incredible time span boggles my mind.

CHAPTER SIX

DANCING FOR LEONARD BERNSTEIN

Leonard Bernstein composed the score for *The Age of Anxiety*, a ballet commissioned by Lincoln Kirstein to be choreographed by Jerome Robbins for the forthcoming London season. Lenny, as everyone called him then before he became the principal conductor of the New York Philharmonic, and Jerome Robbins would arrive for rehearsals together each morning, arm in arm, but their free arms carrying coffee in those awful paper cups that got soggy if you didn't drink the hot liquid quickly enough. They were purchased from the drug store at 59th Street and Madison Ave, conveniently below the School of American Ballet where we rehearsed.

Robbins' subdued little dog scampered along behind him (it never wagged its tail) and then sat on the bench to watch the proceedings. Bernstein played for our rehearsals almost every day for the three weeks prior to the London opening, always wearing a bright red turtleneck sweater, the uniform of a gay man in the 1950s. Robbins also wore a fire-engine red turtleneck, possibly also for its political symbolism. For, as alluded to earlier, he was a card-carrying member of the Communist party, an association that was going to get him into a tsunami of trouble, as well as sweep away those unfortunate enough to have been his so-called friends and colleagues.

"Kids, take your places," Robbins would command. "Lenny, begin." Then Robbins would impatiently pounce on him, "Play faster, cut some measures here, I don't like the rhythm in this passage, this doesn't sound like an iron filing being drawn to a magnet!" That was the image he dredged out constantly to get us to respond to his inarticulate concept.

One after another, the musical change demands were barked out to Bernstein until the composer had had enough of Robbins hacking his creation to smithereens and would slam down the piano cover and stand up and start to walk out. All of us held our breath, for who knew what would happen next?

Robbins would go to Bernstein, try to soothe him somewhat, whisper quietly in his ear, then try to get him to smile. One could only wonder what kind of promises he was making to his Lenny to turn him from *agitato* to *legato*. Jerry and Lenny. Lenny and Jerry. Romeo and Romeo. Perhaps they got the idea of their future *West Side Story* from their own rocky romance. They called each other names and fought like crazy, always in front of others, but it didn't seem to inhibit them at all. When the rehearsal ended, with the dog tucked under Robbins' arm, the two of them always left together, looking at each other with the glow of undiminished love in their eyes.

I was surprised to see that Jerome Robbins showed any capacity at all to express affection, because I had been convinced by his prior behavior that he was only capable of relating heartlessly to others. Someone, Lenny Bernstein, had actually been a rehabilitative influence on him, albeit for a very brief period, all the while taking an alarming amount of abuse from him. We all observed the roller-coaster rise and fall of their union, knowing it would inexorably derail. And, of course, it did, Lenny having no shortage of ambitious young men, straight and gay, to choose from. His later love life, with both his wife and lovers, was to be strewn with broken glass, for even people with the widest choices inevitably gravitate towards the most wounding and destructive.

What the maestro did in his personal life left many to wag reproving fingers at him. Be that as it may, when Lenny Bernstein conducted, he could not be faulted. That is, if you could overlook his bouncing up and down on the podium like a jumping jack to further draw attention to himself. Despite his exhibitionist antics, when he wielded his baton, the high-voltage current of his personality transmitted itself to each member of the orchestra, charging their every nerve ending. Resultantly, to dance under his baton, as we often did in New York, was to be infused with an extraordinary aliveness.

As for the other half of the duo, when did I first catch sight of Jerome Robbins, I asked myself? It must have been during one of Oboukhov's classes when, as luck would have it, he was standing right next to me at the barre. To be in an Oboukhov class was to have entered a temple of sorts, thus you behaved accordingly. Not Robbins, though. Finding the class too demanding, unable to even get into a correct fifth position, he walked out early when it was de rigeur to finish a lesson no matter how tired one may have been. If Oboukhov took offense, he turned a blind eye, for Robbins had a clout about him that allowed him to bend, stretch and break the rules.

As a dancer, and I use the word loosely, his late and haphazard training precluded the acquisition of any technique. He lacked, in consequence, pirouettes, elevation, pointed feet and turn out, thus unequivocally ill-suited for any of Mr. B's choreography. But ill-suited or not, Robbins still wanted to dance. So the red carpet was laid down in front of him so that Mr. B had to use all of his expertise to choreographically camouflage, thereby making Robbins look like he was actually dancing when he wasn't. But if one found his dancing unpalatable to watch, one could always avert one's gaze. Such could not be the case when he chose you to dance in one of his ballets.

After another fraught *Age of Anxiety* rehearsal contending with Robbins' general rudeness, it entered my mind that he was contending with some sort of personality disorder. "Oh, Jerry's a genius," you would hear from those who didn't have to work with him, as if existing in that rarified category exonerated one from unacceptable behavior.

Unable to solve the riddle of his fear-inducing personality, I questioned myself as to why he continued to have me dance in his ballets. Did I serve as a mood stabilizer, or was he curious to see how much I could withstand, like those lunatic contestants who remain in a sizzling Finnish sauna until one of them is severely burned or dies?

My ability to endure was put to the test one late afternoon when I was called in to a private rehearsal for Patricia Wilde, one of the principal dancers of the company. Patty was a superb and very experienced dancer with an effortless elevation. She was, as the public would attest, one of the stars of the company.

I was surprised to be called into the rehearsal when this was supposed to be Patty's solo time with Robbins. I already had my own part in the ballet and, par for the course, was also to understudy all the other ensemble dancers, both male and female. When I entered the studio, Patty was already there in the center of the room, moving her body in readiness for the rehearsal to follow. I went to the barre and started doing some *battements tendu* to warm up a bit.

Then Robbins walked in and announced to us that I was to under-study Patty and learn the entire part with her! This was not the protocol we were used to and we furtively looked at each other with a question-ing glance. I liked Patty personally and admired the polished way she danced. There was no question that she was perfect for the part he wanted her to do. She was to be some sort of dominating force, leading a mass of faceless dancers (we were wearing fencing masks) who were to look like iron filings being drawn to a magnet. The magnet was, if one could decipher Robbins' muddled description, a god of some sort on stilts, Eddie Bigelow. Soon after we started, Robbins, in his rapidly accelerating frustration, became aggressive towards me.

In order to learn the demanding steps he was showing Patty, I was standing well in back of her copying the movements he demonstrated. This is the way understudies learn a role. From one second to the next, Robbins shouted for me to sit down, complaining that I was a distrac-tion and that he couldn't continue with Patty if I was behind her. So I quickly sat down on a chair at the side of the studio, still aware that I was to learn her steps from that disadvantaged perspective.

While drilling Patty, he yelled at her without respite, changing everything over and over again. Then, in a climactic burst of temper he shouted, "Let Bocher do it".

Patty was crushed but tried not to show it. Nerve-wracked, I got up from the chair and did what I thought was his latest version, relieved that at least I remembered the steps, for it is very difficult to learn anything while sitting down. Determined to please him, I did the requested passage repeatedly, I can't recall how many times, but still he wasn't satisfied, screaming at me that I wasn't tough enough!

"Get out of the way," he commanded, then brought poor Patty back to renew his shameful treatment. This wasn't so much a rehearsal as it was an ordeal, an inexplicable punishment inflicted on both of us. And we suffered, both of us on the verge of exhaustion and near tears when he finally stopped abruptly and raged, "Get out, get out, you are no good!" There were several more rehearsals like that before the ballet neared its completion.

Actually, Robbins wanted Melissa Hayden for Patty's role, but Milly, no slouch in the stand-up-for-yourself department, was in no mood to put up with Jerry's flak, nor to play second fiddle to Tanaquil

LeClercq who had been given the principal female part. Besides which, Milly was rehearsing Bill Dollar's new ballet for her, *The Duel*, due to be premiered February 26th, 1950, just two days before *Age of Anxiety*. Knowing which side her bread was buttered on, Milly chose to focus only on that. A wise decision as it turned out, for her success in *The Duel* was to catapult her, along with Nora Kaye, as the stellar dramatic attraction of the New York City Ballet.

In the meanwhile, my head pounding with tension from the *Age of Anxiety* rehearsals, I made the difficult decision to take the bull by the horns and report what was happening to Mr. B himself. Only a quiet desperation could have pushed me to take this drastic step. Bracing myself, I approached Mr. B whose facial tick seemed to move into high gear when he could see by my body language that I was about to unfold some disagreeable news.

With tears welling up in my eyes, for I was trying not to cry, I told him that I didn't know how much longer I could take Robbins' bullying treatment of me, first in *The Cage* rehearsals, and now in *Age of Anxiety*.

"Do not worry, Barbara," he advised. "You remind him of old girlfriend." As if that comparison was going to wipe the slate clean! Nevertheless, I thanked him for listening, then was left totally in the dark as to how his comment was supposed to alleviate the situation. Now the burden was even heavier, for I felt embarrassed that I had interrupted the normally unimpeded flow of Mr. B's cascading thoughts. Why did I have to muddy his pure and crystalline stream of images?

So it was back to the *Age of Anxiety* rehearsals. I said a silent prayer that I would never have to dance Patty's part! Unfortunately, my silent prayer was to go unanswered, for I was indeed to dance the opening at the Royal Opera House in London. Patty had been so overworked that she became injured, no surprise to anyone since the muscles can take just so much maltreatment, not to mention the nerve endings.

I had to step in, dreading every step, for Robbins, whom I was deathly afraid of, loomed large in the wings as he stared at the proceedings, and Bernstein, himself, conducted! I had no fear whatsoever of either the critics, the audience, or Leonard Bernstein, only Robbins!

To this day, I don't understand how Robbins' behavior, witnessed by so many for so long, could have been overlooked, thereby turning the School of American Ballet studios into an early Guantanamo Bay. And I, at only 14 years of age, was the youngest inmate. Was the administration afraid that if you shook the slot machine that was Robbins, it would cease to belch cherried jackpots?

It was transparently clear when Robbins' irritation began to escalate into anger, then to fury. It always started during one of his dry periods, of which there were many. He would stare at the floor for an uncomfortably long period, then he would begin making little circles on the floor with his toe. Since he always wore tennis shoes, they would squeak when he would make the circles. When we heard this warning bell sound, we knew that a sudden attack was imminent, like a thunderstorm that just drops out of the angry skies. I used to studiously avoid making eye contact with him during those all too familiar preliminaries, because it could be you if your eyes were by accident to meet.

"Why isn't there any air in here?" he would whine, or "You useless dancers are lame, crippled, you just don't get it!" His punishing appetite insatiable, he switched his harassment to Roy Tobias, a very gifted, popular and sensitive young dancer. "You call yourself a dancer?" he sneered, "Shit you are! You're just plain dumb and clumsy! Why can't you learn one simple thing? I'm taking you out of the ballet!"

With this kind of public tongue-lashing, and you never really got used to it, Roy had his principal role in *Age of Anxiety* taken away from him about four times during the rehearsal period. Then, in an unexpected decision, Robbins, himself, replaced Roy at the premiere, though he handed back the role to him for the rest of the performances. One of the reasons, I think, Robbins tore into Roy so relentlessly was because Roy was perfectly at home with being gay, whereas Robbins detested his own sexual temperament.

Could Robbins also have been sexually attracted to Roy, a very good-looking boy, and anticipating rejection, turned his desire into persecution? Later on, Roy justifiably had enough, moved far away to Japan, converted to Buddhism and lived with his Japanese lover for the rest of his life. I hope the happiness that eluded Roy in New

York was found by him in that far away refuge, that land of distancing Kabuki, Noh and cherry blossoms.

As cryptic and puzzling as Mr. B's response had been to my problem, to rehearse with him was an antidote to Robbins' steady dose of acid. How we all loved the fulfillment of being the instruments for a Balanchine creation. He always treated us with gentleness and awareness. In looking back, I believe that Robbins was jealous of Mr. B because, despite Robbins' screeching and raging, all he could succeed in doing was eliciting our contempt, never our respect. You can fear a despot, but you can't love him.

When Robbins rehearsed his dancers in the theatre, it was his habit to stand very close to the edge of the front of the stage, his back to the audience, sometimes even stretching his Achilles' tendon over the edge. I had more than one fantasy of pushing him off into the orchestra pit, imagining him flailing about in the tympani, an admission I'm not proud to make. Though I didn't go around making a survey, I know that many of the others spoon-fed their own similar daydreams.

Years after I left the company, I read that Robbins had indeed fallen into an orchestra pit. I wasn't at all surprised, for when you dice with fate as often as he did, you're bound to, at least once, come up a loser. Peter Martins, the present director of the New York City Ballet, relates that not one dancer made a move to help him. They all just stood there, silently exulting in his accident, and hoping for the worst.

Perhaps the most telling comment is from that outstanding former black soloist of the New York City Ballet, Mel Tomlinson. I mention his color only to point out that it served as no protection. "If I go to hell, I will not be afraid of the devil, because I have worked with Jerome Robbins."

In the early 1950s, in America, no one ever thought of reporting such brutal treatment to the union, or, in my case, of taking legal action for what is now termed child abuse. I had to tell myself that everything wonderful has its price, and the price I had to pay for dancing for the greatest choreographic genius of the 20th century, George Balanchine, was to withstand the sadism of Jerome Robbins.

I was raised a Christian and as such we are instructed to forgive our enemies. For years, I was bothered by the fact that, try as I might, I could not forgive Jerome Robbins for terminating my most blossoming career. It was strange, as was the rest of his convoluted personality, because he kept on casting me in his ballets. Though he may well have liked my reliability, what he liked most of all was the convenience of an underage punching bag. Perhaps he liked both, two for the price of one.

Years later, I finally spoke to a trusted member of the clergy about my inability to forgive Robbins, an inability that had haunted me for so long. My counselor told me that there can be no forgiveness without repentance, an important part of the Christian doctrine. Repentance? There was certainly none forthcoming from such a hateful man. The counselor then told me that, in any case, I didn't have to forgive him, for the almighty God would wrestle with that one.

In the meanwhile, I had to adjust to the roller-coaster ride of working with him. Thankfully, he never did teach a class to the company, for I can only imagine the abundance of new opportunities that giving a class would have offered him to crack his snapping whip. Before his rehearsals, you just saw to it that you were sufficiently warmed up. As you waited for him to begin, he seemed devoid of any ideas, so you just hung about, hoping that he would think of something, anything, so that we wouldn't cool down completely and get stiff. Then when it would seem as if the hands of the clock would rotate to the next half hour with nothing as yet accomplished, Robbins would burst forth with very complex choreography to learn in a hurry.

He was almost always deliberately thumbing his nose at the traditional classical style. That, of course, was his prerogative, though in the New York City Ballet, that was like biting the hand that feeds you. It has to be said, though, that when he was choreographing jazz, some of his steps were actually enjoyable to do. Generally, however, he gave us walking improvisations where he wanted us to convey an attitude, rather than actual choreography as such.

And when he did set down actual choreography, he kept discarding it. It was no easy task to assimilate his constantly changing versions, since his temper fits were disconcerting in the extreme. Only when his rehearsal ended, and I moved to the other studio to work with Mr. B, did I reconnect with a true ballet master, a man who provided movement that was always tinged with magic, never ever mania.

One particular class about to be given by Mr B specially resonates in my memory. Everyone was lined up at the barre awaiting him. Then, making a dramatic and last-minute entrance was the ballerina assoluta of our time, the woman whose dancing first awakened me to the celestial beauty of ballet and whose response to my letter altered forever the course of my young life. And there she was, the star of the Serge Diaghilev Ballets Russes, the Ballet Russe de Monte Carlo, featured in the Anne Bancroft, Shirley MacLaine film, *The Turning Point*, the still stunning Alexandra Danilova.

With her perfectly shaped legs in orchid pink tights and a short pink chiffon practice dress, her hair was coiffed in classical style over the ears ("Ears are rarely beautiful", she is quoted as saying) and drawn back into a fashionable chignon. On or off the stage, she personi-fied and exuded the word *star*. When Mr. B entered the studio and saw her, like a moth to the flame he approached her, his old class-mate from St. Petersburg, and gave her a kiss, saying something to her in Russian. "Choura," he began, the rest of their brief interchange inaudible. She responded with a coquettish hint of a smile distilled through the decades' passing parade of husbands, consorts and lovers. It had been two decades since they had lived together in Paris in the early 1930s, but their bond was still intact.

I was standing near enough to the great ballerina to inhale the fragrance of her heavenly perfume and couldn't help but keep my eye on her spellbinding movements at the barre. There was a majes-tic and even imperious aura about Mme Danilova that I had never before seen, to such a degree, in a studio. She was, it could be said, a czarina in exile, an empress without a crown. During the class, Mr. B was extremely attentive to her, inquiring if she was comfortable with each *enchaînement* he gave. I had never before seen Mr. B defer to any dancer, but it was apparent she elicited a very special kind of respect.

When the class ended, I resolutely called upon the remnants of my nerve, for the lowly acolyte was on the verge of communing with the goddess on high.

"Mme Danilova," in trepidation I went up to her, then managed to say, "my name is Barbara Bocher and I would like to thank you for answering my letter from Oklahoma City."

"Oh yes," she smiled charmingly, "you are the Mainbocher niece. How is your uncle? I knew him in Monte Carlo." She then told me that she was happy to see me already a member of the company and wished me all good fortune. Since I had never mentioned Mainbocher to her, I assume she knew that information from another source, probably her long-standing friend, Mme Dubrovska, who also knew Mainbocher in Monaco.

As circumstances decreed, I never did have the opportunity of a further conversation or any contact with Mme Danilova. Nevertheless, if I had not experienced the imperial grandeur of her magnificent dancing when I was a mere six years old, and had she not answered my plaintive and inquiring fan letter at the age of 12, none of the multifarious events set down in this book, from the sadistic to the sublime, would ever have transpired.

Mme Danilova, though I know that you believe a curtsy to the knee should be reserved exclusively for only God and the Czar, permit me the liberty of such a deep curtsy to you as well. For you were, I am ever and gratefully aware, the radiant lodestar of my young life.

CHAPTER SEVEN

Dancing for Frederic Ashton

Igor Stravinsky and Mr. Balanchine often exchanged animated conversations in Russian that included our company pianist, Nicholas Kopeikine. This gifted man, who was also subjected to the foul temper of Robbins, had been a concert pianist in his youth before he jumped from a train and fled from the oncoming Bolsheviks during the sweeping terror of the Revolution.

Stravinsky, Balanchine and Kopeikine had in common the undiluted memories of the majestic Nevsky Prospekt, with its unforgettable melodies of their idolized Tchaikovsky, and unfading images of the Winter Palace. That massive structure, whose tragic inhabitants were to be bullet-holed and bayoneted in that infamous massacre, reminds posterity that such a disparity of wealth and privilege cannot forever coexist side by side.

Moving ahead just over thirty years–that's all the distance there was back in 1949–the dancers learned their parts for *Firebird* quickly, committing the complex score to memory. At the premiere, the theatre was jammed, overflowing with high expectations. Igor Stravinsky himself conducted, and the original Marc Chagall paintings shone forth after their long seclusion in the musty and dusty Paris catacombs.

The triptych of greatness, comprising George Balanchine, Igor Stravinsky and Marc Chagall turned into a quartet with the dazzling performance of Maria Tallchief in the title role. It was she, at the very pinnacle of the totem pole, who galvanized the public and critics. An unforgettable night with the stage piled high with bouquets, there were 14 curtain calls and applause reverberating long after the house lights were hesitantly turned on.

There was no question that it was *Firebird* with Maria Tallchief that put the New York City Ballet prominently on the map. She made the role undeniably her own and although several dancers have performed it since her retirement, no one could compare with her shattered diamond interpretation and overwhelmingly brilliant technique.

At the premiere. Lincoln Kirstein even managed a smile, an unusual occurrence since he never seemed to alter his dour expression of intense preoccupation. And he had plenty of pressures to weight him down since funding the New York City Ballet lightened the bank balance of even a multi-millionaire such as himself.

I have two indelible memories of Mr. Kirstein. One is of him pacing back and forth backstage like a caged lion, rubbing his thumb into the palm of his hand and looking acutely anxious. The second memory is at the front door of his elegant New York penthouse. He and his wife gave a party for the entire cast of musicians and dancers at the close of the 1950 winter season. Topping the guest list was the chubby and jovial Mayor La Guardia, as well as some well-heeled patrons who had contributed funds to support the ballet.

I rang the bell and Mr. Kirstein opened the door himself dressed very smartly, not in his usual navy blue sailor's jacket. Like many born rich people, Mr. Kirstein liked to dress down, so to speak. But unlike most people, rich or poor, and to my utter amazement, right beside him in the hallway was a larger than life-size painting of him completely nude except for, of all things, boxing gloves! It was such a surprise that I couldn't even speak! That image has never gone away; the nude Mr. Kirstein and the tuxedoed Mr. Kirstein juxtaposed! The portrait image of the naked pugilist, I have to say, was not exactly a Michelangelo David! He really did look better with his clothes on.

I breathed a sigh of relief that my mother was not present that night, for her presence would have contributed to my embarrassment. And hers as well, of that I have no doubt. As for the party itself, I recall nothing of it at all!

Bourrée Fantasque was another new ballet premiered that fall season. The scintillating music by Chabrier made it a delightful ballet to dance. In the first movement, we wore black tutus with shining sequins, all of us manipulating fans and wearing chic hats at a rakish angle. This work was a treat for the Francophiles in the audience, of whom there must have been many.

Our costumes were marvelous creations by Mme Barbara Karinska, a well-known couturier in New York. An imposing figure, she was commandingly tall and colored her hair in luminescent purple. When she attended the theatre, all eyes were riveted upon her, for she also wore fabulous jewelry; a czar's ransom of rings, necklaces, bracelets on each arm, chokers and long drop earrings, huge dark amethysts that could have decorated a Fabergé egg.

The gorgeous Ludmila Tcherina, of *The Red Shoes* and *Tales of Hoffmann* fame, always wore white ensembles, trimmed in white fox, and moved about Paris in her white limousine driven by her white-clad chauffeur. For the final touch, her dog, led on a jeweled leash, was inevitably white. So was Mme Karinska always in one color, in her case, purple, set off by her refulgent amethysts.

Underneath her treasure chest of jewels was a heart of gold, for she offered to do the costumes at cost as a favor to Mr. Balanchine. I remember going to my first fitting. She had me try on a half-finished costume and asked me to do some steps so she could see if it looked right when I moved. Mr. B was there and they stood together, he looking rather amused at my self-conscious adjustments. I was barefooted and barely covered up by the tacked together pieces of fabric, but I did a double-time rendition of my part in the first movement while humming the music. Mme Karinska threw back her head smiling, and said in her distinctive Russian Imperial accent, "The costume has passed the test and so have you, my dear-r-r!" We all laughed!

The last five of the *Bourrée* costumes, mine among them, were delivered by taxi seconds before the overture began with administrator Eddie Bigelow and the bejeweled Mme Karinska carrying them.

I was in the first movement and nervously waiting in the wings, dressed with tights and shoes, hat, choker, and fan, but still in my robe, praying that the costumes would arrive! There was always *War and Peace* styled drama when depending on Mme Karinska. It scared Lincoln Kirstein out of his wits but, with her uncanny timing, she always came through at the last minute, like a galloping white horse to the rescue, no, an empurpled and winning racehorse!

The ballet, with its happy and carefree vibrations, bathed the audience in sheer delight. It was considered by all as another resounding hit, and always a joy to dance. Invoking echoes of La Belle Époque, one could imagine the likes of Liane de Pougy, Mistinguette and the Spanish dancing courtesan to kings, La Belle Otéro.

I was also in *Orpheus*, a fury, writhing around the stage, mopping up the floor with grotesque contortions in Hades. Our stunning ballerina, Maria Tallchief, danced Eurydice with Nicholas Magallanes as the doomed Orpheus; Francisco Moncion, the mysterious Dark Angel; Tanaquil LeClercq as the fierce Leader of the Bacchantes; and Herbert Bliss, the handsome Apollo, rising to the heavens at the ballet's mythic apotheosis. It was another Stravinsky-Balanchine collaboration with the famed designer and sculptor Isamu Noguchi creating the netherworld sets and costumes.

Maestro Stravinsky conducted *Orpheus* once during the season, and under his inspiring baton, we all danced beyond our usual capabilities. How could we do otherwise? When he conducted, we had not only descended to Hades but, concurrently, ascended to an artist's heaven.

But all honeymoons, even the most passionate, have to conclude and this one was nearing its end. The New York City Ballet, after being the recipient of almost unanimous rave reviews, began to be criticized by a few carping ballet critics, among them John Martin of the *New York Times*, for not having any American-looking ballets. He thought there was a preponderance of old school Czarist-styled works.

As a rescue device, Jerome Robbins came to Mr. Kirstein's mind. In my view, even though Lincoln Kirstein was almost never wrong, he was dreadfully remiss in this case. Robbins, only five years earlier, was a corps de ballet dancer in Ballet Theatre who, with the success of *Fancy Free*, went on to establish himself on Broadway as a leading choreographer. To tempt him to join the company, since the salary he would be offered was peanuts to what he usually earned, Mr. Kirstein and Mr. B dangled the twin carrots of soloist as well as choreographer. They thought that with such shows as his 1944 musical, *On The Town*, about three sailors on shore leave, and *Billion Dollar Baby* in 1945, he could inject a little Americana into the post-Russian Imperial repertoire.

What he injected, however, as painfully alluded to earlier in this book, was a virulent poison that infected the entire company. Back in 1950, all of us who had trusted Mr. B now had to withstand the tortured outbursts of a man whose viciousness had pulped many a dancer, both on Broadway, then later terrifyingly in *West Side Story*, and now within the company. Ridicule was one of Jerome Robbins' lesser weapons. I, however, found him not funny, but, conversely, shockingly uncouth and contemptuous. All I wanted was to be far away from him. Unfortunately, it was not to be, for he chose me to appear in his new ballet, *Age of Anxiety*.

Irene Sharaff, the extraordinarily successful Hollywood designer, was commissioned to create the costumes. Among her future roll call of screen credits would be *Cleopatra* with Elizabeth Taylor in 1963, and *Hello, Dolly!* with Barbra Streisand in 1969. I remember at one fitting she paid undue attention to my earlobes. I had an uneasy feeling and was relieved to get away from the fitting, later learning that she was a lesbian. I had never heard the word before until another young dancer in the company, Doris Breckenridge, gave me an explanation. Apparently her ears, too, were some sort of attraction for Ms. Sharaff and, with this awareness, she, too, felt the need to keep her distance.

Nevertheless, my artistic respect for Ms. Sharaff was completely maintained, for she was the queen of Hollywood costume design and merited all her accolades. But I just reasoned that, though I was accustomed to and totally comfortable with gay boys, lesbians were another aspect of diverse sexuality that was new to me. I decided that it would be prudent not to tread water too close to the isle of Lesbos.

Robbins was relatively civil to Maria Tallchief, then Mr. B's wife, for he knew which side his bread was buttered on. I would like to think that had he maltreated that great dancer, she would have scalped him, or the contemporary equivalent. But Maria, a ballerina to the role born, was comfortable with toe shoes, not tomahawks. Be that as it may, he minded his P's and Q's with the respected wife of George Balanchine when he partnered her in the new ballet, *Jones Beach*.

In the ballet, designed to be a crowd-pleaser, we all had to wear sticky bronze body make-up applied with dripping sponges, our costumes various colors of Jantzen bathing suits. The make-up was nearly impossible to remove so the ballet was always last on the program so that we could take the time needed to scour the make-up off with soap and brush.

By this time, Maria was just about a household name in America. The future Hollywood film star, the exceptionally handsome Richard Chamberlain, recounts how, as a teenager, Maria had been his neighbor in California and that once she had thrown a pair of her worn pink toe shoes, replete with frayed ribbons, into the garbage can. Hastily, he retrieved them, took them home and tried them on and began to hobble around on them when his father unexpectedly paraded in. "Take those things off!" his father bellowed.

"They're Maria Tallchief's," his young son protested.

"I don't care if they belonged to Pocahontas, take those goddamn things off!"

Of course, had TV's future Dr. Kildare retrieved Joe DiMaggio's old baseball mitt, his father would have grabbed it and put it on himself!

Jones Beach was to be a collaboration with Mr. B and Robbins working together on the choreography. Mr. B wound up doing nearly all of it, with Robbins' name listed as co-choreographer. Going back in history, in the 1895 production of the revised *Swan Lake*, Marius Petipa, to ease his work pressures, allocated the second act, the famous white act, in addition to the poetic fourth act, to his assistant, Lev Ivanov. He himself choreographed the third act featuring the duplicitous Odile. Yet in almost every production one sees today, even when some attention-getting choreographer adds roller skates to supposedly enliven the proceedings, it is always stated in the programme, After Petipa. And what about Lev Ivanov? Even a master choreographer, such as he was, had his credit shredded by future generations.

The same dishonest division of credit took place in the future *West Side Story* when Peter Gennaro, who had choreographed the winning Latin segments, took a camouflaging back seat regarding program acknowledgment, resultantly giving the impression that it was all of Robbins' choreography.

Robbins, as stomach-churning as ever, did not succeed in steamrolling Nora Kaye during *The Cage* rehearsals, though it was not for want of trying. She was a tough, no-nonsense girl from Brooklyn with a nasal New York accent that you could slice with a knife. Her father, Gregory Koreff, had been a Yiddish Theatre actor, so she came by her abundant dramatic genes biologically. Nora, named after Ibsen's heroine in *The Doll's House*, would take none of his shit (as she referred to it). She screamed back at him and had shouting matches threatening to walk out. Rushing to my defense after one of his abusive name-calling sessions, she hissed at him, "You know, Jerry, sometimes you stink!"

Robbins would be amiable one moment then, without warning, a fearful and raging fiend. He began to gradually wear me down and I began to have recurring doubts about how long I could withstand his relentless persecution, the price, I reasoned, that I had to pay in order to dance for Mr. B.

Since Robbins allowed no observers, my mother wasn't able to be present and I feared to tell her what was happening. A perceptive woman, by my mood and the expressions on the faces of the exiting dancers, she knew that something ugly was taking place behind that closed door.

Mr. B revived *Prodigal Son* with Jerome Robbins playing the role of the Prodigal and Balanchine, himself, enacting the part of the long-suffering father. Maria, as the Siren, again paired with him, but I sensed, reluctantly. Shortly thereafter, she donated the role to Yvonne Mounsey, the tall, charming South African dancer. Mr. Balanchine, who originally choreographed the ballet for Serge Lifar and our own Felia Dubrovska in the Diaghilev Ballet, did manage to give the impression that Robbins was dancing, but such was not the case. Mr B was so skillful a magician that he could falsify an illusion that made even a non-dancer look otherwise.

Antony Tudor was engaged to stage his *Lilac Garden* to Chausson's music as a vehicle for Nora Kaye. Not everyone, however, was happy with Nora having joined the company. On her first night with the New York City Ballet, someone seething with uncontainable resentment sent her a gift-wrapped box, looking no different than the endless floral gifts showered upon ballerinas. But this one was different, for it was an artfully disguised container that was, when opened with anticipatory pleasure, the cardboard coffin of a rotting, dead snake.

Hatred and intrigue notwithstanding, the banquet of ballets continued with William Dollar's *The Duel* for Melissa Hayden to Raffaello de Banfield's music. It was a spectacular vehicle for Milly and she thrilled the audiences with her sharp staccato attack while dueling on pointe.

Milly, whose father had been a pushcart vegetable peddler in Toronto, had started studying at 16, an unheard of age for a girl.

But with her ferocious and unremitting drive, she rose to the very top. Every major choreographer of the mid-twentieth century loved to work with her.

Her own favorite was, not surprisingly, George Balanchine, around whom, for all his dancers, the planets spun. Genius has its untouchable way of defining itself and few people in its glowing presence are unaware of its emissions. I always felt this in his orbit, or even just as a peripheral observer, seeing him in action.

Then came the ballet event of many a year, the Sadler's Wells Ballet's first appearance in New York at the old Met, a huge triumph. New Yorkers, until then, had never seen the full-length *Sleeping Beauty*. Such was its impact that, simultaneously, Margot Fonteyn appeared on the cover of *Time Magazine* and *Newsweek*, catapulted into super-stardom, as famous as any movie star. The future Dame Margot kept everyone spellbound with her enchanting Princess Aurora.

Still floating on air after one of the Sadler's Wells Ballet performances, I went backstage hoping to meet the lustrous pearl that was Margot Fonteyn. This was the woman whose roles were danced with such honesty and integrity, that her interpretations became the yardstick for which future dancers would be judged. The media never lost their fascination for Dame Margot, for they recorded her off-stage life no less than they do nowadays with the likes of Angelina Jolie or Madonna. From attempting on her yacht to help her husband overthrow the existing Panamanian government, to being imprisoned in the presidential cell overnight, to being arrested in San Francisco for being proximate with Nureyev to a noisy party, to being raked over the coals for dancing in a stadium in Chile; wherever Margot went, whether in practice clothes, tutus or her Dior and Saint Laurent wardrobe, the newsreel cameras were never far behind.

As is often the case with the press, they remained on the scent for controversy, but ignored her huge humanitarian contributions, such as when she, at least once, paid for the funeral of a former poverty-struck colleague.

And there she was in front of me, so warm, unassuming and friendly, so generous with her time following her exhausting and demanding performance of *Sleeping Beauty*. We chatted for a while and she gave me her photograph with the inscription, "Good Luck in your

Covent Garden Season, Margot". It is among the most cherished of my lovingly packed memorabilia.

The entire New York City Ballet now looked forward to our forthcoming five-week season at the Royal Opera House, scheduled for July and August, 1950.

Frederick Ashton, then principal choreographer for the Sadler's Wells Ballet, was commissioned by Lincoln Kirstein to create a new work for us. It was to be *Illuminations*, an impressionistic ballet based on the short and violent life of the French symbolist poet, Arthur Rimbaud. The haunting music would be by one of the greatest British composers, Benjamin Britten, while the inimitable Cecil Beaton would design the ravishing scenery and costumes. The entire ballet would all be in stunning black and white (this was before *My Fair Lady*). At the dress rehearsal he went to each dancer, whose face was covered in white greasepaint, and hand-painted each face, with black and red surrealistic lines. He reminded us to remember and duplicate the pattern for every performance.

There was no way then, unless I had been prophetic, which I wasn't, to foresee that my own life would, to a degree, parallel Arthur Rimbaud's. He, of course, wrote his untouchable and divine poetry, *Les Illuminations* and *Une saison en enfer (A Season in Hell)*, when only 16 years old, and then disappeared, while still in his teens, into the escapist wilds of Africa, to re-emerge and die at the age of 37. I, though, without one iota of his literary genius, made a splash as an early teen-aged dancer, apparently en route to Balanchine ballerina-dom, until circumstances beyond my defenseless control toppled me off that precarious pedestal so that I was finished at the age of 18, a mere footnote in the history pages of the New York City Ballet.

But in that bittersweet period of 1949–1954, blinkers, as on a cane-whipped horse, kept at arm's length the imminent reality. And so I immersed myself in the phantasmagoria of Rimbaud's hallucinatory poems, the *Illuminations* rehearsals taking on their own special fascination.

Ashton, the future Sir Frederic, didn't teach a single class, for he had crossed the Atlantic to call upon our techniques, not to improve them. A loving and very creative choreographer, he also drew on his observant eye, incorporating small details that he happened to see, perhaps a dancer just stretching a certain way, and then he would impulsively place that movement in his ballet. I was an example of how he transplanted the activity surrounding him. Given the small role of The Baker, Mr. Ashton was quite taken with my being able to bring my arms with hands clasped from behind my back to the front without unclasping my hands. He incorporated it into the ballet and it gave the desired effect of a tormented soul dragging itself through the fiery grottos of hell. All of my hard work in ballet classes was not necessary for this anatomical trick, but to please "the Shakespeare of the dance" as Dame Margot was to refer to him when he died, was indeed a rewarding surprise.

He was mild-mannered and very considerate to all of his dancers, listening to them much more than any other choreographer with whom I've ever worked. For example, after a new passage, he would ask us what we thought! Eliciting our opinions absolutely amazed us, a democratic approach we had never ever come across!

Furthermore, during a break in one of our *Illuminations* rehearsals, he came over to our group sitting on the floor, then joined all the dancers to regale us with tittle-tattle of Buckingham Palace, of which he was a frequent visitor. It seems that Queen Elizabeth, the future Queen Mother, found his imitations terribly amusing and she would prevail upon him to give one of his inimitable take-offs. He was bitingly accurate in his depiction of dowager society ladies, duchesses and other highborn ladies of the aristocracy. Anyone who saw Sir Fred portray one of the ugly stepsisters in his own ballet, *Cinderella*, knows how achingly comical he could be.

The Queen, whenever she was in residence at Buckingham Palace, invariably invited Sir Fred for tea. She was a wonderful audience, for she would laugh unrestrictedly while fingering the strands of pearls dangling on her ample and heaving bosom. Always in the midst of his sidesplitting parodies, she never failed to request his imitation of the malevolent Carabosse, a role I saw him do with uncanny believability. What, it is reasonable to ask, drew the regal and always charming Queen to relish an encore of a role that transfixed audiences with its Bela Lugosi styled horror? Possibly this *Sleeping Beauty* character, as danced and mimed by Sir Fred, reminded the Queen of the Duchess of Windsor, a woman she absolutely loathed. "The lowest of the low" was how she described her in one of her tongue-loosened moods. Perhaps while being tickled pink by her favorite court jester, Sir Fred, as Carabosse, she was safely letting off steam in the direction of Wallis Simpson.

Once when questioned about the enormously high percentage of homosexual personnel employed by the House of Windsor, the future Queen Mother sagely commented, "If we were to lose all gay staff, Buckingham Palace would at once become self-service."

Mr. Ashton was a most lovable man and we all worked so hard to fulfill his artistic vision, for he was not only molding on us a masterpiece in the making, he treated us as sensitive human beings.

My dear mother, who had long become a kind of human fixture in the building, watched every rehearsal with total focus, including Sir Fred's just concluded impromptu entertainment. He frequently asked her if she liked what he was doing! As high a pinnacle as he inhabited, he craved reassurance, almost seeming to depend on her for encouragement. My beloved mom had become a pillar of strength for the likes of the future Sir Frederic Ashton. Not only did I have the greatest respect for him as a supreme artist, but, on a personal level, I couldn't help but like him immensely.

As for Mom, she had ridden a long road from her golf-playing days in Oklahoma to being supportive of an Ashton, Britten and Beaton collaboration. She always provided Sir Fred with encouragement, telling him, in all truth, that he and *Illuminations* were wonderful.

On opening night, March 3, 1950, he was in a state of panic, a veritable basket case in fear of a hostile reception. Backstage just before the curtain, afraid to go out front, he asked my mother, yet again, trembling, what she really thought. She told him it would be well received by American audiences and not to worry one bit! He hugged her then summoned up his nerve and, thus fortified, went out to view his new work from the front.

The ballet was indeed more than well received, it was acclaimed, even described as a masterpiece by the majority. Nevertheless, its more provocative aspects raised a few eyebrows here and there in those more circumspect days. Melissa Hayden had quite a controversial role, dancing with one pointe shoe and the other foot bare. Her role of Profane Love required her, in one section, to lie on her back on the floor undulating, while Nicholas Magallanes as Rimbaud, doing push-ups above her, simulated sexual intercourse.

This is where, as anyone conversant with history, will know, that Sir Fred took artistic liberties, since Rimbaud was not only homosexual, but involved in the most notorious sex scandal of the time, his lover, the poet Paul Verlaine, going to prison for shooting him in the wrist during a quarrel. This scandal reverberated across the English Channel, for when Oscar Wilde was, some years later, on trial for his affair with Lord Alfred Douglas, the book was thrown at poor Wilde, as if his punishment had to encompass not only his own "crime", but that of Paul Verlaine as well.

Tanaquil LeClercq, in sharp contrast to Melissa Hayden, danced the role of Sacred Love, wafting white tulle and carried aloft by four male partners. Tanny, as we all called her, was later to be married to Mr B and, at the age of 25, was mercilessly struck down for life by polio, never to leave her wheelchair to walk again, let alone to dance. But that most dreadful of curses was five years into the future.

When we all appeared in London in 1950, the distinguished ballet critic and author Cyril Beaumont, watching *Illuminations*, wagged his finger at Sir Fred, chiding him that ballet would fall into disrepute if such graphic scenes were to be depicted. What, may I ask, about the orgy scene in *Schéhérazade*? Subsequent generations seemed to have survived that intact. And so did Mr. Beaumont, who actually saw Nijinsky dance the role of the sex-deprived Golden Slave.

Closer to home, in New York, the authoritarian ballet author and editor Anatole Chujoy advised people to "leave the children at home for this one", which I think added to the ballet's popularity. The old "banned in Boston" warning was as titillating as ever. It not only sold books and films, it sold this ballet, witness the sold-out City Center for just about every performance!

Once the contracts were signed with Covent Garden and it was official that we would be going to London, Mr. Balanchine made every day an unrelenting effort to shape a larger repertoire and bring out all the best in us. Since London was one of the world's major ballet capitals, we knew we had to surpass ourselves. And so, all of us were inflamed with a passion to excel, to do justice to Mr. B's magnificent dancescape.

Once in a blue moon, there were times of comic relief during some of the grueling rehearsal days at the theatre. One afternoon, we had about two hours between rehearsals and I decided to venture onto the forbidden staircase. When we first started to go to the theatre we were told never to go up those particular stairs! It made me so curious I just had to at least peek at what was up there! I opened the door and started up the dim passage. It was definitely creepy, but my curiosity was getting the better of my fear. Finally, I came to a blank wall in which there was a small panel of wood at eye level.

I tried to push the panel but it didn't budge. Then, it gave way a little so I could peek into the next room. There, and instantly recognizable, was the famous face of comedian Sid Caesar rehearsing for his wildly popular television series, *Show of Shows!* I surreptitiously watched for a while, chuckling at the humor, thinking I was not noticed, when suddenly Sid Caesar's face was inches away from mine, glaring straight at me, eye to eye, with irritated puzzlement.

All I heard was, "What the hell?" I let out a yell and raced down the stairs as fast as I could get my legs to carry me. Luckily, because of my quick *batterie*, my legs obeyed my cornered brain and I was off like a shot! Another reason I didn't get caught was because the opening was too small for anyone to get through to chase me! Chastened, I never went back, having belatedly learned my lesson.

But not long afterwards, at the invitation of the leading Ballet Russe male star Frederic Franklin, whom I had first seen in Oklahoma as a child, partnering the great Danilova, I was invited to dance on the Sid Caesar show. During rehearsals, I actually saw the panel opening, though now from the other side.

The nationally acclaimed comedian, who at birth must have made even the doctors and nurses laugh, waiting for the opportune moment, approached me. Then, with a baffled look, his eyes narrowing, he said, "Haven't we met before? You look familiar!"

Now fortified with my special guest status, I just smiled enigmatically and said, "I don't think, Mr. Caesar, that we were ever introduced!"

CHAPTER EIGHT

THE GIRL IN THE PAINTING

At the close of the 1950 winter season of the New York City Ballet, there was a period of some eight weeks before our rehearsals were to begin for the forthcoming Covent Garden season in London. For all of us, this interim period was our preparation for the Olympics. Although no gold medals would be awarded, the hoped-for triumph of the company would be our highest and truest recompense. During that time, I took every class given at the school as well as Mr. B's additional classes.

It was during one of the most demanding classes taught by Anatole Oboukhov that I first became aware of a slender curly-haired youth who always stood at the barre by the large windows overlooking Madison Avenue. There was an aura about him of total dedication, of complete immersion in his efforts. As committed as I was to my own improvement, I couldn't help but notice him, fascinated by the fine bone structure of his face and noble profile. The respect he showed Mr. Oboukhov was, as I look back, no less than a disciple to his guru. That also impressed me.

We had never spoken, but some sort of connection had already begun to be forged. During the *adage*, his passion to dance was clear in his every expressive movement. As young as I was, I had already worked with enough major artists to recognize that this adolescent youth was clearly destined for greatness. Looking back, it was an accurate glimpse of the future, for the youth, still a teenager, was Adam Darius, American of Turkish and Russian Jewish ancestry.

During the sixty years that Adam and I were separated, he became the world's most travelled dancer and mime artist, appearing in over 85 countries. He also became the choreographer of *The Anne Frank Ballet,* and, resultantly, a friend of Anne's father, Otto Frank. Among his many future honors was the Premio Positano Léonide Massine, Italy's highest medal for the dance, and, twice, the Noor Al Hussein Award from the Hashemite Kingdom of Jordan.

Let us, for a few moments, leap ahead half a century. Through the wonders of YouTube, Adam's 1967 production of his *Anne Frank Ballet* on Italian Television is being screened after an absence of 44 years. After viewing it, Shimon Samuels, President of the Simon Wiesenthal Center in Paris, wrote:

"Thank you for your magnificent gift...It is an excellent global pedagogical tool transcending language...Your own performance, especially in the Hatikvah finale as the destroyed patriarch, is a heartrending masterpiece."

The boy at the barre also became the dance world's most prolific author, for he was to write a score of plays and 15 published books, from novels, philosophy, autobiography to his teaching methods.

Back in 1949, a student at Columbia University, Adam was struggling to nurture his embattled dancing vision, for his lawyer father was less than enthusiastic about his dancing plans. Fortunately, Adam's father lived long enough to proudly see his son adorning the walls of the Gothenburg Theatre Museum in Sweden, adjacent to photographs of Greta Garbo.

But that was some way into the future. One day, in that still turning point year of 1949, after a particularly strenuous class, Adam stopped me in the hall and introduced himself. I was delighted to finally meet him. He began enthusiastically telling me about the ballet he was choreographing, *Antigone*, based on the Greek tragedy by Sophocles. To my delight and amazement, he wanted me to dance the leading role! It was such a thrilling moment for me and I thought it such a compliment. I readily accepted his invitation. Mom and I immediately rushed to the New York Public Library to read *Antigone* in order to better understand the character I was to dance.

One sad day, Adam told me that, due to a recurring knee injury, his leg was going to be placed in a plaster cast. There and then, that was the end of our dancing together. John Mandia, from the school, was hastily recruited to do the role of Haemon. Despite the cast on his leg, Adam managed the steps up and down the BMT's cavernous subway station at 14th Street, adjacent to where the rehearsal studio was located. His tenacity and persistence were already abundantly in evidence.

I found Adam's work to be inspiring, particularly the striking pas de deux between Antigone and Haemon. The rehearsals went well, for he choreographed quickly and, always, despite the discomfort of the cast on his leg, exuded an incipient holy fire. The original music for the ballet was played by the composer himself, a young student named Russell Smith.

Like Balanchine, Adam Darius's choreography was classical and based on the Imperial Russian tradition, but with something more. There was an original creativity with every phrase he choreographed, contributing to the further unfolding of the narrative. Long before the word came into dance world usage, Adam was already an intuitive dramaturgist. And beyond that theatrical instinct, the pas de deux between John Mandia and myself owed no allegiance to any other choreographer, no small achievement for such a young and impressionable youth.

At Adam's request, Mr. B came to one of our rehearsals held at the School of American Ballet. He stayed for a time but then with apologies left early in order to greet his old friend Igor Stravinsky, arriving by ship from Europe. It was a further compliment to Adam that several days later Mr. B spoke to him for some 20 minutes, revealing his thoughts on choreography and ballet in general, an almost stream of consciousness monologue that made Adam almost miss the beginning of Arthur Miller's new play, *Death of a Salesman.* But as Adam dashed across mid-town traffic to get to the matinee, taking precedence in his thoughts was the latest ballet of George Balanchine, not the latest play of Arthur Miller, albeit his masterpiece.

Ever enterprising, Adam had persuaded an organization called Theatre Dance to fund and present his ballet. And so it was seen at the Humphrey-Weidman Studio Theatre in Greenwich Village, the studio belonging to the highly respected contemporary choreographers Doris Humphrey (Martha Graham's arch rival) and Charles Weidman. At the end of *Antigone*, during the appreciative applause, a fragrant bouquet of roses was presented to me. As the attached card had become dislodged from the flowers, it was only recently that I learned they were from Adam. I sent him what must be the most belated thank-you note of all time, sixty years after the event!

That ballet was the first ballet ever created for me and, as such, occupies a very special niche in my, until now, locked drawer of memories.

After *Antigone,* Adam disappeared, seemingly forever, from my life. I went on to perform and tour with the New York City Ballet and he went to Europe where he worked under the celebrated Ingmar Bergman's direction and scored early successes as a choreographer. As the Wikipedia records in some 15 languages, from Japanese to Arabic, he evolved into the peerless mime tragedian that he still is today. Even at the age of 82, he continues to dance throughout the world, and at an amazingly high level technically, his latest port of call in the Nepalese capital of Kathmandu. There, in the foothills of the Himalayas, Adam continues to echo the vulnerability of displaced humankind.

Long a guru himself, he has shaped the lives and careers of many luminaries, including Hollywood film star Kate Beckinsale, rock star Kate Bush, Shakespearean actor Clarke Peters, and dancer, actor and mime artist, Kazimir Kolesnik. As the creator of his own system, the Adam Darius Method, he has contoured the careers of several generations of Syrian actors in Damascus, as well as Finnish circus artists, among a steady stream of others from Argentina to Afghanistan. Who can count the flowers of generously sprinkled seeds?

How, the reader may well ask at this point, did Adam and I reconnect after sixty years? This reconnection has persuaded me to believe in synchronicity and perhaps a voice calling from beyond the grave!

In 1950, there was a young and gifted art student, Lester Chace, initially from Illinois, but then also a student at Columbia University. He was a friend of Adam's. On the shy side, one noticed immediately his bright red hair as he attended some of the *Antigone* rehearsals. He had already done a large oil painting of Adam, looking soulfully towards some far horizon.

Lester wanted to do a portrait of me, which he did and then exhibited as a final exam application to the prestigious Portraits Incorporated in New York. The painting completed, Lester invited me to go to the reception at the exhibit where the judges would review a number of submitted paintings, his portrait of me among them.

Wearing the same dress as I did in the painting, Lester asked me to stand next to the portrait so that the judges could see how accurately the painting resembled me. The judges were sufficiently impressed because Lester was accepted at once into their organization. He later gave my parents the portrait where it proudly hung in their living room until they passed away. That painting now adorns my own home, with its happy early vibrations, but also a reminder that time tramples all underfoot.

Several years ago Lester Chace died in his home state of Illinois, a semi-recluse surrounded by squeezed-dry tubes of oil, stiffened paintbrushes and canvases in various states of completion. A woman named Anne Phipps, his devoted friend and dedicated curator, began collecting what she could find of his past body of works, donating them to the Illinois State Museum in Springfield. Included in her donation was that long ago sensitive portrait of the young Adam Darius.

In her ceaseless quest to locate Lester's lost paintings, Anne discovered that he had painted me as well. Not leaving a stone unturned, she found out my address and telephone number, mentioning this to Adam with whom she was in regular overseas contact, though they had never met personally.

Adam then wrote to me, a surprise, to say the least, out of the blue! So was life's jumbled jigsaw puzzle reassembled.

Understandably, Adam, asked me what I had been doing since 1950. My reply was that I would need to write a book to tell him. He replied, "Then do so!" As I followed his choreographic instructions in 1949, so do I now follow his literary instructions in 2011. This is a project I could not have even begun, let alone kept on writing without his guidance as the immensely experienced writer that he is. He also helped me to overcome the depression I would inevitably undergo when reliving certain dreaded episodes now safely set down and expunged within these pages.

Writing this book serves as a remarkable purification, a catharsis and I trust an eye-opening view of the cloistered world of ballet as I, personally, experienced it. So securely locked in my private attic were my years with the New York City Ballet that not even my own now middle-aged children, and growing grandchildren, were ever aware that once their mother and grandmother had been a ballet dancer on the stages of Europe's leading opera houses.

As for Lester Chace, I am so grateful to him for reuniting me with Adam, albeit posthumously. I thank him as he paints on whatever celestial canvas now occupying his gaze.

There are many words in the Greek language for the gradations of love, but in English we have only one, an umbrella term that covers loving your mother and loving a local restaurant. They, of course, are not equal.

Despite the passage of the speeding almanac, and our having lost contact for longer than many lifetimes, I now feel closer to Adam than ever. Call it love, call it what you will; a rose by any other name will smell as sweet. His home is in Espoo, Finland and mine in Santa Barbara, California and it is entirely possible that we will never again meet face to face. But as that tragic queen, Marie Antoinette, once said, "Many miles and many countries can never separate hearts."

In Joan Rivers' recent film, *Rivers*, she has a soliloquy in which she laments losing her publicity agent of 25 years. Tearfully, she struggles to say that she has no one now with whom to remember, no one to share the memories of the early years when she was just beginning to gain a foothold.

Mme Danilova, when Mr. B died, said something quite parallel, that he was the last of her beloved friends and colleagues with whom she grew up in St. Petersburg. Such is the lonely plight of the last survivor.

Those friends who remember you from years past have steadily dwindled and are precious, indeed. To again quote the Bard, "Grapple them to thy soul with hoops of steel, for they shall be numbered by the very digits of one hand".

No longer fearful of opening the floodgates of memory, how accurately prophetic was my perception of future greatness in the young man at that distant New York barre.

Among the future stages that Adam would skim across was the Cultural Center of the Philippines in Manila. Shortly before his solo appearance there in 1976, President Ferdinand Marcos and first lady Imelda Marcos hosted an awards ceremony honoring national artists. Their words, spoken with the luminous silver of eternal truth, are excerpted here, for they are applicable to Adam and a few other supreme artists with whom I was once privileged to work.

"It is our artists who add value and dignity to our times. They have made themselves the nerve-endings of our sensibilities, the carriers of our dreams, the articulators of our yearnings, forging in the smithy of their souls the conscience of the race.

"They guide without the arrogance of political leaders, they direct without the ostentation of the social scientist, and they unite without coercion. They give purpose to the despairing and nobility to the dishonored.

"And so, since the artist, by his creativity, defines, documents and memorializes the past, the present and future of the race, to that extent he becomes a leader of man. For he indeed articulates in palpable form the vague, groping yearnings of his people. And by thus defining the past and the present, he forecasts our future.

"True and great artists are the noblest among us. Their achievements shine in the midst of our own common endeavors. Long after material acquisition of goods and property will have crumbled, the work and the beauty they have created will remain."

To conclude these pervasive thoughts on Adam Darius, I am also profoundly grateful to him for his abundant qualities as a human being. It was he alone who prompted me, without pause; it was he who urged me, without respite, to share, in this book, my long hidden years of pain and glory.

CHAPTER NINE

HIGH TEA WITH LORD MOUNTBATTEN

The day had finally arrived for the entire New York City Ballet to depart for London, our first trip abroad! With the Royal Opera House in Covent Garden to be our home for a five-week engagement, the excitement in the air was palpable. If we were going to the moon, I couldn't have been more excited! Mr. B had augmented the company with more dancers so as to add quantity to the quality already embedded in the ballets themselves.

Lincoln Kirstein, as always, provided the very best he could for all of us, chartering British Overseas Airways' newest plane, the Stratocruiser. It was to travel at the then unheard-of altitude of 14,000 feet, taking off from New York and landing for refueling, three times, in Goose Bay, Labrador, then Reykjavik, Iceland, followed by the final refueling in Shannon, Ireland, before arriving in London itself.

Prior to our leaving New York, the company's publicity manager, Phil Bloom, had been asked to send some promotional material to be used by the British press upon our arrival in London. Then he arranged for members of the press to be at the airport to meet the plane, take photographs and interview some of the members of the company. I had gotten to know Mr. Bloom fairly well because, while in New York, he was always looking for someone willing to volunteer to go to an interview or have pictures taken, with no payment, but as a favor to him. I was always eager to go and thought it was fun to talk to people who were from "the real world," as we called it. Mom called me "the original volunteer"!

Mr. B had instructed us to be dressed very stylishly at all times while we were in London so that we could present ourselves to advantage. When the Sadler's Wells Ballet first came to New York, the leading London clothing shops had outfitted all the dancers so that the girls and boys of the company looked like fashion plates. Since neither Saks Fifth Avenue nor Bloomingdales, nor any other department store, had offered to dress us as if we had stepped out of a display window, we, ourselves had to be responsible for looking presentable. So did Mr. B remind us. He wanted us to impress Londoners not only with our dancing, but also with our appearance.

The week before we left, Mom and I went shopping at Gimbels Department Store on 34th Street, next to the famous Macy's. I purchased a very tasteful pale beige suit, high-heeled shoes, a hat with a veil, and tan kid gloves to round out a smart look. I had never worn such an outfit, but I felt a need to look and act more grown-up in order to fit in with the other dancers in the company, all older.

After all the hours spent *sur les pointes*, walking in high-heeled shoes was a cinch to master! The veil was another matter because my eyelashes would stick in the veil, and move the veil up and down every time I blinked! Some of my favorite movie stars had hats with veils and I wondered how they avoided the eyelash problem. I felt like a little girl playing "dressing up" and hoped that I wouldn't draw attention as such. I did so want to look chic and follow Mr. B's advice.

Checking in at the airport and before we boarded our plane, we each had to step on a scale with a huge round numbered face, weighing us, along with our luggage. It was part of the BOAC requirement for the airline to know exactly how much weight the plane was carrying. Mr. B watched with pride as every single dancer complied with the mandatory weigh-in for the flight. In my non-existent knowledge of aircraft, I could not begin to fathom how this huge aircraft would ever get off the ground, let alone stay in the air!

Passport in clammy hand, and with some serious nerves and repeated and deliberate delays, I finally said goodbye to Mom. I tried to hold back the tears that I knew Mom was also suppressing, for I didn't want my sadness to become contagious. Actually I felt as if I was being wrenched from the loving anchor I had known all my young life. This was to be the first time I had ever been away without her. How could I not help but miss her terribly? In those days, of course, there were no emails or mobile phones with which to stay in constant and immediate touch.

Tomi Wortham, one of the dancers' mothers, was a nurse, and she had been chosen to be our chaperone. The management thought it prudent to have one who could fulfill the dual role of nurse and chaperone for the teen-age girls who were members of the company, of which I was the youngest. She was a native of Arkansas with a very thick accent, some would call it hillbilly, which the British could not readily understand. More than once, I acted as interpreter for Mrs. Wortham. She was a warm and caring woman and she must have always been torn between having a great time with all of the young dancers and trying to keep track of us! We just did our own thing and she almost never knew where any of us were! In her defense, how could she, without being a harsh, schoolmistress type, and that she was not? Also, the dancers stayed in different hotels scattered around the area of Covent Garden, so looking out for all of us was nigh on impossible.

Once we boarded the plane we received instructions from the smartly uniformed flight crew. We were warned about the constant loud buzz of the propeller engines, the non-stop vibrations, and that we would experience pain in our ears both taking off and landing until the air pressure had stabilized. Barley sugar was on offer to help us combat the symptoms. By this time, I was fit to be tied, but I tried to give the impression of an experienced air traveler, though I had never flown before. When they went through the safety instructions, the possibilities of crash landing, landing on the sea or however, I was in an ill-concealed state of tension. I was ready to live, not die.

After take-off, and we were settled in for the long flight ahead, I noticed a card game going on with the players sitting on the floor in front of the emergency escape hatch. As I passed them in the aisle, I could see that they were playing canasta. Jerome Robbins was one of the players along with Frank Moncion and other principals of the company. Noticing that I looked at them with interest, they asked if I wanted to join them. Since Robbins had me understudy everyone in his ballet, *Age of Anxiety*, as well as giving me my own part to dance, I hesitated before daring to join him on a social level. Then I thought if I refused, he would take umbrage, interpreting my refusal as a rejection. I was caught between the devil and the deep blue sea!

Since Mom and I had played quite a lot of canasta between rehearsals, I thought I could hold my own in the game. So I agreed. By this time, I was all too familiar with Robbins' moods and knew that they were without transition, changing without warning as tropical weather. Nevertheless, he seemed in a pleasant enough mood, laughing and joking with everyone. I was dealt extraordinarily good cards and, to my surprise, I won the game!

Winners are usually exultant, but not this one! Jerome Robbins, beaten in a card game by a girl who had barely left childhood, was visibly upset. He began to complain loudly about losing to some stupid little kid! He slammed down his cards and all the other players, most of all, I, froze! There, within a few seconds, he went from fun and games to dark and ominously sullen. He stood up aggressively and if looks could kill, I would have been dead. Then, in his latest bout of emotional diarrhea, he abruptly quit the game and stomped away.

Mr. B then came along, and noting the funereal quiet among the players, patted me on the shoulder, having already noticed the atmosphere turning sour. Sensing my distress, I think via telepathy, which was usually the way we communicated, he seemed to know what I was feeling.

Mr. B later gave me the leading role of the Queen of Hearts in his Stravinsky collaboration, *Card Game*. I alternated performances with the delightful Janet Reed in the part. To this day, I wonder if Mr. B, aware of my emotional displacement after that game of cards had so abruptly ended, cast me, as a consolation prize, in the role of the Queen of Hearts! To dance a lead in a Balanchine/Stravinsky ballet, under the personal guidance of the creators themselves, was surely a way to pick up anyone's spirits! I loved dancing the ballet and fairly romped through it with Todd Bolender dancing the part of the Joker.

On very special occasions, Igor Stravinsky would conduct the performance. What a tempo and thrilling sounds came from the orchestra when he conducted his own work. So perhaps I should thank Jerome Robbins for his infantile and snarling response to a girl barely into her teens beating him at a mere game of canasta! The news of my "victory" and Robbins's "defeat" had passed around the plane like wildfire, such news doing little to further endear me to him.

With each one of the refueling take-offs and landings, I was in held-breath wonder as to how such a monumental mechanical feat was going to be accomplished, yet again. I think even among the agnostics and atheists on board, there were a few who managed to discover God as they nervously buckled their seat belts, then surreptitiously fingered their gold crosses and Stars of David. I thought of my parents and how they would suffer if disaster were to befall me.

The landing at Heathrow Airport, then called London Airport, was smooth, thank goodness, and, safe, sound and still alive, we were finally asked to descend the steps to the tarmac. As we stepped onto British soil, hordes of reporters rushed towards the plane from seemingly nowhere, flash bulbs popping without respite.

I assumed the press was rushing towards George Balanchine and Maria Tallchief, two illustrious names, or possibly our conductor, the distinguished Leon Barzin, who was to be awarded the French Legion of Honor, but, no, they whizzed right past them and descended onto insignificant little me! I couldn't believe what was happening; they were all asking for Miss Bocher. How could this be? Was this a mistake, a joke or was I groggy and dehydrated from such a long haul flight? Not only was I astonished, so was everyone else in the company! At that moment, the communal daggers were drawn in my direction. Jealousy, though sometimes masked, was, from that time on, always present.

It seems that Phil Bloom, our publicity agent in New York, had turned me into a loose cannon, for by letting the British press know that there was a fourteen-year old girl dancing with the company at Covent Garden, that information obscured all the combined credits of the others. So, aware of the baby ballerina in their midst, as I was labeled, they rushed towards me for pictures and interviews. Being surrounded by cameras, flash bulbs, notebooks and microphones, I pulled myself together in a hurry.

"Which is your favorite movie? Who is your favorite movie star? Do you wear nail polish? How much money do you earn per week?" The barrage of questions was taking place even before we checked in at the Customs counter. Greedy for more than my impromptu responses, they were requesting further appointments to interview me. At this point, my being amazed at the attention was being replaced by embarrassment and discomfort, for I knew there would be fall-out from this excessive interest.

Phil Bloom, remembering that I was always willing to talk to reporters, thought I might facilitate the publicity needed for the season. Little did he realize the trouble it would cause me with the other members of the company. Or perhaps he didn't care, as long as he fulfilled his function of promoting the company for its Covent Garden season. The result was that I found myself isolated from the others, with no possibility of any kind of female friendship.

Due to the tarmac interviews, I was the last to get to the customs counter to go through what I thought was a mere formality. Then, like a short circuit shock, it was made clear to me that I was going to be put straight back on a plane for the USA because I had no permission to work as a child in the British Isles! They had strict child labor laws and no one in the company had been informed that it was a neces- sity to obtain a special work permit for me before they would even allow me to enter the country! I plunged into an instant depression and barely heard the urgent pleadings of Betty Cage, the company manager. She begged them, she implored them, each and every civil servant, to use their influence to give me this permit. If I were to be sent back, she explained, the entire season would be severely jeopar- dized since I was dancing in all of the ballets, some of them in soloist roles. In no way could I be replaced in such a short time.

After what seemed like hours, with each succeeding minute ticking away like a primed hand grenade, I was finally told that I was to report to a physician's office the next morning. There, I would undergo a complete physical examination. If the doctor were to find me healthy and sign the proper documents attesting to that fact, then the Ministry of Labor would grant me the permission to stay and perform as scheduled. Betty Cage, bless her many times over, had wrought a mini-miracle!

The next morning, in a state of nerves, and after a cuticle-picking wait in the doctor's office, I was perfunctorily examined by some physician who determined that I was indeed "quite healthy" and, in consequence, gave his authorization for me to stay in England and dance! But the authorities were not quite through with me, yet! There was a stipulation that I must have a private dressing room (heaven forbid that I should be contaminated by the salacious conversations of the older dancers)! I was also to be out of the theatre before 10:00 p.m. after each evening performance.

That enormous hurdle managed, the morning after our arrival on July 5th, 1950, my picture was on the front page of the *London*

Evening News with the caption, Barbara (14) is a Girl with Poise by Gwen Robyns. In her article, she described me as "the luckiest young person I have met. She knows exactly where she is going and what she wants from life!" Ms. Robyns continued, "Take a look at that pretty little head with its honey-gold Hottentot hair-do, tilting green eyes, dimpled cheeks, and rosy lips; there is all the wisdom of Solomon in it!

"From her uncle, Mainbocher, the famous American couturier, she has inherited a flair for clothes. There is nothing of the bobbysoxer about her. She prefers simple elegant dresses in subdued colors, a dozen silk scarves and tiny floral posies to tuck in her hair."

The *Daily Mirror* carried a picture with a caption, *And she is Only 14 Years Old.* The *News Chronicle* had Dancing Girl under my picture and the *Daily Express* featured a photograph with Jacques d'Amboise, then 15 years old, and a caption, They Dance While You Sleep! I sent the clippings to my father and he was so proud that he immediately bought a scrapbook the same size as the front page of the *London Evening News.*

I was on a conveyor belt of continuous publicity with no immediate end in sight. There were also trips to historic Hampton Court for photo shoots, and a feature in *Debutante Magazine*, all sandwiched in between some very intensive rehearsals in preparation for the imminent opening on July 10th, only five days away. Just as Eric von Stroheim was "the man you love to hate", I was fast becoming, among the girls in the company, "the girl you love to hate." Not only could I beat the likes of Jerome Robbins at canasta, I could also handle with dexterity the usually blasé British press corps. In my own eyes, I was only doing my best to fulfill my obligations. But after that onslaught of publicity, I was persona non grata among the girls in the company.

The Ministry of Labor, with still no let-up in my strict supervision, had also assigned me an "inspector" who was to be backstage at every performance to see that I was in compliance with the stringent rules. Like a cartoon character, he wore a black derby hat and a black suit every night and always carried a furled black umbrella. I felt sorry for him as he just sat on a box in the very back of the wings, looking neither left nor right, but always miserably straight ahead. I would smile at him but never received even a semblance of a smile in return. Never did he once say a word to me, nor did he talk to Mrs. Wortham. If I hadn't known better, I could have sworn my inspector was an effigy from Madame Tussaud's famous Wax Museum. In fact, the waxworks were much more lifelike than he was!

Despite the permit problems, I absolutely loved everything about London; the theatre, the friendly people, and their love and respect for their some thousand years of tradition. London, in those far-off days, was still outwardly tranquil, for it was long before politician Enoch Powell's rivers of blood speech, long before the IRA "troubles", and years before terrorist bombs were to be planted in the London underground and buses.

In that unforgettable summer of 1950, it was thrilling for me to be able to dance at the historic Royal Opera House, Covent Garden, the stage that the impassioned Anna Pavlova and the mystical Vaslav Nijinsky had both emblazoned, and the stage where Dame Nellie Melba had bade her final and tearful farewell to opera. History vibrated in that building, freezing a pantheon of unsurpassable artists at their very summit.

In that period, the Opera House was home to the Sadler's Wells Ballet, with the likes of Margot Fonteyn, Beryl Grey, Robert Helpmann and Frederick Ashton, all of them to be ennobled in the near future, showering the knowledgeable London audiences with their exceptional artistry. What an honor to be invited to dance there!

The stage at Covent Garden had a rake, that is, it slanted toward the audience. The Opera House, built for opera, had the floor raised in the back, enabling the audience to see the singers at the rear of the stage. Though wonderful for opera, it was very difficult for dancers.

Constructed of large planks of wood, the stage, due to age and heavy use, was subject to splintering. Our pink satin pointe slippers took a real beating on that floor, but we felt confident in our ability to cope. I learned quickly how to adjust my center of balance while dancing on that threatening rake. When doing the circle of rapid *piqué* turns in *Serenade*, the opening ballet, we had to turn very quickly going uphill, and then to slow up going downhill. By altering our speed in this way, we managed to remain with the music.

As if these obstacles weren't enough to contend with, the Covent Garden stage was almost twice the size of our City Center stage. We needed to adjust our spacing and cover considerably more ground with our jumps. This expansion of the choreography took priority in our five-day period of rehearsal.

Then, from out of the frying pan into the fire, the Labor Ministry's edict that I have my own dressing room was to aggravate an already tense situation. For my assigned place was right next to the "Corps Room", written in large letters, where all the female dancers who were not major soloists were assigned.

One of them, Helen Kramer, had come from the old Ballet Russe de Monte Carlo after it had closed. Although she was very beautiful outwardly, the lovely exterior masked a spitfire temperament. I became her private punching bag, fueled by her resentment and jealousy of my youth and all the media attention being lavished on me (through no doing of my own). Even a beautiful woman, when enraged, becomes ugly, as did Helen Kramer.

She lost no opportunity in letting me know how unhappy she was at every chance she got. Once, she poked her head in my dressing room door and screamed at me at the top of her lungs, "Who do you think you are, you little shit, with your own private dressing room?" The bile released, she continued ranting, "I danced soloist roles with Ballet Russe and here I am in the room labeled, Corps!" Her eyes were fiery and she reminded me of the wicked witch in the *Wizard of Oz*, hate oozing out of her every pore.

I hesitate to use the word, bitch, but it definitely comes to mind. Mrs. Wortham was in the room with me when she lashed out at me, and she was a big help at the time, saying that it was hard for Helen Kramer to adjust to not being able to dance well anymore. After that ugly outburst, I kept my distance from Helen and realized it was better to know who your enemies were than to be deceived by fake friendship!

Fortunately, Mrs. Wortham's wise council enabled me to feel vaguely sorry for Helen, for she was indeed to be pitied in the last gasps of her dancing career. To watch her having difficulty executing Mr B's seamless steps, even in the corps de ballet, was a warning to others. Ballet is for the very young. To be still struggling in the corps as you push the rusted gates of 50 is to invite the bacterium of tetanus, or its emotional equivalent.

In Helen's case, I feel Mr. B had hired her, along with Vida Brown, another ex-Ballet Russe dancer, since both of them had been Maria's close friends in that company. Mr B thought by hiring them, though neither could do justice to his technically demanding choreography, he was providing Maria with the security of long-standing friends.

Thanks to the avalanche of publicity that had been showered on me, it was hard to know whom to trust; certainly no female, for my private dressing room seemed to be the last straw among the girls in the company. It's just as well that the other dancers hadn't an inkling that my isolated changing room actually belonged to Britain's ranking choreographer and chief character dancer, Frederic Ashton, who occupied it while in London. This was his private inner sanctum in which he painted his face, hands and brain to become Cinderella's grotesque stepsister and the blood-lusting Carabosse, nemesis of the innocent Princess Aurora.

Though female friends were now out of the question, that left all the boys in the company, most of whom were gay. I could confide in them and I could safely trust them. In no way was I a threat to them, not artistically and not in the romance arena. All the boys, including the minority of straights, were always kind to me. They encouraged me in class and bolstered me when I was down for one reason or another. So was I adopted by the whole community of gay guys in the company. With them, I could be offered moral support, laughter and friendship. They saw me as their little sister!

Looking back at the resentment caused by all the newspaper stories about me, I have come to believe that the attaching of such importance to media publicity is way out of proportion to its impact. For the very next day, the pages of newspapers are to be found in the muddy gutter, sopping up the rain, or being swept by dustmen into the garbage can.

Nevertheless, I remained the bête noire of Helen Kramer's existence. Her next and expected outburst always hovered over me in the theatre. For like an epileptic, who knew when her next attack would take place? Nicky Magallanes did the most devastating and hilarious impersonation of her, his each imitation serving as a sedative for me. That was the best medicine at the time, for ridicule really is a great tension fuser.

Pandora's box had not yet been fully emptied. It was the dress rehearsal the morning of opening night, July 10th, 1950. We were rehearsing *Age of Anxiety* with costumes and full orchestra. Leonard Bernstein was conducting. Patricia Wilde had injured her leg and was not sure she could dance that evening, a very worrying proposition since she had a major role in the ballet, a tour de force solo. Because Robbins had made me learn her role a few months earlier in New York, as I have already recounted, I knew her part.

He had me dance the dress rehearsal full out on *pointe*. After the rehearsal, he assured me that I would not be doing it that night, and that I just had given Patty a rest so she could dance that evening. The ballet was second on the program, right after *Serenade* in which I danced.

Just before *Serenade* that night, I was told by Robbins that I would be dancing for Patty Wilde in the first movement! What a responsibility had been thrust on my shoulders, still at the age of 14, to do a major soloist role on opening night in a Robbins/Bernstein ballet in one of the grandest opera houses in the world!

The music, in all deference to the composer, Maestro Bernstein, sounded like a traffic jam at rush hour and, resultantly, was very difficult to count. As the unheeding clock ticked away, the fear I felt continued to escalate. Standing in the wings, I had a talk with myself and gradually a relative tranquility replaced the turbulence. Taking my place on stage at the Royal Opera House, when the curtain went up I danced with everything I had; heart, soul, mind and muscle. The waves of applause at the conclusion confirmed that I had sailed with the vessel, not capsized it.

There had been no announcement of a cast change in the program, or any front of curtain announcement. As far as the press and public were concerned, they had been watching Patricia Wilde. With or without credit, I had seen it as a victory, for it had been achieved despite the obstacles.

After the ballet, I was on my way to the dressing room to quickly change for the third ballet of the evening, *Symphony in C*, when I passed Jerome Robbins in the corridor. He didn't stop walking, nor did he slow down, but as an aside, barely looking at me, he said begrudgingly, "Thanks, Bocher" and kept on walking. Good manners remind us not to speak ill of the dead, but to paraphrase Gertrude Stein, "An ingrate is an ingrate is an ingrate!" It would have cost nothing for him to smile at me, I thought, as I painfully removed my frayed and bloodied *pointe* shoes.

Our *Symphony in C* was such a beautiful ballet and a perfect choice to close the opening night program. The applause was tumultuous. We were a success! London balletgoers flooded the street outside the stage door waiting for autographs and a glimpse of Maria Tallchief, the Indian princess and the queen of American ballet. Many of us received fan mail, something very foreign to us since in New York this rarely happened. I answered every one of mine. What a loyal group of stage door fans!

The theatre was dark on Sundays and Arnold Haskell, the distinguished ballet author, critic, and head of the Sadler's Wells Ballet School, had been to the opening performance. He sent a note backstage inviting me to go for an afternoon drive to his alma mater, Kings College in Cambridge, and then go punting on the River Cam.

Punting, I looked up, was poling a small square-ended boat along a waterway. This nautical excursion would be followed by dinner at his home. I knew who he was and was eager to go.

Mrs. Wortham had some reservations about letting me go for a day on my own with a middle-aged man she didn't even know. Though Vladimir Nabokov's controversial novel *Lolita* was not to be published until 1955, the attraction of older men to pre-pubescent youngsters was not unheard of. Mrs. Wortham, a nurse and a mother herself of a young girl, was not unfamiliar with such situations. She suspiciously wondered why he hadn't invited one of the older soloists, more prominently featured than I.

As for my own thoughts, I was totally oblivious that such psychiatric undercurrents even existed. All I knew was that Arnold Haskell was a ranking ballet author and a major influence in the appreciation of ballet in both Australia and Britain. As an historian, his biography of Diaghilev was considered definitive. I began begging Mrs. Wortham, like a child, to please, please, please, let me go, assuring her that this distinguished man was trustworthy, that I had some of his books, and that I was to meet Mrs. Haskell during the same visit. Finally, she relented and agreed, though without any visible enthusiasm.

The car to collect me was at our door right on time, and Mr. Haskell and his friend, ballet-loving Captain Lakin, were there to greet me, whisking me off to Cambridge. The English countryside was velvet green with idyllic weather after all the artificial and blinding lights of the opera house. At Kings College in Cambridge, we walked along the hall where Sir Isaac Newton had tested his theory of gravity. And then we glided along the River Cam, the men taking turns punting. I just loved drifting along the calm, clear water. What a contrast and antidote to all the tensions of the opera house!

After the delightful time in Cambridge, we drove back to Mr. Haskell's home where his charming and hospitable Russian wife had a scrumptious meal waiting and ready for us. The table was set with fine embroidered linen, sparkling crystal and delicate bone china. She made it a truly festive occasion.

During dinner, Mr. Haskell, no stranger to baby ballerinas, having famously described the young Tamara Toumanova as "the black pearl of Russian ballet", told me that, after researching, I was the youngest person ever to dance a soloist role on the stage of the Royal Opera House. I was younger, he explained, than even the then child prodigy, Dame Alicia Markova, had been when she first appeared at Covent Garden. As for the majestic Dame Beryl Grey, her first *Swan Lake,* at the age of 14, was danced in Oxford. When, several months later, she danced her first full-length *Swan Lake* at what is now London's Albery Theatre, he took Dame Beryl and her parents for a celebratory tea. It was, coincidentally, Dame Beryl's 15th birthday!

After dinner, my head spinning circles from Mr. Haskell's comparative examples, he took me to his library and proceeded to give me books he had authored; *Ballet Annuals #1, 2, 3* and *4*, inscribing them all. In his *Ballet Annual #7*, which I later purchased in New York, Mr. Haskell had an extensive spread about the New York City Ballet's London engagement. I felt honored to find my picture in it.

And so I returned later that day to Mrs. Wortham, none the worse for wear and, above all, immeasurably enriched.

We were in the midst of a social whirl, with London's most prominent hostesses vying to entertain us. In a welcoming party given at the Crush bar of the Royal Opera House to toast the first appearance of the New York City Ballet in London, Arnold Haskell spotted me.

Without hesitation, he invited me to join him at his table at which sat Ninette de Valois, Margot Fonteyn and Alicia Markova, a future triptych of Dames of the British Empire, and already three reigning queens of the ballet world.

I looked at Alicia Markova, dressed to perfection in a very feminine flowing dress with mauve roses decorating the pastel print. Strands of pearls adorned her slender neck and she was wearing a large brimmed picture book hat to complete her fashionable attire. As I fixed my gaze on her, I saw concurrently the greatest Giselle I had ever seen, so carefree in her untroubled joy in the first act, then rapidly deteriorating in the mad scene, yanking at her hair in her crushed disbelief, dragging the sword around the stage until she fell upon it, then surviving for a few more staggering steps until she stumbled into her mother's desperate arms to die. At her every performance of *Giselle* during those 1949 and 1950 appearances in New York, I would unfailingly shed tears for her Giselle, for the destruction of her once trusting innocence.

In the second act, when she returned as a pale and pasty ghost maiden, she was exquisite, effortless and ethereal as she barely seemed to touch the ground, skimming the cold earth and flitting from the vengeful Myrtha to comfort her guilt-burdened Albrecht. Has there ever been another ballerina so at home in the very realm of intangible air?

I also saw Dame Alicia dance Fokine's *Les Sylphides* and reincarnate the floating Marie Taglioni in Anton Dolin's *Pas de Quatre*. In whatever she danced, her fleetness of foot and lithograph lightness were unparalleled.

And there she was, the Giselle of my dreams, sitting next to me, so gracious and devoid of airs of any kind. I was so much in awe of her that I said very little, just hanging on her every word and trying to give her intelligible answers to her questions.

"How are you getting on as the youngest dancer in the company?" she queried. She then told me that when she was the same age, 14 in 1924, the youngest dancer in the legendary Diaghilev Ballets Russes, the rehearsal schedules were posted in Russian, which she couldn't read, the Cyrillic alphabet giving her no clue whatsoever. So when she asked one of the Russian dancers to translate for her, she often was deliberately given the wrong information causing her to miss that intended rehearsal. Sabotage, fuelled by jealousy and resentment, doesn't seem to go out of fashion, as I was to discover!

Life had been no bed of roses for Dame Alicia. With her father's suicide, precipitated by bankruptcy, she had been propelled into the role of family breadwinner to help support her mother and younger sisters. At the age of 11, a bout of diphtheria precluded her joining the Diaghilev Ballets Russes and it was not until three years later that she was able to accept the great impresario's invitation.

How this woman, Alicia Markova, sitting next to me, was the flight of history telescoped. For in Diaghilev's youth, he tried, but failed, to become a student of the legendary composer Rimsky-Korsakov. Eventually, as all the chroniclers of art well know, Diaghilev discovered his true niche, not as a composer, but as the 20th century's most impacting cultural catalyst.

I continued, in awe, to be transfixed by Markova, born Lillian Alicia Marks, asking myself if ethnicity was an ingredient in the magic recipe of greatness. Like her own goddess, Anna Pavlova, for whom she had danced as a child, Markova was half Jewish, sharing with the Swan an aquiline profile and, more importantly, a missionary zeal.

Dame Alicia was to die the day after her 94th birthday, never having married, her total allegiance having been all her long life to the all-consuming and gluttonous art of ballet. Serge Diaghilev had kept a strict paternal eye on her and then, after his death in 1929, Markova's dancing partner, Anton Dolin, hovered over her possessively (in her own words) as a jealous older brother. But as incomplete as her personal life may have been, she did become Britain's first prima ballerina assoluta, no small achievement in the ongoing marathon of determined aspirants.

Princess Margaret, the King's younger daughter, came to one of our performances and sat in the Royal Box. Still only 19 years old, she was the same age as many of the corps de ballet. After the performance, we all stood lined up on stage waiting to be presented to her. Instructions had been meticulously given us that we were to neither touch her, nor shake her hand, just curtsey, or bow in the boys' case. This royal protocol ruffled the feathers of a good half of the company, all of them having grown up in backslapping and egalitarian America.

They thought such bowing and scraping was belittling, outmoded and demeaning and, as such, refused to join the line-up. As for myself, I was something of a traditionalist and responded to the protocol, perhaps due to my Russian teachers' reverential relationship with the Romanovs.

Her Royal Highness, the Princess Margaret, was wearing a sky-blue silk dress and a hat with a veil. Her eyelashes, I noticed, did not stick to her veil and I was curious to know how she managed that. Of course, if you weren't permitted to touch her royal personage, or shake her hand, to ask her to explain a make-up secret was certainly off-limits! Perhaps if I had had the temerity to pose the question, I'd have found my head on the chopping block or, less radically, cooped up indefinitely in the Tower!

Despite her privileged existence, Princess Margaret did not have a happy life.

One early morning I decided to venture out to Vera Volkova's ballet class on nearby West Street. I had heard so much about her extraordinary pedagogy, and was eager to take some of her classes. Perhaps she was having an off day, but I found her rather cold and aloof. As for her class, it was one of the hardest I had ever taken, outside of Oboukhov's. The combinations were very long and she demonstrated them so quickly that you had to be on extra alert to learn them. I regretted that I didn't find her teaching inspiring. It could have been that, after such a relentless schedule, I was too fatigued to be fully on the receiving end. As Mr. B was teaching class almost on a daily basis, I decided to stick to those.

One unforgettable Sunday afternoon, we were entertained at Lord and Lady Mountbatten's country estate, Broadlands, at Romsey in Hampshire. Lord Mountbatten was the great-grandson of Queen Victoria, the history books showing a photograph of him sitting on her lap in 1901, the year of her death. He grew up to become Earl Mountbatten of Burma, then, subsequently, the last Viceroy of India. Though his public life was wreathed in glory, his private life was less so, his wife Edwina having been heavily rumored to have had a relationship with Jawaharlal Nehru, India's first Prime Minister.

Lord Mountbatten was very tall, commanding and handsome, groomed to be a leader of men. He and his wife stood at the door of their estate, greeting and shaking hands with each of us. Though all the soloists had been invited, so few accepted, disinterest ruling the roost, that the rest of the company was quickly invited to fill in the embarrassing gap. That is how I found myself there.

I could not understand how disengaged so many of the company were with such a rare opportunity to encounter such historical figures. Be that as it may, Maria Tallchief, Nicky Magallanes, Roy Tobias, Bea Tompkins and a few others did realize this moment would not replicate itself so quickly, if ever again, and were present.

Lord Mountbatten was, it must be realized, a product of his time, when Britannia really did rule the waves. Vestiges of the colonial mentality, as was to be expected, prevailed. Nowadays it might be called racism. So when he asked me, within earshot of Maria Tallchief herself, if there was still "an Indian problem" in Oklahoma (having read in the advance publicity that I hailed from that state), I assured him that things had noticeably calmed down, that they were loyal American citizens, many of them having served in the Second World War, and that "the situation with the Indians" that he inquired about no longer existed.

Thankfully, Lord Mountbatten had not asked Maria, herself, those questions, for if he had, I dread to think what her answers might have been. In actual fact, there are still justified grievances among many Native Americans against the federal American government. But baby ballerina of the London season that I was, I was the last person in the world qualified to enter into a political discussion with the likes of Lord Louis Mountbatten, one of the most decorated statesmen of the British empire.

Both Lord and Lady Mountbatten were faultless hosts, pleased to show us the rolling and verdant green hills of their estate. They were both genuine ballet lovers, asking many questions about Mr B and whether the American success of the Sadler's Wells Ballet was really as great as they had read. I confirmed to them that the success was nothing less than monumental. Lord Mountbatten was a great admirer of Margot Fonteyn, and when I told him that she had sent me opening night good wishes, he said such thoughtfulness was typical of her.

To stand next to Lord Mountbatten, who even in my high heels towered above me, was to hear the ceremonial bugle calls of a vanished era. Despite those echoes of his pageant-filled past, I had no difficulty conversing with him, finding him to be a very engaging, open and friendly gentleman. What a memorable day that was, mingling with the last Viceroy of India, the final ruler of the fading Raj, when the fluttering Union Jack had been lowered there for the very last time, and when the Imperial sun of the British Empire was rapidly sinking into the horizon.

When, so many years later, in 1979, I heard the news of Lord Mountbatten's assassination in Ireland by the IRA, his legs blown off before death released him from his agony, I shed tears of shock and incomprehension. Dying with him were his pet dog and his grandson, Nicholas; his eldest daughter's mother-in-law, the Dowager Lady Brabourne; and the boat boy Paul Maxwell.

We finished our Covent Garden season and went on to give several performances in what they called the provinces; Manchester, Liverpool and Croydon. Then, five weeks after we had first arrived in excited apprehension, we returned home, crowned and festooned with new and hard- won laurels.

Though one could safely say that I was artistically in advance of my years, my emotional development had not yet caught up. But that age of cocooned innocence was soon to draw to a halt. For once back on American soil, I was to find myself becoming more and more attached to a young man who, though he loved me in his own fashion, did not and could not respond in a way that I would have wanted. There was no way in which I could have distanced myself from him, since we were dancing partners on stage. Several years later, he was to occupy that special niche in memory reserved for those we have loved, but lost to indiscriminate death.

CHAPTER TEN

THE APOLLO OF MY LOVE'S AWAKENING

U pon our triumphant return to New York, we had little more than three weeks to rehearse before our fall season. The discriminating London audience had roared their approval and David Webster, Covent Garden's administrator, was so impressed with our reception that arrangements were immediately made for our return engagement in 1952.

Author Arnold Haskell, who had taken me punting on the Cam in King's College, Cambridge, wrote in his 1951 *Ballet Annual*:

"Very welcome visitors have been the New York City Ballet...Here is an Englishman indulging in the national pastime of seeking dollars, but for an American company this time. If any wealthy American happens to read this, and I believe that men of wealth still exist in America, I would like to assure him that the New York City Ballet has done more for the artistic prestige of his country than a carload of crooners, ten years run of musicals, a high-powered comedian, and a million reels of Hollywood celluloid all added together."

The unsolicited plea for funds was welcomed by Morton Baum of the City Center, for he discovered, to his dismay, that the deficit upon return was $40,000, not the expected $25,000. Again, the difference was made up by generous devotees of the ballet with the unwavering Mr. Kirstein at the front of the line.

We were all saddened to learn that Maria Tallchief had decided to ask for an annulment from Mr. B, her publicly stated reason, splashing the tabloids, that she wanted children whereas he wasn't prepared to lose her to pregnancy, albeit temporarily. "Any woman can be a mother, few can be ballerinas" he famously commented. Appraising the break-up realistically, the schism had to happen sooner or later, for such was the pattern of Mr. B's need to renew the arterial flow, the very heartbeat of his ceaseless creativity.

Some believed that her marriage to Mr. B was never consummated, that he married his ballerinas in order to give them 24-hour a day private coaching. From breakfast table to boudoir, the latest wife was inundated with his non-stop thoughts and philosophy on music and the dance. I, myself, am inclined to believe this interpretation.

Most of the men in the company were gay, a few were straight, while Mr. B, I sensed, though he loved women, remained impervious to other men's more primal needs. The sexual urge manifested in him, though I can't prove it as such, not in the act of physical coupling, but in the torrential outpouring that drenched, non-stop, his dancers through the generations. I remember hugging him when, at a low point, I was pouring out my woes to him. I recall that it was like embracing a lamppost.

Not that I should use myself as a barometer of response, for gay boys obviously had their reasons for showing me no interest, while straight men perhaps perceived me, due to my age, as jail bait, most, but not all.

André Eglevsky, very handsome and virile, once grabbed me in the stairwell on my way down to watch Maria and him dance the *Sylvia pas de deux*. He then forcefully soul-kissed me when I barely had heard of such tongue-colliding expressions of sexual desire. Then he speedily withdrew his tongue, slackened his grip on me and continued racing down the stairs to dance at his usual virtuosic level.

I was so dumbfounded I could hardly stand on my two feet! But I didn't want to miss the pas de deux and also wanted to be sure André made it to the wings on time. Maria would not have taken kindly to me waylaying her partner en route to the wings! Jezebel, Salomé I was not, more the young girl in Ingmar Bergman's *The Virgin Spring*.

That was the only encounter I ever had with him. Perhaps he kissed me, as young as I was, to pump up his adrenalin before the pas de deux. The risk factor often excites otherwise conventional men, and women, too.

André was married and no decent girl would then go for a married man and ever have a clear conscience. That was then, this is now! Today, gay and straight, male or female, married or not, people meet in bars for the first time and, without further preliminaries, get down to the business of the day, or night, as the case may be. Not in those more circumspect days!

Maria had more than the *Sylvia pas de deux* on her mind. Another reason for her annulment was that Mr. B was clearly besotted with a new muse, the tall, thin and angular Tanaquil LeClercq. As with all of Mr. B's past muses, Maria was to care deeply for him until the day he died and then without respite after. Regardless of her new status as ex-wife, she continued to dance all of her roles for the company

Soon after the annulment Maria married a hunky and dashing airplane pilot who seemed to adore her! He would stand backstage in the wings during a performance, his eyes glued to her every air-slicing move, while every girl in the corps de ballet would be besieged by thoughts inappropriate to performance focus. On the scoreboard of physical attraction, he was a winner, so it was no mystery what drew Maria to him. Unfortunately, the marriage did not survive a travelling ballerina's airborne itinerary. Maria was to eventually find emotional fulfillment in her third marriage to a Chicago lawyer with whom she had a daughter.

Frederic Ashton once again returned to the company to create his new ballet, *Picnic at Tintagel*. With the apt period music of Sir Arnold Bax and the as always exquisite costumes and decor by Cecil Beaton, this was an Edwardian ballet of delicate pastoral setting. Without effort, one could visualize the vaporous clouds of sky-pink and sea-blue hue, canopying the genteel figures.

Diana Adams and Jacques d'Amboise were cast in the plum roles of tourists visiting the Cornish castle of Tintagel. There they imagine themselves to be the medieval lovers, Tristram and Iseult, better known through Wagner's opera as *Tristan and Isolde.* As the picnic comes to an end, so does their flirtation, with daytime fantasy reverting back to late afternoon reality. Frank Moncion was King Mark, another role in his gallery of portrayals that he imbued, as always, with the conviction of etched belief. As for Diana, she brought to her role the unadorned sincerity that was the essence of her own character. Regarding Jacques, though he was still a teenager, he was a seasoned and totally reliable old pro, carrying off his huge responsibility with aplomb and effortless honor.

By this time, Mr. B was in thrall to Tanny and choreographed *La Valse* for her to the haunting score of Maurice Ravel. It was a gift to the woman he was now in love with, just as Aristotle Onassis once gave jewels to Maria Callas during his trophy-hunting period of wooing her. There was a difference, though; Tanny, through her marriage to Balanchine, became a star, while Maria Callas, through her long yacht-sailing years with Onassis, dismantled the machinery that had made her the prima donna of the century.

Mme Karinska, not as philanthropic this time as in the past, created the most lavish costumes, but charged $1,700 for each corps de ballet outfit. We felt beautiful and looked beautiful. As for the expense, there is a story about the early Broadway showman, Florenz Ziegfeld, and his annual *Ziegfeld Follies.* When questioned as to why he had the gorgeous chorus girls costumed with the most outrageously expensive silk underskirts that the audience couldn't even see, he retorted, "Ah, but the girls know the difference!" So did we Balanchine girls feel and look as lovely as our Ziegfeld forebears.

The men looked noble and elegant in their tuxedo-styled costumes, partnering us in the rhythmically sweeping waltzes. The ballet was a big favorite with not only the dancers, but also with the audiences in New York and, later, in Europe.

The dress rehearsal went without any hitches with Mr. B and Lincoln Kirstein out front watching the ballet. Even Lincoln Kirstein looked pleased, a rare occurrence. I was among the last to leave the stage after the rehearsal and heard Mr. B say, "Is fine, but we need chandelier."

Mr. Kirstein answered, "But George! We don't have any time or any money!"

Mr. B just stared off into space saying, "Yes, chandelier...real crystal," nodding his head into space while wandering away.

I could hear Mr. Kirstein still saying, "But George, but George!"

At the opening that night, hours later, hanging from the center of the stage was a huge Waterford Crystal chandelier! Mr. Kirstein had whipped out his checkbook and had purchased, no time at all later, a massive crystal chandelier at the Waterford showroom on 57th Street. Money talks and within hours, the splendiferous chandelier had been transported, assembled and hung, ready to be lit by Jeannie

Rosenthal. That opulent chandelier was the final sumptuous touch for Tanny's priceless gift from Mr. B.

In addition to supplying Mr. B with whatever he required to fulfill his cascading visions, such as the luxuriant crystal chandelier, Mr. Kirstein also kept his eye out on Mr. B's more practical needs. Once at a train station in Europe, the entire company was assembled and ready to board the train. Mr. Kirstein came up to Mr. B and said, "Now George, here is your ticket! Just hold on to it until I get back and don't move! Don't go anywhere!" Mr. B. looked like a 5-year-old boy following the instructions of his daddy, clinging to the ticket whose purpose he couldn't quite decipher. Watching him, I was prepared to go after him if he started to wander off.

Another time I heard Maria ask him if he had had any breakfast, and after a long pause of bewilderment, he answered that he didn't quite remember. Luckily, Mr. B had guides and minders if he seemed to be disoriented, for he lived, as does everyone else, in a world of planes and trains that waited for no one.

George Balanchine struck me as something of a master astronomer, his mind functioning like a Hubble Space Telescope, sorting out the super-celestial patterns of galaxies and exploding stars, but not straightforward timetables. Such pedestrian details as shopping lists, appointment books, changing time zones and budgets didn't fully register in his exploding mind. Nevertheless, even a master astronomer needs to be reminded to hold onto his train ticket, as Leonardo da Vinci's cook had to remind him, the supreme universal genius, that his soup was getting cold!

Shopping in the supermarket for new dancers, Mr. B was more comfortable, hiring some new principals from the American Ballet Theatre; Hugh Laing, Diana Adams, Janet Reed, and Nora Kaye.

Hugh was actually past his sell-by date, but, in his favor, still had a strikingly good-looking face with the most defined bone structure. In the 1930s and 40s, in England, then later at Ballet Theatre, he had been the inamorata of choreographer Antony Tudor. The absence of any technique counted for little since he was the beloved of the choreographer. Taking his limitations into consideration, Tudor created works in which Hugh's dark, handsome looks and presence could compensate for his complete lack of technical command, roles such as Romeo in the Delius *Romeo and Juliet, Undertow* and *Pillar of Fire*, the ballet that made Nora Kaye a star.

In his Ballet Theatre days, after the performance, Hugh used to be seen leaving the old Met stage door with a small parrot perched on his shoulder, the applause and attention of the audience insufficient to carry him through the rest of the day. For some people, no amount of attention is sufficient, their need insatiable. Where does this craving begin and why? Perhaps birth can be viewed as the first environmental insult, that sudden withdrawal from the mother's body, with the rest of one's life a futile pursuit of that abrupt departure from the womb. Hugh may have been one of those people whose appetite for attention, in consequence, could never be appeased.

By the time he had joined the New York City Ballet, he was no longer with Tudor, having inexplicably married Diana Adams, a union that predictably did not survive. Well, no one could accuse Diana of being gullible, for she certainly knew the score upside down on the subject of gay men. But as far as Mr B and Kirstein were concerned, Diana was a very good dancer and Hugh came along with the package. Another added factor was the circulating rumor that Mr. Kirstein, also decorated with a wife on his arm, was attracted to Hugh. If so, that stands to reason why he hired him to dance in a repertoire that didn't suit him, and to be among dancers whose ankles alone he could never hope to reach.

Mr. B, dipping into his bag of magic tricks, again pulled out *Prodigal Son*, the ballet that serviced non-dancers such as Jerome Robbins. Thus cast, Hugh would be less likely to elicit criticism.

As for Nora Kaye, she was a strong dancer with a good enough technique to dance *Swan Lake, Giselle* and the *Black Swan pas de deux* replete with 32 machine-gunned *fouettés*, but to tackle the Balanchine repertoire was another kettle of fish, an aquarium unsuited to her. She was now out of her depth, simply not having the speed and scissor-sharp attack required to do Mr. B's ballets. When she attempted Maria's role in the first movement of *Symphony in C*, Nora ended up gasping for air and just averted falling a few times. Her failure made us all cringe, wince and feel for her plight. To her credit, she was a magnificent dramatic dancer who just could not manage the demanding Balanchine ballets. But not one to take a failure lying down, she pushed herself in class and rehearsal to acquire the speed and attack needed to do justice to any of Mr. B's work. With the addition of Tudor's *Lilac Garden*, her situation began to change. And with the creation of Robbins' *The Cage*, she created a sensation.

How? Nora, in all frankness, was not without her hang-ups, one of them being that she was addicted to collecting, not seashells or first edition stamps, but gay men. With the exception of one of her husbands, straight violinist Isaac Stern, she tried to corner for the marriage market the likes of playwright Arthur Laurents and choreographers Robbins, Ashton and Kenneth MacMillan. What, one might ask, was so wrong with straight men? Did they have measles, boils or dandruff? For the record, Nora's final marriage was to former dancer and choreographer Herbert Ross. Together they went on to become top Hollywood producers, generating many films including *Funny Girl* with Barbra Streisand, *The Turning Point* with Shirley MacLaine and Anne Bancroft, and the well-intentioned but stillborn *Nijinsky*.

But to return to Nora's dancing days, she was able, in the studio and on stage, to be as grotesque as we poor girls, as hard we tried, could not. Robbins, without one iota of directorial ability, was able to tap into Nora combustive ingredients. Make no mistake about it, he was a helluva chef, taking the witches' brew of his own disordered juices, stirring thoroughly, then adding, in generous portions, Nora's cumulative neuroses. Abracadabra, a screaming exorcism, for out of Hell's Kitchen came the slimy infant devil that was Rosemary's baby, no, Jerry's baby, *The Cage!*

The pure and uncluttered *Concerto Barocco*, with Mr. Balanchine's choreography and music by Johann Sebastian Bach, the *Concerto in D minor for Two Violins*, was another ballet in which I was so happy to be dancing. In the coda, we were required to jump on *pointe* to the syncopated Bach music, thereby wearing out a pair of *pointe* slippers at almost every performance. But Marquis de Sade styled sadism was not part of Mr. B's style, so we fulfilled his vision without victimization. What a breath of fresh air to dance for him!

Mr. B. revived *Le Baiser de la Fée* that returning season, a charming work except for the blonde wig worn by Maria, an accessory she soon discarded when she read John Martin's critical review. I was a peasant girl, although on *pointe*, with some very interesting dancing to do. How gratifying it was to again be part of another Stravinsky/ Balanchine collaboration.

The *Sylvia pas de deux* was created for Maria and Herbert Bliss, but Herbie strained his back just before the opening and missed the first performance. The role was then handed down to Nicky Magallanes before being inherited by André Eglevsky, a world-class premier danseur. André, on his entrance with his first *cabriole*, suspended himself in the air evoking the audience's gasps and cheers. Along with his 12 pirouettes, he was something to behold. With his handsome face and beautiful body, how could anyone expect him to be reserved for only one gender? And he wasn't. André was bisexual. His wife, Leda Anchutina, preferred his boyfriends for fear that a transient girlfriend would steal him from her, though she didn't feel the threat of that theft from men. Leda and André, as it happened, stayed securely married until his relatively early death from a heart attack.

Well, Mrs. Eglevsky never had to worry about me being love's thief; I was too busy with my schoolwork. As we prepared for our next trip abroad, I still had lessons to contend with, carrying books around between rehearsals so that I could study for those Friday exams. Mr. B. advised me to take French, "So when you go there, you will be able to speak!" That was just what I needed to hear because I then threw myself into learning that most lyrical language with renewed effort.

Mr. B was on fire with ideas. His creativity burst forth encouraged by the artistic success in London. I felt his watchful eye on me and he gave me a tremendous opportunity to shine, arranging new choreography for Herbert Bliss and me to dance the opening pas de deux, Melancholic, in the revised first movement of his *The Four Temperaments*. The music was composed by the well-known Paul Hindemith who occasionally came down from Yale to guest conduct for us. It was always an occasion to dance to the music of a composer being conducted by himself.

The Four Temperaments was a ballet based on the belief of ancient Greek medicine that associated earth, water, fire, and air with the four temperaments that constitute the basic moods of people. The curtains opened to reveal Herbie and me on a bare stage waiting for Paul Hindemith to conduct. With his first precise gesture to the musicians, we started to dance.

During this period, a new feeling was beginning to envelop me, not learning new choreography, which I was accustomed to, but a congestion of my mind that had until then been free of romantic traffic. When we first started working on the ballet with Mr B, I saw Herbie as a big brother, but when we started moving to the music together, I began to relate to him as much more than a substitute family member. As I danced with him, I began to be stirred by a desire to touch and be touched by him, to expand our emotional proximity into physical closeness. Erotic, carnal, sexual, there are many words in the dictionary to define the longing of one person for another. The feelings I was having for Herbie were entirely new to me, for I had never before felt the desire for a man. I had never even gone on a date, and here I was in the closest physical proximity with a beautiful young man in body tights, with not even thick jeans to camouflage the contours of our bodies from each other.

He was so sensitive and kind, always helping me with balance and support when I needed it, but over and above that, seemingly attuned to me evolving as a young human being. I felt myself drawn to him physically and would deliberately let my cheek touch his when we were practicing as a sort of affectionate flirtation. He didn't even have a beard, no bristles that could be felt on touch, only soft, smooth and almost transparent skin. With his considerable androgynous beauty, he could have stepped out of a medieval canvas, a Botticelli angel or a Leonardo shepherd. As it happened, he was a Balanchine Apollo, ideally cast as the radiant Greek sun god in *Orpheus*.

Herbie was older than I by several years, but it didn't deter me from flirting with him and hoping for some kind of positive reaction. Was there something wrong with me? Why couldn't I at least get him to squeeze my hand or give me a peck on the cheek? When we finished a difficult series of steps we hugged in excitement that we had made it through a demanding part of the pas de deux. It was spontaneous and natural, but I held on just a little longer than correctness dictated so that I could feel his sinewy arms around me and his lithe body proximate to my own.

Is there a female corps de ballet dancer who has never been in love with one of the gay boys in the company? If there is, then point her out to me. To fall in love for the first time is enough of a topsy-turvy experience, but to fall in love with the unattainable is doubly hard. One's flimsy and fragile self-esteem takes a beating. Staring at the mirror, mirror on the wall, you seek confirmation that you look presentable. One panel of glass assures you that you do, then moving to another panel or glass, you seem to be gazing at one of those funhouse mirrors of zany distortion! Which is me, you ask, the lopsided one, of course.

My relationship with some of the girls had somewhat improved when we got back to New York since I no longer had the private dressing room, inspector, chaperone and, above all, that avalanche of London publicity. But still, New York teen magazines featured me, and that continued coverage did nothing at all to win me new backstage friends. On top of which, I was beginning to be highlighted in various ballets.

After a rehearsal, and in an unguarded moment, I made the foolish mistake of confiding in two of my dancing colleagues (both of whom had been persistently infiltrating my protective reserve), that I was suffering my first romantic involvement, falling for Herbie Bliss! Wasting no time, like Cinderella's spiteful stepsisters, the two young ladies immediately sashayed over to Herbie and told him, betraying my confidence with tongue-wagging glee. This left me to face a very awkward situation, for the next rehearsal was coming up.

I was blanketed by embarrassment, for by their calculatedly spilling the beans, so to speak, they also made it uncomfortable for him since he now felt obliged to share his otherwise guarded private life with me. After all, this was decades before Gay Pride and all those carnival-styled floats that defiantly parade your libido.

Herbie tenderly took me aside and in the quiet and privacy of a studio corner, told me that he did love me, but regretted having to tell me that he was gay. As such, he had no capacity to feel that same spark toward me that I was feeling towards him, explaining that it was men who ignited him in that regard, not women, no matter how sweet and pretty he found me.

So I was pretty, after all! A lot of good it did me! His diplomatic and psychological explanation didn't succeed in extinguishing the sparks that had by now grown within me into an early flame. I loved him anyway! Who ever labeled youthful yearning as puppy love? After all, dogs love for life, and the love of babies and children for their parents is very powerful, not even reduced in memory as age distances us from its early and needful source.

No matter how I tried to unravel the confusing threads, I wished that Herbie could feel what I was feeling. Though it was a one-sided romance, I continued to love him for as long as he lived. What I loved was his very being, his soul. The physical part was left to be rerouted as I intertwined my body with his in Mr. B's masterful choreography. Taking on board his explanation of neutrality, I ceased flirting with him, for I didn't want him to feel uncomfortable in my presence. I masked my longing and always acted the role of the smiling little sister, while yearning inwardly whenever we danced together.

Was I really that naive insofar as gay men were concerned? Did I have any excuse, even in 1950, to be so unaware as were the young innocents in Frank Wedekind's distant play, *A Spring Awakening?* Not really by this time, but perhaps, subconsciously, I was hoping to reach Herbie, despite the locks and bolts that closed his door, that vaulted door that otherwise had been accessible only to men. How little I then understood the compulsive aspects of sexuality.

Gay men, I was to discover, when they "perform", that euphemism for having sex, are doing just that, performing. In other words, they are surrendering, obliging the woman that they love, albeit only on an emotional level. The parallel is found, I was to note, when a gay man falls in love with a straight man, and the straight man acquiesces, though the sexual link will end, if not the deep feeling.

All human beings, of whatever inclination, seek escape from the prison of their own solitude. Those who remain locked up often re-route themselves into charitable work, religious pursuit, creative art, or war, the killing instinct legitimized.

And so, though my thwarted romance had ground to a halt, artistically we were conquering new ground. There was a short engagement at the Chicago Opera House when I danced the lead in Lew Christensen's ballet, *Jinx,* in place of Janet Reed who had to tend her sick six-year-old son. Having already danced the lead in this ballet at London's Covent Garden, I had digested the role, so was acclimatized to its requirements. One's best roles, I discovered, do not look like roles, rather they emerge as emanation of spirit.

This time my name was on the program and I was reviewed by Ann Barzel, the foremost Chicago ballet critic.

Jinx Circus Ballet Shows Striking Skill

"The romance of a wirewalker and equestrian is danced very well by Barbara Bocher and Herbert Bliss. Blonde little Miss Bocher has an engaging manner and like everyone else in the company she can dance very well!"

That was my first review, and though Miss Barzel's repetitive writing would not win any prizes, I was grateful for her praise. Never look a gift horse in the mouth! What pleased me most was that in *Jinx*, as well as in *The Four Temperaments*, I could also dance with my secret love, Herbie.

Well, perhaps not so secret with those gossipy blabbermouths, the two deceptive friends at the ready to torpedo my romantic efforts. In addition to the blood, sweat and twisted tendons of the dancing life, there was now the maelstrom of intrigue in which I found myself. For there I was, the company's youngest dancer, barely into my teens, and already favored with soloist roles and international media attention. The jealousy would escalate into a hateful campaign of opportunistic damage, a strategy I was ill equipped to fight.

As for the late and lamented Herbert Bliss, the Apollo of my love's awakening, even now I often wear the shimmering gold-chained necklace with the turquoise and gold pendant he and his boyfriend gave me. It was a gift to commemorate my dancing the lead in the tennis ballet by Mr. B, *A La Françaix*, with André Eglevsky as my partner. The presentation of the gift took place in Trieste, at the opera house, after a long journey on the fabled Orient Express.

A conventional trio we were not, for the necklace seemed almost an engagement present, but there was no marriage in the viewfinder, and the betrothed were two lovely gay boys in love with each other, not me. Who was I fooling? No one, and by this late date, not even myself. The necklace, though anything but a diamond engagement ring, was no less precious to me.

My dear, sweet and lamented Herbie was to die violently in a late-night high-speed automobile accident on a Los Angeles freeway, a gentle light and life extinguished in a flaming crash at the age of only 37. This was six years after I married and left the company, and a short time after his Trieste lover had left him to marry a woman. No one will ever be able to answer the question if, disillusioned and crushed, perhaps one too many relationships terminated, a corner of his brain wanted to flee. And what better way than sudden death from which there could be no return? Was he driving carelessly or, conversely, did he know exactly what he was doing?

I still love him and always will. Perhaps Herbert Bliss and I will meet again, if after death, a new life, without pain, awaits us. And if such a world does not exist, then to feed such fervent fantasies does help smooth, to a degree, the ankle-twisting and heart-breaking terrain before us.

There was an elegiac poem written in 1913 by the British poet, Richard LeGallienne, father of the noted American actress, Eva LeGallienne. Entitled *The Lonely Dancer*, it could have been spoken by the distant voice of George Balanchine, himself, eulogizing Herbert from afar.

And what if all the meaning lies
Just in the music, not in those
Who dance this, with transfigured eyes,
Holding in vain each other close;
Only the music never dies.
The dance goes on, the dancer goes.

CHAPTER ELEVEN

SWAN LAKE AND BENNY GOODMAN

The year 1951 was the most prolific period of choreography in Mr. Balanchine's lifetime. Phenomenal in his ability to work with focus, precision and speed, he created a multitude of diverse ballets to suit a variety of dancers. Always kind and soft-spoken, and without ever raising his voice, he commanded absolute respect from one and all.

Until then, I had only one issue with Mr. B and that was that he never ever had a conversation with me about anything. Occasionally, he would come up with one-liners while teaching a class, but no personal conversations. Yet I must have found favor with him because, firstly, I was his scholarship student when scholarships were few and far between. Secondly, and more importantly, I was dancing more and more as an alternate for soloists in the ballets and he, alone, controlled everything regarding casting. Never, though, did I get any assistance from him regarding the treatment Robbins meted out to me during *The Cage* and *Age of Anxiety* rehearsals and, to a far lesser degree, while preparing *The Pied Piper*.

"Barbara, be patient," he once said to me, "Stalin waited forty years!"

Forty years? For what did Stalin wait so long - to starve millions of peasants to death? Understandably, I didn't get any reassurance from Mr. B's most cryptic comment.

Nathalie Branitzka, who was one of the two servants in the 1929 Diaghilev premiere of Mr. B's *Prodigal Son*, once stated that both Balanchine and Stalin came from Georgia, adding caustically, "and both of them were dictators!"

And I will add, "Yes, but Balanchine, unlike Stalin, was a benevolent dictator. And Mr. B didn't take life; rather he gave life. He was our supreme master and we were his devoted acolytes and non-question-ing followers. His word prevailed, the ultimate law as such, not to be changed or challenged, Working with Mr. B was no deportation to Gulag. No barbed wire kept us there. And with Lincoln Kirstein continuing to drain his vast fortune to fulfill Mr. B's choreographic revelations, there was no danger that Mr. B would be deposed as, sooner or later, are other ballet directors.

The New York City Ballet was soon to embark on its next European tour. To say I was excited would be an extreme understatement. In that year of 1951, I was alternating on a regular basis as soloist in *Jinx*, as well as a lead in *A La Françaix* and *Card Game*. I was one of the four cygnets in *Swan Lake* and occasionally danced one of the special waltz variations in *La Valse*. Also, I, from time to time, danced the lead in the rousing third movement in the Bizet *Symphony in C* with either Harold Lang, before he left to do *Guys and Dolls* on Broadway, or Bobby Barnett. Though few girls were up to it, the technical hurdles of doing double *saut de basque* were no deterrent. I didn't even want to know how I did it. I was just grateful that I could, and did.

The dream I had of dancing had become a vibrant reality, way beyond my expectations. Happiness was my constant companion! Looking at the orchestra in a thoughtful moment, I reflected, with respect, on those fifty or so musicians taking non-stop lessons as children, to one day play in a major symphony orchestra. They were a fine ensemble with Leon Barzin as our regular conductor and Hugo Fiorato, our accomplished first violinist. There were many guest conductors often conducting their own compositions.

Though you couldn't quite call him a guest, I remember Mr. B conducted *Symphony in C* with a speed demon tempo. He looked like a gleeful little boy grinning from ear to ear while our feet reached near horse-racing speed. How we galloped through that performance and to such roaring approval!

Capriccio Brilliante was the only ballet in which Mr. B choreographed a part especially for me. The role pushed the body to its limits and then some. With Mme Karinska designing the elegant costumes, to paraphrase George Gershwin in the song he wrote for Ethel Merman, who could ask for anything more? And while touching upon that song, *I've Got Rhythm*, Miss Merman said that when she, at the outset of her career, auditioned for Gershwin, it was like auditioning for God. Who, in the New York City Ballet, couldn't understand such a worshipping sentiment?

As a complete change of pace, Ruthanna Boris was commissioned to create a vintage American-styled ballet, dipping back into the country's heritage of the Deep South's minstrel shows. It was called *Cakewalk*, after one of the typical dances of that Mississippi steamboat era, and was as merrily southern as Aunt Jemima pancakes. Ruthanna herself danced the opening, her leading role then taken over by Janet Reed, after which I was honored to alternate with Janet.

I had never essayed a comic role before. As Hortense, Queen of the Swamp Lilies, I entered the stage on a swing, the stagehands releasing me from the wings already perched on the swing. Then I sailed above the stage. With my Mary Pickford curls on either side of my head secured with oversized roses, I wore a long Romantic era length pink tutu. Lowered to the ground, I was a syrupy sweet southern belle unhinged from being left a wallflower at a ball, the damsel no one wants to dance with.

After the first entrance there would be a little giggle from some in the audience at the unexpected sight of a dancer entering the stage from a swing. As the dance progressed and the comedy broadened, there were actually belly laughs coming from out front, a brand new experience for me!

Considering the fact that I was just 15, Ruthanna's choosing me to alternate the lead showed considerable belief on her part. Tanny, Herbie Bliss, Patty Wilde, Bobby Barnett and Frank Hobi, also paraded their dancing wares, helping to evoke the long-ago charm of composer Stephen Foster, author Mark Twain and, of course, the man who wrote the infectious music to *Cakewalk*, the inimitable Louis Gottschalk.

A former leading ballerina with the Ballet Russe de Monte Carlo, Ruthanna Boris was American of Russian-Jewish heritage. On leaving the company, she concentrated on choreography. When she died, there wasn't even a mention in the *New York Times* Internet pages. This glaring omission brought to mind the death of Carlotta Grisi in 1899, the woman who created the title role in *Giselle* so much earlier in 1841. By the time of Grisi's death, she was only recalled in the obituary of the day for having once been adored by the distinguished French writer Théophile Gautier. Not a word about her *Giselle*. Ruthanna, like Carlotta, had long outlived her celebrity.

Mainbocher, my uncle and top costume and dress designer, was attending performances regularly then, always sending me flowers when I danced a leading role. Now, looking back I wish I had been able to spend more time with him, for he was a fascinating man and such a morale booster whenever I did manage to see him. But I was knee-deep and mired in classes, rehearsals and performances from morning to night. Time, time, why is it so sparingly doled out?

On top of which, I had to garner my forces as my nemesis, Jerome Robbins, renewed his assaults on me. For the moment, he chose just to trespass on psychological territory that should have been strictly off-limits. I was chosen to dance in nearly every one of his ballets, often with my own very good part but with the added responsibility to understudy everyone else. That assignment necessitated my attending many more rehearsals than all the other dancers, also providing Robbins with my continued proximity to him.

"Why don't you get rid of your mother?" he would harangue me, a question that shocked me, for it was a query dipped in poison. Was there nothing sacred in his priorities? My mother loved me unconditionally and I depended on her for everything at that time when I was in New York. She accompanied me on the bus ride home from the theatre to make sure I was safe in the shadowy streets of New York at midnight. She knit me beautiful soft woolen leg warmers; she cooked for me, did my laundry and was constant companion and my best friend. Just because Robbins detested his father, and perhaps his mother, too (for threatening to give him away when he misbehaved as a child), was no reason for me to feel likewise towards my own wonderful mother. As Margot Fonteyn answered when someone was criticizing *her* mother, "No, stop."

"Why?" the obstinate faultfinder continued.

"Because she's my mother." That answer said it all.

Variations of Robbins' bulldozing question were asked me by him on a regular basis. He was concurrently working on the Broadway show, *Gypsy*, with Ethel Merman. I now wonder if his work and research for Gypsy Rose Lee's archetypical pushy, no-holds barred stage mother made him transfer his negative thoughts to my mother, the reverse of the famous stripper's parent. In actual fact, my mom never shoved me, but kept loving watch on my own driven pursuit of becoming a good dancer.

Robbins said, "Go out with kids your own age." How could I follow such advice? What kids? The ones I used to know were all back in Oklahoma. I didn't know any kids in New York and even if I did, I didn't have a spare minute in my entire week. As for the few girls in the company who were just a few years older than I, they were not to be trusted, a lesson I had yet to fully learn.

"You're taking too many classes!" Robbins further needled. What a perverse observation and criticism, for anyone worth his salt knew that intensive training should not and could not be sidetracked ever, let alone at my age and stage. Could he, I wracked my brain, be jealous that I had the technique I already had, when he didn't take his first lesson until the very end of his teens, and then only sporadically?

All the time he was choreographing *Pied Piper*, he never stopped chipping away with his puzzling and damaging daily lectures. Had I been older, I could have ignored his erosive methods, but I had not developed the thick skin needed as armory in his presence. Yes, he was a bullying creature, taking such cruel advantage of the youngest girl in the company. Prudently, I noticed that he kept his distance from the more macho members of the company, such as Jacques and, later, Eddie Villella.

I was caught in a contradictory situation; Robbins obviously liked my dancing, though I think he liked even more my convenience as his own and mobile punching bag.

All of us, not just myself, were invariably subjected to his oft-repeated mantra:

"SHIT, SHIT, SHIT! You are all shit! You look like shit, you dance like shit, you are all shit!" This was heard so often, it almost lost its shock impact, bouncing off our eardrums, if not our perforated nerve endings.

"There he goes, again," we thought, steeling ourselves for the next festering explosion of his nastiness.

The young reader should bear in mind that that scatological expletive was as jarring then as the F-word is when publicly used today. Perhaps even more so, since the F-word is called upon so freely nowadays in countless films and television programs.

Yet, despite Robbins' besmirching language, as strange and paradoxical as it may seem, I somehow enjoyed doing *The Pied Piper*. The prominent part he gave me in the new ballet, with its jazzy style of dancing, was refreshing to learn, calling on me to do an acrobatic walkover in the opening. Surprisingly, I was the only one who could manage that. Towards the end of the ballet, there was a vigorous Charleston with Frank Moncion, reminding me of doing that 1920s dance with my Dad as a four-year old girl. Oh, how rehearsing that dance made me miss him and his protective love! Dad, help me, I thought often, but there was no way he could have, because I never breathed a word to him of what was happening behind closed doors with Robbins. Had I, Dad would have taken me straight back to Oklahoma City.

Tanaquil LeClercq, in *Pied Piper*, was a terrific lead, with Janet Reed a bubbly funhouse of movement. Jill Ann Zimmerman, a year older than I, was now a member of the company, that year changing her name to Jillana. She had a pleasing opening section with Roy Tobias.

For me, the most memorable part of the ballet was the solo clarinet passage played at the front of the stage adjacent to the front black wing. The clarinetist would be seated on s stool playing Aaron Copland's *Clarinet Concerto*, a virtuoso vehicle. It was a showstopper and how could it not be, played by the likes of none other than the King of Swing, Benny Goodman, one of American's most celebrated popular jazz musicians. Along with Harry James, Tommy and Jimmy Dorsey, Peter Duchin and Gene Krupa, Benny Goodman was a household name throughout America of the 1930s, 40s and 50's. Under the aegis of the ubiquitous Sol Hurok, Benny Goodman bridged the gap between jazz and classical acceptance by appearing in the hallowed corridors of Carnegie Hall where Tchaikovsky himself conducted at its opening.

Benny Goodman's clarinet, I once in a while fantasized, would have made a perfect instrument with which to fend off Robbins as he was trying to dislodge me from my fragile security. I don't think, however, that Benny would have appreciated his rather expensive clarinet being turned into a weapon of defense! Unlike Lenny, Benny was unused to the coarse language so favored by Robbins, and once the rehearsals were over, scooted right out of the studio. He had, I sensed, felt that he and the ballet world made strange bedfellows.

Composer Aaron Copland himself, of *Appalachian Spring* and *Rodeo* fame, conducted the score for *Pied Piper* several times during that first season. The story line was slight, almost non-existent, showing how dancers moved, even involuntarily, to the impetus of the sound of music. It was Robbins in one of his rare, carefree moods, a ballet performed in practice clothes on an empty stage with a few stray ladders propped up against the bare back wall.

At the end of the final note played by the clarinet, there was a bright flash of light and a puff of white smoke from under the stool where the clarinetist had been sitting. Suddenly, there was a blackout for a split second during which time the clarinetist had vanished! It was a theatrical ending, but it scared the daylights out of Benny Goodman and he, at first, said he would not under any circumstances stay on the stool when the dreaded explosion took place. He insisted that he would exit the stage before the dynamite went off. After all, he was a musician, not part of a magic act; Benny Goodman he was, Houdini he was not!

Jerry somehow smooth-talked him into changing his mind, reassuring him that it was perfectly safe, lighting designer Jean Rosenthal further reassuring him of his guaranteed safety. Finally, between the two of them, they wore him down and Benny did, indeed, stay put on the stool during the loud pop with its attendant blast of smoke, resembling those fireworks going off every year on the Fourth of July! The audience loved it, but whoever played the clarinet at subsequent performances had to be persistently coaxed to keep sitting on that stool and remain there until after the explosion had taken place!

There was always a bet among the dancers to see if our guest artist would chicken out, for several guest clarinetists did run for their lives before the explosion, and who could blame them? Their fears were fully justified because when Margaret Hamilton played the Wicked Witch of the West in *The Wizard of Oz,* after a bungled explosion in a take where she was supposed to disappear in a puff of smoke, she suffered a second-degree burn on her face and third-degree burns on her hand! Those injuries necessitated her hospitalization and six weeks of recuperation.

To move from medical struggles to financial struggles, how, one can ask, did we all survive economically, considering the fact of the company always being in debt and always extending the begging bowl? We somehow managed, but just, paid a lump sum of $40 a week for the rehearsal period, and $60 a week for the performance weeks.

I learned a ballet very quickly and when anyone was sick or injured, soloist, or corps de ballet, I usually knew the part or could learn it in a few minutes, jumping in at the last moment. There had been a performance in London when, filling in for people who were either sick or injured, I danced all three movements of *Symphony in C.* That pressure was minimal, however, compared to emergency sessions in New York when I sometimes danced all three ballets in a matinee, and then all four ballets in the evening, all on the same day! Ah, the passion of youth and its attendant vigor, muses the now great-grand-mother thinking back!

Just before the departure for our European tour, there was a ballet ball held at New York's most de luxe hotel, the Waldorf-Astoria. It was organized as a fundraiser to help offset the $20,000 debt we had incurred, despite all cost-saving procedures. Presenting ballet, like opera, is as addictive as gambling and betting on the horses. Despite the deceptive winning streaks, bankruptcy lies just around the corner.

The Waldorf-Astoria evening was a very upmarket affair with fragrant white flowers patterning the walls and ceilings. Both ladies and gentlemen were the last word in haute couture, looking as if they had emerged from those fashion advertisements in Broadway playbills, circa 1950s.

While most youngsters my age in Oklahoma City were attending their end of school dances in the local high school gymnasium, I was at my first social dance at the Waldorf Astoria! Though I could face opera house audiences dancing George Balanchine at over-the-limit speed, I didn't know how to foxtrot! I really didn't, but I learned quickly and, in the process, just let my partner lead. I was reminded of the joke that when some businessman was ballroom dancing with a ballerina, he said to her, "Now I know why you're a toe dancer."

"Why?" she asked, still trying to keep up with him.

"You're a toe dancer, because you haven't stopped stepping on my toes, for crying out loud!"

In retrospect, I couldn't have been that bad, for I had a great evening! And the company's deficit had been considerably reduced.

When people in Oklahoma asked my mom if she regretted that I wasn't leading a normal teenager's life, she always answered that she wasn't at all sorry, adding that it wasn't so much what I was missing, as what I was gaining.

As far as my own thoughts on this subject were concerned, the life I was leading was, for me, a normal life; dancing under the batons of Stravinsky, Bernstein, Copland and Barzin and to the accompaniment of Benny Goodman, interpreting the choreography of masters such as Balanchine and Frederic Ashton, being costumed by Cecil Beaton and Mme Karinska, meeting British aristocracy and royalty – that for me had become the norm. I didn't miss smoking on late-night Oklahoma City street corners, secret beer guzzling, or speeding around town in broken-down jalopies. If I had missed those teenaged thrills, so be it. I'm actually grateful to have avoided them.

Only one sickly microbe kept returning, the disease for which no antibiotics had yet been discovered, namely, Mr. Robbins.

In the meanwhile, our minds were full of anticipation as we all boarded the plane for Barcelona, the first stop on our European tour. Once again, Phil Bloom, our ever-enterprising publicist, arranged for the Spanish press to meet us on arrival. When we landed, reporters made a beeline for Mr. B, Maria, and, this time I wasn't as taken aback, me! No longer 14, now 15, in Mr. Bloom's bag of bright ideas, I was still a newsworthy peg upon which to hang the local media's interest. The next day in the Barcelona newspaper, there was a headline in Spanish: *Balanchine, Maria y Barbara!* There was a little caricature of the three of us, with me wearing my old faithful Gimbels suit and hat with the veil that still stuck in my eyelashes! Looking back with the objectivity accrued by time, what did America's prima ballerina, Maria Tallchief, think when circumstances forced her to share her limelight with the likes of a youngster who, just a few years earlier, was still playing with dolls?

Betty Cage had organized an older dancer, Edwina Fontaine, to share a hotel room with me on tour, an arrangement that worked out fine. We were so exhilarated to find that our room had a balcony that overlooked the flowerbeds of the boulevard below. When we opened the French door that led to the sun-drenched balcony, the scent of the flowers filled the room with the fragrance of lilacs and magnolias. I knew then and there that I was going to love Spain!

After quickly unpacking at the hotel, we took a leisurely stroll along the delightful Las Ramblas promenade, shaded with inviting lime trees, until we reached the Gran Teatro del Liceo. What an awe-inspiring and splendiferous opera house that was!

On this trip, I had no chaperone and that bit of extra breathing space was a bonus. I was an experienced enough traveler by now not to get lost or in trouble. Besides which, there were so many people in the company that I never felt alone. I did feel that, in an unconventional way, the New York City Ballet was my family with Mr. B as Big Daddy, the head of the entire sprawling household.

Often seasoned artists are asked to cite the performance they look back on as coming closest to completeness, even touching upon perfection. Well, though I was experienced by now in terms of my artistic alliances and major event performances, in terms of time span I couldn't call upon extended memory. Still, there was a single performance that did stand out as the kind one dreams about, happens rarely, and even more rarely, repeats itself.

Without hesitation, that performance was our first *Swan Lake*, given in Barcelona. It was the new second act choreographed by George Balanchine and danced by Maria Tallchief and André Eglevsky at the Gran Teatro del Liceo. Traditionally designed, the theatre was built in 1847. Decorated with gilded gold and red velvet seats, it had a grand horseshoe with five tiers and an ornate royal box in the center of the first tier. Enormous chandeliers hung from the ceiling and I was told that the acoustics left nothing to be desired. The stage did have the usual European rake, so all of the balance adjustments we had made for Covent Garden had to be made for the Liceo. We had a rehearsal on stage the same day we arrived and class with Mr. B. early the next morning, needing to work out the kinks in our muscles from the long, cramped flight.

The dressing room was barely large enough for all of us, so all the girls were claustrophobically squeezed together in the very limited space. With no other choice but to manage, we set up a dressing table for make up, practice clothes and *pointe* shoes. Though we used every square inch of space, it was still so congested that I slipped out onto the rickety fire escape to tie my ribbons.

Then, once we were warmed up and later ready to change into our costumes, the metamorphosis began, for we were dressed in the Cecil Beaton swan tutus with feathered wings, feathered headdresses and an iridescent jewel on each of our foreheads.

When the overture began with the familiar strains of Tchaikovsky's elegiac score, it was as if a spell had been cast on the proceedings. So inspired was Maria, she just melted into the role of Odette, her every movement part of one extended musical and emotive phrase. She seemed even to be listening to the silences. When she finished the pas de deux, there were tears in her eyes, bringing to mind the advice that to be able to move an audience, one must first be moved oneself.

André was at his superlative best, the most attentive of handsome and romance-consumed princes. The corps danced as a single breathing unit, while the lighting magic-carpeted us to a bittersweet land of fairy tale fantasy. The musicians, too, were infused with the same rhapsodic transport as everyone else in the production.

At the closing curtain, I was later told, tears were shed by tuxedo-clad men in the audience, as well as by the bejeweled and ravishingly dressed ladies, many of them fluttering their exquisite black lace and gold embroidered fans. After a worrying pause, there was a unanimous standing ovation with thundering shouts of "Bravo"! That evening, there were 28 curtain calls, I know because I counted them!

As if some celestial garden had released its bloom, a flurry of rose petals cascaded down upon us, while six white doves were released from the stage to circle above the audience before returning. All of the dancers were profoundly moved, sensing prophetically that such an occasion would not again be repeated. Yes, that Spanish night of pure bewitchment was the most perfect ballet performance of my life. I'm so very grateful to have been part of it.

Many years later, in 1994, I read that the Gran Teatro del Liceo in Barcelona had burned to the ground, the latest of Europe's historical opera houses to be reduced to a mass of ashes. I was shocked that that magnificent building, a structure that had played host to more than a century and a half of the world's greatest ballet dancers, opera singers and classical musicians, had been consumed by flame. I could hardly reconcile myself to such an irreparable loss! I wept for what was no more, for that blazing funeral pyre of vanished art and artists.

CHAPTER TWELVE

Post Paris Opera Scandal

Before I relate the puzzling encounter I had when Mr. B entered my Orient Express carriage en route from Barcelona to Paris, I must first explain to the young reader the history of this legendary train. What transpired in that luxurious carriage was only an unsettling breach of ethics, but what it indicated was patently an indication of the master/devotee environment in which I was now entrenched.

The Orient Express had once been the most elegant way to travel through Europe in the 1920s and 30s. During the Second World War, the train was dismantled to be used for carrying troops and military equipment. In the single restored carriage in which I sat, one could easily imagine this ultimate status symbol of long dead millionaires and crowned heads travelling in this very same rail car. Whatever those royal personages were doing to keep themselves occupied during those trips, none of them, I'm sure, was taking two and a half hours to darn a pair of *pointe* shoes, as I was, for that's how long each pair took. Above my head on the rack was a bag full of undarned *pointe* shoes awaiting their turn.

The entire carriage in which I was traveling was a resplendent example of art deco design. Remnants of faded grandeur stared at us from threadbare velvet covered benches and flame mahogany wooden panels. Though electric engines were coming into use, we were still pulled by a puffing old steam engine that emitted a shrill whistle as we raced though darkened tunnels. The train rocked on the tracks in sharp contrast to the hurtling and zooming trains of today.

There was another reason this ride had an added significance, namely, nostalgia. Ten years earlier, as a five-year-old, I was given a miniature toy train that my parents, annually, would set up to wind its way around the Christmas tree, illuminated by colored fairy lights, hovering angels and delicious red and white peppermint sticks. My toy train had a whistle and puffed smoke just like the Orient Express engine that was at the front of the train in which I was now riding.

If Mom and Dad could see me now, I mused, for there I was in the real McCoy, sharing a compartment with the two corps de ballet dancers, by now attached to me like Velcro. They had even persuaded Betty Cage to assign hotel rooms on tour for the three of us together. So between the extended train journey and the very proximate arrangements of always sharing a hotel room, they had access to me day and night.

The train continued its huffing, puffing and hooting. "What do you feel about Hugh joining the company?" they probed, their casual demeanor belying their mentally tape-recording a suitable sound bite.

Hugh Laing, originally from the island of Barbados, had been a principal dancer of Ballet Theatre, the favorite on and off stage of choreographer Antony Tudor. Within the confines of his modest technique, Hugh had a noticeable stage presence. But he certainly was nowhere in the same league as Jacques d'Amboise, Frank Moncion, Herbie Bliss and, least of all, André Eglevsky.

"We heard, via the grapevine," the two girls went on, "that Mr. Kirstein is, well, sort of taken by Hugh and, you know, invited him to join the company..." Their pseudo-hesitant bit of gossip petered out into a cryptic ellipsis.

Then they continued, though I very quickly understood what they were driving at. "Well, by accepting Mr. Kirstein's invitation, Hugh will be, you know, obliged to return the favor. What do you think?"

"Yes, It makes sense," I answered, "because outside of *Prodigal Son,* which of Mr. B's ballets could he dance? None," I ventured to state in my adolescent know-it-all way. "He's just riding on Diana's back. If Mr. B hadn't wanted her, they wouldn't have given him a second glance."

"You think so?" they prodded further.

"Oh, yes," I responded, oblivious of the explosive potion then being brewed.

I had, admittedly, no respect for Hugh artistically, and was, even more, put off by his publicly superior manner. And that is where the matter should have ended, with my trite and worthless opinion. For to my everlasting shame, I was at the age where my evaluation of other dancers was jet black or snow white; they were either wonderful, or unworthy of working with the magician that was Mr. B.

No sooner had I dispensed with my negative responses, than I wondered if I perhaps had been too spontaneous, for my mother used to say that if you had nothing nice to say about someone, then say nothing at all. I should have heeded her counsel, but, but to my discredit, didn't. Then I told myself not to give it a second thought, since you couldn't walk around perpetually suspicious of everyone. Misguided babe in the woods that I was! For with hindsight, a sprinkling of suspicion might have averted what was to happen.

How welcome were the brief stops en route to Paris, for food vendors would run up and down the platform selling fruit, rolls and ice cream. We bought food quickly while leaning far out of the train windows, for there was no disembarking allowed and no dining car accessible to us. Fortunately, I had a small amount of currency for each country we visited during our tour, provided by my practical father. Back in 1952, the euro as the monetary unit for all of Europe was not even dreamed of. There were, however, the "don't leave home without it" American Express Traveler's Checks which helped me out of more than one empty wallet circumstance. Mr. B always kept a watchful eye on all of us, but as I was to soon and painfully realize, not for our welfare as might meet the eye. He walked up and down the narrow corridor of the train peeking in the windows of each compartment. At one point, en route, he completely took me by surprise when he slipped into our compartment and, wordlessly, motioned for me to take off my stockings and shoes! Nonplussed, but ever obedient, I obeyed his bare feet order.

He then made another motion for me to give him that by now stockingless and shoeless foot, gesturing for me to press as hard as I could against the palm of his hand. So I pushed with my bare toes against his extended palm, first with one foot, then the other. I pushed with all my might until each foot in turn shook; he nodded, whatever that meant, and then just walked away without uttering a sound! Silently he had walked in and just as silently he had walked out! It was left for me to find some reason for such peculiar behavior. Not one word of explanation. Even more disconcerting, he didn't test the other girls.

This little episode, to be followed by the implosion that was to take place at the American Embassy reception, was the first light to be shed into my hitherto blinded eyes insofar as my quasi-religious worship of George Balanchine.

The train rushed by villages and farms of the sprawling French countryside. Some minutes before we arrived at the Gare Saint-Lazare in Paris, a uniformed guard suddenly appeared. He was there, he informed us, in terse and unintelligible French, to collect our passports. In America, I was told never to give up my passport to anyone, so I put up a real battle about handing it over to the uniformed man who was speaking French at a very rapid rate of which only a few words here and there were familiar. Then when I saw everyone else obligingly surrendering their passports, did I reluctantly comply. Gruffly, he instructed all of us to collect them at a specified police station in Paris the following day. What a time-consuming hassle when all I wanted to have on my mind was the soon-to-be appearance on that hallowed stage of the Paris Opera!

When, the next day, I found my way to the police station, I was informed that they wanted a $20 fee. That was unexpected, but even more so was the rough pinch on my backside from one of the on duty policemen while I was waiting at the front desk. Mr. B could get away with pressing my bare feet, but under no circumstances whatsoever would my strict upbringing permit me to ignore the bottom pincher. What was next, a strip search? I withheld a strong urge to do a Fanny Elssler and kick the assailant where it would hurt most, a makeshift and early vasectomy. And I could have, because I was at the peak of my muscular power. The moment of anger passed, thank goodness, just as well, because one can't fight City Hall, or a man in uniform with a gun. You can complain, but only after the fact.

They accepted my American Express Traveler's Checks and perfunctorily returned my passport. Then and there, I resolved never to have anything to do with the Parisian police force, that is, if I could help it, seriously doubting any protection could be forthcoming from any of them!

Upon arrival in Paris, we were taken directly to the opulent Paris Opera House, built in 1875 in neo-baroque style by the competition-winning architect, Charles Garnier. With its lavish decorations of intricate gold leaf, marble friezes and sculptured deities inspired by the myths of ancient Greece, the first impression of the building was that it was the ultimate temple of both opera and ballet, fit for the aesthetic palates of kings, queens and emperors. Such a profusion of pink and white marble, translucent crystal and gilt that was even more in abundance than the Teatro del Liceo in Barcelona, and certainly more sumptuous than anything to be found at the Royal Opera House in London.

The vast stage accommodated up to 450 dancers at any one time, while the lush auditorium was overhung by a massive six-ton crystal chandelier. If that chandelier fell, I thought, for a man had been killed at the end of the 19th century when one of the counterweights dropped from its moorings. I immediately recalled the classic novel, *The Phantom of the Opera,* and two of the film versions, one with silent screen star Lon Chaney, the other with the suave British actor Claude Rains. Andrew Lloyd Webber, no child prodigy as was Mozart, hadn't, at the age of five, yet composed his musical.

True to its danger-ridden associations, the opera house was constructed over swampland and a subterranean lake that had to be pumped and drained before the actual construction of the building could begin. But glory and grandeur ruled the roost in Garnier's architectural masterpiece, with an unrivalled assemblage of composers, opera singers and ballet dancers adorning its stage since 1875.

The next day we were notified to report to the famous Foyer de la Danse where Mr. B was to teach a class. This was an enormous area directly behind the stage and with the same dimensions, adorned with palatial chandeliers and velvet-lined benches. It was here that the influential libertines of the day selected their future paramours. For such wealthy men, no sleazy bordello women as painted by Toulouse-Lautrec, but, instead, for their slaked taste the fresh young blood of the Paris Opera dancers.

Such assignations did not then even enter my mind, for all I could think of was that I would be dancing in the same fabled Foyer where ballet icons Carlotta Zambelli, Serge Lifar, Lysette Darsonval and Nina Vyroubova had practiced. I was thrilled and chilled at this face-to-face confrontation with French ballet history.

As for the immense stage, it was sharply raked. Many adjustments were needed in order to dance well, so a grueling two days of muscle-cramping labor followed. The stage floor, as at Covent Garden, had wide and worn wooden planks, pitted and splintered with holes drilled in it from the shifting of over seventy-five years of massive opera and ballet scenery.

Then there were the metal frames of fearful trapdoors. Would one of them open as in the 1937 classic ballet film *La Mort du Cygne?* In that haunting film of a pre-war Paris Opera Ballet, Rose Souris, played by the 12-year old Janine Charrat, aims to ensure the supremacy of her idol, Mlle Beaupré, danced by Yvette Chauviré. Deliberately opening a trapdoor to incapacitate the visiting ballerina, Mlle Karine, danced by Mia Slavenska, the child's sabotage unexpectedly results in the guest star being crippled for life.

Between the rumored ghost of the *Phantom of the Opera* and trapdoors suddenly activating, there was, more realistically, the raked stage sloping towards the cavernous orchestra pit. With swans rapidly weaving in and out of each other, a slip from that slanting stage into the pit could prove fatal.

The rehearsals were over and backstage we were steeling ourselves with every speeding minute to face the notoriously difficult Parisian public, no strangers to hissing, booing and displaying their aggressive distaste at less than what they considered perfection.

The call came over the tannoy, *Mesdames et messieurs, cinq minutes, s'il vous plaît. Tout le monde sur la scène. Merci.* Then, in anachronistic English, *five minutes please!* Silently, with only the swish of our Cecil Beaton tutus and muffled sounds of broken-in but intricately darned *pointe* shoes, we assembled like a military platoon ready to do battle, and that's exactly what it was going to be. In such august surroundings, we were on tenterhooks, calling upon our wordlessly mouthed prayers, incantations, perhaps even a touch of voodoo thrown in, and whatever other rituals we could seize upon to deliver us from failure and public disgrace. So did the bloodless swans, pallid from the makeup and keyed nerves combined, assemble onto the stage, each one filled with parallel thoughts. In the wings, the equally tensed hunters were doing last-minute *pliés* and *relevés*.

The house lights, including the colossal chandelier, slowly dimmed after which our conductor, Leon Barzin, entered and commandingly took his place in the orchestra pit. The stirring *Star Spangled Banner* was played first, followed by the majestic *Marseillaise*. With a respectful pause for the national anthems to be digested, the tragically poetic strains of Tchaikovsky's *Swan Lake* began.

For one split second, I panicked, having made the mistake of mentally trying to go over the opening choreography. I couldn't remember even one step! My mind had gone terrifyingly blank, that is, until the curtains of the great opera house opened and the surging music sparked my memory. Thankfully! Never again did I do such-last second reviewing.

The program consisted of four diverse ballets, Mr. B's version of *Swan Lake,* with Maria who, fresh from her Barcelona triumph, delivered a remarkable portrayal. This was followed by Ravel's sweeping *La Valse* with Tanny superb in the role created for her by Mr. B. Then came the hideous and highly controversial *The Cage* by Robbins, providing Nora with a sordid but memorable vehicle, with, as the closing ballet, the buoyant *Bourrée Fantasque.* Two French composers had aptly been recruited, Maurice Ravel for *La Valse* and Emmanuel Chabrier for *Bourrée Fantasque.*

I danced in all four ballets and afterwards felt that I had done justice to all of them. What a relief that was! We were met by thunderous applause and we sensed that Mr. B. was proud of us although, as was his wont, he never did express it verbally. We had to guess at his approval.

Never in my wildest flights of fancy back in Oklahoma did I, even for a fleeting moment, daydream that I would one day, at the age of 16, or any age, be dancing at the Paris Opera! In that distant period, the most exciting dancing I had ever seen was that first performance of the Ballet Russe de Monte Carlo.

In a totally divergent style, it was thrilling to watch the annual Indian Fair in Anadarko, when all the tribes gathered to dance around campfires, re-enacting their archaic history The men, dressed in red, blue and white dyed eagle feathers highlighted by tiny mirrors, were also adorned by bells strapped to their ankles, knees and elbows. Stomping through a frenzied war dance, they yelped throughout while pounding the dust percussively with their earth-hardened feet. As a child, I was fascinated but frightened simultaneously, because I saw it not as a performance, but as an actual ritual for preparatory battle.

What an exciting panorama of early American history that was! As for the child that I was watching in awe from the sidelines, a few short years later I was successfully winning my own battle, not with eagle feathers, but with swan feathers, for I had glided across the stage of the opulent Palais Garnier, the Académie Nationale de Musique! From the land of cowboys and Indians to the lakes of sylphs and swans, I was a world away, but now amazingly conjoined!

The euphoria of that incredible evening, unfortunately, abruptly ground to a halt. The two corps de ballet members, seething with resentment at my dancing leading roles in *Jinx, Cakewalk, Age of Anxiety, Card Game* and a solo in *Capriccio Brilliante*, choreographed specially for me by Mr. B, had been plotting on how to derail my blossoming career. Luring me into their confidence, they had, as mentioned earlier, pried out of me my involvement with Herbert Bliss, then wasted not a moment in exposing my most private thoughts to him.

But then, having achieved that devious though minor victory, they were determined to inflict additional and actual damage. With their latest plan, they more than succeeded. Having extracted from me my negative response to Hugh Laing, they then planted the Judas kiss on either cheek. Gloating, they swam off like those South American piranhas to attack Hugh where it hurt him most, his failing and flailing ego.

Following our performance at the Théâtre des Champs-Élysées, the American Embassy, hosted by United States Ambassador James C. Dunn, gave a sumptuous party for the entire company as well as many other high-ranking diplomats and the cream of Parisian society. Not to have been invited was as big a public slap in the face in Paris in 1952 as it was to be excluded, fourteen years later, in 1966, by author Truman Capote for his much-publicized New York City black and white ball.

Chauffeured cars were waiting at the stage entrance to transport us to the Embassy, and although I had danced in all four ballets, I was not the least bit tired because of the thrill of dancing at the famed Paris Opera House.

Crystal goblets, countless glowing candles and an imposing white marble fireplace adorned the spacious room. I was wearing a newly purchased Helen Rose Original white lace dress with long white gloves. It was my one and only designer outfit, for which I had scrimped and saved nickels and dimes and hoped that I would blend into the tout Paris buzzing ambience. Holding a crystal and gold goblet in my hand, I began tentatively sipping my first taste of champagne. Though it provided a new and uncertain experience for me, I adapted an immediate air of nonchalance.

In the midst of my savoir-faire projection, from across the room I noticed that Hugh Laing had fixed his gaze upon me, squinting, as if trying to read the bottom line of an eye chart. By now, he was getting more and more inebriated by the minute. Just when I was most enjoying the party, nibbling on delicious little hors-d'oeuvre and engaging in snippets of conversation with the glitterati of the French haut monde, there was a shout that shot across the reception room.

"Bocher!" the voice thundered in my direction.

An instant hush descended over the social proceedings. The furious voice belonged to Hugh! Flushed, he had become uncontrollably drunk, yelling at the top of his lungs at me while trying to keep his balance! I froze to the spot as he continued to hurl invectives at me with the force of thunderbolts. As he swore and cursed me in slurred foul language, I turned rigid, mortified by the sudden attack. Remembering my mother's advice to take the high road in a contentious situation, I cut off, though wishing the floor would open up so I could escape his screeching onslaught. Instantly, Hugh's wife, Diana Adams, rushed up to me, imploring me to ignore him since he was clearly dead drunk.

Then Maria Tallchief, fresh from conquering Paris with her limpid Odette, hastened to my side, telling me to ignore him as he was clearly out of his senses. Trying to restore my spirits, she complimented me on being able to retain my cool. Other dancers in the company crowded around me, offering their highly disturbed sympathies.

Though my senses were swirling, I could see Hugh's mouth still gyrating in fury, his eyes flashing with hatred. Diana was now next to him pulling on his arm saying, "Stop Hugh, stop, stop!" a litany of pleas that did no good whatsoever.

And where was the director of the New York City Ballet? All the while, strangely enough, Mr. B stood close by, but not budging an inch, his waterfall of choreographic images having been irritatingly blocked and suspended by the outburst. Because I understood and appreciated the ever-flowing geyser of cascading creativity that poured forth from George Balanchine, I didn't condemn him for not coming to my rescue, the youngest of his flock. But not everyone overlooked the erring shepherd that was Mr. B, the majority of people believing that to turn a blind eye to a crime being committed adjacent to you makes one guilty of collusion.

I could see Mr. B, surveying the scene as if he were watching an in-flight movie, content to leave me at the mercy of the attack. There was no question that that attack ruined the post-performance happiness that would otherwise have been everyone's. Diana, who was humiliated by extension, finally dragged Hugh out of the room with her, depositing him somewhere out of sight, then returning to me to again profusely apologize.

Diana was not only a great asset as a dancer, for who could forget how funny she was dancing with that side-splitting comedian, Danny Kaye, in the film *Knock on Wood*, and lovely in the Gene Kelly film *Invitation to the Dance*? She was also an outstanding human being. When Tanny, at the age of 25, was to be struck down by lifelong crippling polio, it was only Diana whom the paralyzed victim wanted to see from the company. And, of course, Mr. B, Tanny's husband, was ostensibly present when rehearsals and performances of the company were over.

What, kind of karma, one may well ask, was it that Mr. B, who adored the beautiful and muscle-toned young female body, was to be married to a woman confined to a wheelchair for life? But Mr. B's invalidic habitat was to end when he divorced the tragic Tanny in order to be free to marry Suzanne Farrell, his next major all-consuming muse. But it was a union not to be, for Suzanne resisted it with all the force of her young being, a refusal strengthened by her staunch Catholicism. Her escape clause was her marriage to dancer Paul Mejia, an act that incited Mr. B's most vindictive response. But I have travelled to a future that had not yet transpired.

At that fiasco of a party that was taking place at the Embassy, Jerome Robbins was also present, naturally not moving a finger to assist me. There they were, Jerry and Hugh, birds of a feather in sleazy foul-mouthing. Any second, I expected my assailant to pour red wine over my Helen Rose white lace dress, but he didn't, so at least my hard-earned outfit remained intact.

I glanced again at Mr. B who, for all intents and purposes, could have been in another country. What did this complete distancing signify? This absence of action from my revered Mr. Balanchine was the first cracked pane in my stained glass window view of him. Had my father not been in far away Oklahoma, but in that same sumptuous room, would he have stood by and watched his 16-year-old daughter being mauled by the pouncing panther that Hugh had turned into? That rhetorical question needs no answer, since even strangers risk themselves to help unknown victims of public assault.

Luckily my father wasn't there, for had he been, my attacker would have tasted kangaroo court justice. But, fortunately for me, 17-year-old Jacques d'Amboise was there and rushed over to rescue me. "Let's get out of here!" he ordered, leading me by the arm straight out of the party. His arms protectively around my shoulders, he led me out to a fin-de-siècle horse-drawn carriage parked at the curb. We climbed in, as the driver, following Jacques' instructions, had the horses begin to trot around post-midnight Paris.

In a night of topsy-turvy emotions, Jacques' protectiveness soon escalated into desire, for he gave me the first passionate kiss I had ever experienced. With his muscled arms enveloping me, I felt rescued by a hero, for that is what he was that tumultuous evening. The kiss subsided, but not his loving reassurance that I didn't deserve any of my assailant's alcoholic bile.

There are times in our lives when we would dearly love to freeze time, to stop it in its runaway tracks, so as to preserve the evanescent beauty of the moment. That horse-drawn carriage ride was one of them. I didn't want it to end, but within a few hours, we had a rehearsal, besides which neither one of us had unlimited funds to pay an all-night driver.

Though I had long left the building, I could imagine the two jubilant young ladies still enjoying themselves at the almost vacated party. There is no way that Hugh Laing could have been spoonfed that worthless appraisal by me, except by those two hate-filled dancers, for I never shared with anyone else my response to him.

Back at the hotel, after snatching a few hours sleep, but carefully avoiding any conversation with my roommates, I reflected on the numberless intrigues that have littered the ballet world through time, from enemies placing crunched tiny pieces of glass in *pointe* shoes, to inserting slivers of glass in Giselle's second act veil. So, still in one piece, I had to consider myself lucky, for I had not fallen through any deliberately released trapdoors at the Opera!

As for that disastrous reception, I learned a lesson for life, castigating myself for the stupidity of such misplaced trust. The lesson? Don't share less than positive thoughts with so-called bosom friends, for the vipers in their satin bodices will uncoil to release their poison. A night of spite; not *Swan Lake*, but *Snake Lake!*

Some forty years afterwards, the frenzy to eliminate competition reached its nadir in the American figure skating championship that preceded selection for the 1994 Olympics. The ex-husband of a top female competitor hired thugs to smash, with a collapsible police truncheon, the leg of the rival contender. With hindsight now, Hugh Laing's soapbox tirade against me was insignificant compared to being deliberately disabled.

But that night had deeper and extended repercussions, for it began a turning point in my subconscious, an imperceptible shift in my thought process. I fought with every fiber of my being the gradual realization that Mr. Balanchine was less than perfect, that he could be utterly selfish and self-centered, and that we, his dancers, were only human fodder for the cannons of his huge creativity.

And so I fed, ravenously, my self-protective delusions. I was in denial, for Mr. Balanchine dwelled at the apex of his Great Pyramid; he was the ultimate pharaoh, we were the obedient and grateful slaves who had built his structure and maintained it day and night through all the astrological seasons.

Years later, long after I had stopped dancing, I discovered that on the company's first visit to Russia, after a lifetime of separation, Balanchine was reunited with his younger brother, the composer Andrei Balanchivadze. Upon hearing his body of music for the first time, Mr. B dismissed it with the harshest of criticisms.

Tell me, do not younger siblings have sensibilities just as much as their older and more acclaimed ones?

Now, in 2012, as I review decades of experience in the medical and psychiatric fields, with all due respect to George Balanchine's choreographic brilliance, other people's feelings were irrelevant to him. He could have, with the snap of his fingers, removed me from the cast of Robbins' ballets, but he didn't.

Barely into my teens, I never should have been allowed to dance in *The Cage,* its degenerate subject matter shocking even to liberal Europeans. Why, then, did Mr. B permit it?

His weird behavior in the Orient Express carriage would have been totally unacceptable in any office if perpetrated by the top executive on a secretary. But that was minor compared to Balanchine standing by at the Embassy party, watching me being verbally mauled by a drunken Rottweiler.

I looked here and there to find excuses for Mr. B's behavior. But finding none, I began to ask myself the most dislodging questions. Had I become a supplicant kneeling at the feet of a human being I perceived as a deity? Why was I for so long so blinded to his acute shortcomings?

Whatever the answer might have been then, today I am left with the unbalancing thought that the worship of Balanchine had unhealthy repercussions. Of course, I could have just left the company, but that was easier said than done, for I was caught, like a fox in a trap, by my own dancing passion and until then impenetrable belief that George Balanchine was a demigod. You served a god, you didn't question one.

Many gifted young people are prime targets for the predatory leaders of this world, whether they are directors of athletic teams, drama schools or ballet companies. Driven by pipe dreams, scholarships and concocted false promises, young people submit, completely unaware of how to recognize the symptoms of manipulation. Ambitious parents are also blinded by their desire to see their children become stars, thereby able to live in their reflected glory. I know because I, myself, was a victim, so trusting and eager to offer anything that would serve the master.

With none of my self-questioning finding an answer, I began to feel guilty that I was perhaps betraying the artist I most admired. Was I callously throwing George Balanchine to the baying wolves? No, I answered myself in sharp rebuttal, not by a long shot. If I was remiss in anything, it was the inexcusable fact that it took me almost six decades to finally come to my senses, to be able, at long last, to sift the silkworms from the maggots.

There is no question that George Balanchine exerted an all-powerful pull on just about all those within his orbit. All his ex-wives and muses, except one, remembered him reverentially, nurturing his mystique and dedicating their later years to the preservation of his legacy. The one exception? That, as any reader of *Dancing on my Grave* knows, is Gelsey Kirkland. For, in that autobiography, Kirkland squarely puts the blame on Balanchine for initiating her squalid years of drug addiction, feeding her the first of the drugs that would overcome her exhaustion in Russia. That she took so long to break the habit was her own fault, no one else's.

The 1986 suicide of principal dancer Joseph Duell shocked the New York City Ballet. Never endingly self-dissecting, prone to dungeon-deep depression, not overcome by even psychiatric help, the 29-year-old soloist, as a last resort, had gone to Mr. Balanchine for advice. The advice, as I knew from personal experience, was made light of, brushed under the carpet; not to worry, just get on with it.

With no suggested course of conduct forthcoming from Mr. Balanchine, Joseph Duell made his own decision, and that was to kill himself by throwing himself out of the window, hurtling to his certain death. Though Mr. Balanchine couldn't be blamed for Joseph's suicide, why hadn't he listened constructively to a highly disturbed young man, clearly at a crossroads?

Once, years earlier, unable to resolve my own acute and pounding harassment in Robbins' *The Cage,* I looked out of a window on to the street below, but froze. Tragically, Joseph Duell's own last-stand solution was to look out of his fifth-story window, and jump.

Returning to 1952, there were to be five more days in Paris, with the remainder of our performances at the Théâtre des Champs-Élysées. It was in that theatre, vibrating with legend, that I found myself in a predicament where, to extricate myself, I brainlessly put my life at risk. But that, in retrospect, was par for the course, for obediently and willingly brainwashed as I was, I didn't think twice about jeopardizing my life, the better to serve our undisputed leader, the living apostle of the dance, George Balanchine.

CHAPTER THIRTEEN

Eternity Five Floors Below

I t was a new morning and time to put aside the tensions of the previous days. Leaving the Left Bank where my hotel was located, I walked across the medieval Pont Neuf, completed in 1606, to find the Théâtre des Champs-Élysées. Once I would find my way to the theatre, I would then focus on the scheduled full orchestra rehearsal, for I was so looking forward to it. Checking the street signs, the potent and fragrant charms of Paris vied with the pressures and responsibilities awaiting me.

I might have taken a wrong turn, for suddenly I found myself on the rue Le Peletier, the same street that had once been the site of the previous Paris Opera. That former opera house, the Salle Le Peletier, had held 1,900 spectators. Before it had been completely ravaged by fire in 1873, it had played host to the premieres of such operas as Rossini's *Guillaume Tell,* Meyerbeer's *Robert le Diable* and Verdi's *Don Carlos,* alternating with the first performances of such balletic masterworks as *Giselle, Paquita* and *Coppélia.*

Among the pantheon of superb dancers who had skimmed across that stage was Marie Taglioni, the supreme sylphide of the Romantic Ballet's diaphanous blue moonlight. As I began to drift backwards into that far-distant era, my mind's eye paused to imagine those gutted gates of greatness.

Thinking of that 27-hour raging inferno, Emma Livry came to mind, Taglioni's protégée for whom she choreographed her only ballet, *Le Papillon.* But fate was to deny the fruition of Emma's enormous promise for, during a rehearsal, the young ballerina's billowing tulle skirt caught fire from an exposed gas light. Pandemonium engulfed the stage as co-workers frantically tried to extinguish the human torch that Emma had instantaneously turned into. Eight months of intense suffering were to follow before Emma Livry was released from her agony, dying at the age of 21.

That, I told myself, was a tragedy of dreadful dimensions, and it put into perspective the ill-willed arrows being aimed in my direction. I had no right to complain, for I was alive and well, but what was next, I couldn't help but wonder?

Recently, in one of our airport stopovers, I had bought a book on major philosophers, one of them being the 18th-century German thinker, Immanuel Kant. "People should always be treated as valuable, as an end in themselves, and not be used in order to achieve something else." Well, Herr Kant had obviously not been a dancer in a major ballet company where the reverse philosophy prevailed.

I tried to put myself in a positive and enthusiastic state of mind for when would I ever have such a repeat opportunity of relishing the history-soaked boulevards of Paris? Along with Taglioni and Emma Livry, I thought of the soul-impacting and unforgettable Fanny Elssler, as well as the new cluster of stars including Adèle Dumilâtre, the first Queen of the Wilis, Carolina Rosati, and Amalia Ferraris.

As uncomfortable as it was to accept, each generation rapidly succeeded in swallowing up the preceding one. Nowhere was this clearer than in Paris where history seemed to emanate from every corner and cobblestone.

How I yearned to become a better and better dancer, to achieve higher and higher degrees of excellence, to become a fully-fledged ballerina in the New York City Ballet. What would I do, I asked myself, to achieve this? Would I, like Faust, sell my soul to the devil, if not for eternal life, then to become a great ballerina? What, I asked myself, would I choose to do, so as not to disappoint George Balanchine? Where would the limits lie? Within a few racing hours, totally unforeseen circumstances would provide the unexpected and shocking answer.

Mr. Balanchine had increasing demands placed upon him while he was in Paris, so once our considerable success in the city of light was established, he didn't feel the necessity of teaching a daily company class. We were given, in his place, Lew Christensen.

Lew, in his youth, had been a virtuoso classical dancer and if such technical equipment was not already a blessing, he was further smiled upon by the gods with a pulse-accelerating, blond Greek god beauty. It was heavily rumored that Lincoln Kirstein's libido had been turned into a raging bonfire by the unattainable Lew who had married the dancer Gisela Caccialanza.

Passions aside, released or thwarted, I was very grateful to Lew Christensen, the choreographer of *Jinx*, for of all the huge choice of girls to choose from, he had given me the leading role in his ballet – in which I alternated with the much older and very experienced Janet Reed.

But by Mr. Balanchine appointing Maria's best friend, Vida Brown, the former Ballet Russe dancer, to be our ballet mistress, my life in the company was to be made more difficult. For it was Vida and Helen Kramer who were the most vindictive towards me when the London authorities ordered my private dressing room at the Royal Opera House. And why? So that the 14-year-old that I was that earlier summer would be protected against the possibly foul language of the older girls. That, as it happened, turned out to be a sick joke, for following the lead of Helen and Vida, some of the other girls would, as they passed my dressing room, open the door, loudly shouting, "Shit!" Well, aside from their obvious attempt to hurt me, I was quite accustomed to hearing that expletive since Robbins used it as frequently as a preposition. With, to, shit, those words were for him interchangeable.

Conventional wisdom spreads the idea that the ballet world is pristine and chaste, inhabited by the likes of Snow White characters and placid flocks of pure white swans. What a gross misconception of the actuality! Shit, shit, shit, they hurled that word at me, such well-directed imprecations of hate!

It was my firm belief that Vida was lacking the qualifications for the position of ballet mistress for the New York City Ballet. Her duties, among other administrative details, included the responsibility of teaching company classes and scheduling rehearsals. Sometimes she would point out where a swan's spacing was misjudged in *Swan Lake*, or if someone was not quite on the music. Her classes, much to my disappointment, were downright dull and lifeless. When we were seeking real instruction to strengthen and refine our techniques, she was offering a series of the most mundane exercises. I avoided her classes, as did many of the better dancers who, instead, chose to do their own warm-up and barre.

I am sure that on top of her contempt for me stemming from my private Covent Garden dressing room, my non-participation in her classes consolidated her aversion to me. Being in a position of undoubted power, she grew accustomed to the currying favor type who provided her with little gifts. I was never one of her fake and sycophantic fans, for they were, in my view, hypocritical and fawning.

My introspection suddenly came to an end when I at last found and entered the Théâtre des Champs-Élysées. Once in the backstage area, the next search was to find the dressing room, set up my make-up table and lay out my *pointe* shoes in readiness for the evening performance. The dressing room, I found, was on the fourth floor above the stage, while the wardrobe room was up another flight of stairs on the fifth floor.

That fifth floor! As long as I live, I will never forget the single bathroom down the hall.

I located Mme Miranova, Dunya, as we called her, our devoted Russian wardrobe mistress. She was in the large wardrobe room unpacking and hanging our tutus upside down from the bars suspended from the ceiling. It was her enormous responsibility to keep track of all of the costumes worn by all the members of the company. A tiny white-haired woman, her exact age wasn't known for sure, though it could be approximated since she had once been a dresser for Anna Pavlova, accompanying her on her many tours of the world. Dunya, as so many of her generation, had fled St. Petersburg during the Bolshevik uprising.

Though she sounded dictatorial and out of sorts all the time, I knew Dunya to be a woman of compassion. I grew to have deep affection for her, and we would laugh and exchange short conversations with some added animated gestures, for her heavily accented English was limited. In one of those conversations, she told me that she had been a seamstress for my uncle, Mainbocher. Because she was always shouting, she frightened many of the dancers. But she wasn't angry, just very hard of hearing.

All seemed to be well as she was counting the costumes. A single costume was missing, but she had accounted for that since she had sent one of our *Symphony in C* tutus to be cleaned, a test to see how efficient the service was. If she were to be pleased, only then would she entrust all of the hundreds of costumes to the unknown Paris cleaner. The test costume was to be delivered that afternoon, well in time for the evening performance.

There were four ballets to dance that evening which meant climbing up and down four flights, four times, to quickly change. This was hard on our legs but there was nothing to be done since the old theatre had no elevators. Though I knew my muscles could take it, I wasn't that sure about my satin *pointe* shoes. We were given a very limited number of *pointe* shoes for the tour and, like bottles of water on a drifting lifeboat, we had to make them last as long as possible.

This evening's performance was to be another grand occasion. The reviews from the Paris Opera gala opening had been superlative and the Théâtre des Champs-Élysées had been sold out in advance for the entire five days ahead. Mr. Kirstein was on hand, pacing and rubbing his hands, looking his usual doom and gloom self. I thought he should have looked relatively content because things were going wonderfully well. We could, thankfully, anticipate breaking even financially. But, to justify his somber expression, each performance is a risk. That risk, if not one of life and death, for this was not the Barnum and Bailey circus, then the risk of success or failure. So, I thought. So brood, Mr, Kirstein, brood, if it serves you as a sedative.

The rehearsal went well and we had a bit of free time to relax before the evening's warm up, make-up, hair styling, and getting into costumes.

I was keyed up, as I always was, before the curtain. To this day, when I hear an orchestra tuning up, I get butterflies, not quite stage fright, but a feeling of high alert excitement and anticipation.

The first ballet was *Bourrée Fantasque*, a festive and colorful opener. Its first movement was particularly funny because Jerome Robbins, short in stature, was partnering the elongated Tanaquil LeClerq, well over six feet tall on *pointe*. She looked striking and her usual loose-limbed self, while Robbins appeared, not intentionally comical, but absurd. I couldn't help but think that it was Mr. Balanchine's private little joke on his associate director, so that Robbins' sense of power would be kept in check. For there was an unspoken arm's distance between the two.

Bart Cook, in the future to become a principal dancer of the company, then subsequently *repetiteur* for both Balanchine and Robbins, stated, as quoted in Wikipedia:

"Neither one understood what the audience saw in the other's work...both were jealous of each other and found the other to be 'an enigma'... Mr. B hired Robbins to provide variety and relief from his own ballets: 'You can't eat steak every night.' "

As well as *Bourrée Fantasque*, the opening ballet, and *Symphony in C*, the closing work, there were two more ballets in between, but I'm sorry to say I can't, for the life of me, remember what they were. As it happened, the upheaval of what I was to soon endure blanked out their names.

As for the Bizet/Balanchine *Symphony in C*, for which I was now readying myself, that was the ballet in which I made my debut in New York as a demi-soloist. Mr. Balanchine had entrusted me to do an adagio in the celestial second movement, partnered by Bobby Barnett. Bizet's sublimely beautiful music required skimming *bourrées* and an aura of radiant calm.

I went upstairs to the fifth floor wardrobe room in sufficient time to get my costume, silk tights, *pointe* shoes and hair all in place. Ballet mistress Vida Brown was standing next to Dunya, both of them gesticulating wildly and shouting. The single costume that had been sent to the dry cleaners, to test their efficiency, had not been returned as arranged! That meant that we were missing a costume for one of the girls in the first movement.

When the dancers came to the wardrobe room and immediately heard about the absentee costume, a commotion ensued. Some of the girls started grabbing the nearest costume on the wardrobe rail, even if it was not their own. The panic escalated as the hubbub of desperate voices kept on increasing.

In the midst of the din, Vida started barking orders for anyone who was wearing someone else's costume to immediately remove it and place it back on the rack. "Do not leave this room!" she commanded in no uncertain terms. By then, some of the dancers in the first movement had grabbed a costume and made a dash for it.

Vida then made the pronouncement that one of the girls from the second movement would give up her costume to a first movement girl, then be in the wings to take it from the first movement girl after she came offstage. In other words, the 30-second switch was to take place just before the second movement began.

Vida looked at me but I didn't wait to find out what she was going to ask! It was clear that she had picked me to be the near-naked dancer in the wings! I had found my own costume and had it on, so I decided to run away from the general tumult and go down the hall to hide in the bathroom until just before the curtain. In my plan, it would be certain that I would not forfeit my costume to another dancer with the dubious hopes of pulling it off her sweating body in order get it on my own, then fly on to the stage to dance my part in the second movement! Had I had any respect for Vida, I would have obeyed her harebrained scheme, but I didn't, so I made my own contingency plan.

I raced down the hall to the bathroom, opened the door, then shut it and remained there, breathless with my heart pounding until I heard the orchestra tuning up for the first movement. This, I thought, was the moment to exit the bathroom, slip past the wardrobe room, now presumably empty, and get to the wings well in time for the second movement.

I took hold of the antique brass doorknob, and to my utter dismay, it wouldn't turn! I tried again, but the heavy wooden door wouldn't budge. An instant panic set in as I pulled, pushed, rattled, twisted and yanked at the door handle! The large door was made of heavy wood and it resisted my every effort to make it open. During my losing wrestling match with the handle, I could faintly hear the first movement music.

I tried not to let my escalating panic clog the decision-making area of my brain. Desperately thinking of an alternative way to get out, I climbed up on the grimy and ancient porcelain sink, hoping it wouldn't fall off the wall, then put my head through the transom while repeatedly shouting, "Help, help, help!" No one was in the hall so my urgent calls all went unheeded. Everyone was either in the wings or on stage, and that is where I would have given anything to be myself.

I thought of squeezing through the transom, but couldn't get up high enough to even attempt it. The transom, framed by wood, had a glass panel suspended on a thin chain that I was unable to break or unfasten! I shouted again and again and kept pounding on the door as forcefully as I could. Again, there was no response. The corridor was as silent as a morgue, so that hope of being rescued went out the window.

There had to be another way out! The firmly locked door and the transom were no longer possibilities for escape, nor was yelling for help at the top of my lungs. I looked at the casement window, made of milk-colored glass with wires in an octagonal design secured inside it. The hinge was very rusty, as if no one in decades had tried to open it. I stood on the toilet seat and frantically tried to open the window, but it only opened a few inches. I was running out of time by the second! I knew I had to, at whatever cost, make that entrance! Kicking the window to open it completely, it fell down to the alley far below. Along with the music from the orchestra, I could hear the sound of shattering glass seconds after the window had broken loose.

There was only one option left. I shuddered and took a deep breath, willing myself not to look down, remembering that it was what all the mountain climbers strongly advised. With this do or die decision, I placed one pink satin *pointe* shoe firmly on to the granite ledge. With a quick swing out the window, I was standing on that narrow ledge, simultaneously clinging to the wall of the building. Though determined not to look down, my peripheral vision took in the people five-stories below, looking no larger than ants, and the automobiles that looked like miniature toy cars. I inched my way along the ledge, my hands hanging on to the walls of the building, until I reached the next window. Grabbing it, I felt at once that it was stuck, though open about an inch.

To get on to that stage in time, I was daring death to take me, for pink satin *pointe* shoes were not designed for inching one's way on a narrow granite ledge five stories above the busy Paris traffic. Holding on for dear life to the window frame, I balanced on one foot and kicked the window open. Thankfully, it didn't break as the other one, for if it had, it could have toppled me from my precarious perch. The window open, I quickly jumped through it on to a desk and saw that I was in some sort of office.

I tore across the room and yanked the door open that led to the hallway and then I recognized where I was! Running faster than I have ever run in my life before or since, I flew down five flights of stairs sliding down the handrail for several flights before arriving in the wings just as the second movement was beginning. Speeding across the stage behind the back curtain to the other side, I arrived in the nick of time to take my partner's hand – it was Bobby Barnett – abruptly moving the astonished Vida Brown to one side. She was in costume and had been holding Bobby's hand, ready to dance my part. With my heart still thumping from the terror of heel-toeing my way across the ledge, followed by the demon flight down the five flights of stairs, I registered the peculiar expression on Vida's face. Obviously, she knew I wasn't in the wings where I should have been, and contending with the missing costume and now an absent dancer, she was at her wit's end. To her credit, she was ready to salvage the second movement by dancing unrehearsed with Bobby. .

I entered the stage and was met by a look of utter incredulity on the face of one of the six corps de ballet girls! How can I further describe that expression? I will say that the look of astonishment was quickly replaced by one of resignation, of one who very reluctantly accepts last-second defeat at what was thought to be a foolproof scheme.

I began the *bourrées* forward in a diagonal line, the elegant entrance to the second movement of *Symphony in C*. Wearing my slightly dusty tutu, now less than pristine white from the grime of the fifth story wall, I called upon an emergency reservoir of calm. While we were dancing, Bobby tensely whispered to me, "What happened?" Whispering back, I answered through gritted teeth, "I'm sorry I was late".

Thankful to have managed to get on stage despite certain death one false step away, when the ballet concluded I returned to the dressing room and noticed that my tights weren't even torn. That is more than I can say for my nerve endings, for they had been completely shredded. Somehow, I had, against all odds, succeeded in turning Mary Wigman's *Totentanz*, her dance of death, into my own reaffirming dance of life!

How, though, in heaven's name, could I have done what I did? Why was I so willing to risk my life, no, forfeit it, rather than disappoint George Balanchine? Or did I do what I did to honor my own commitment to my self? Whichever the reason was, lunacy had replaced the inborn instinct of survival. My determination to get on that stage, that historic stage where *Le Sacre du Printemps* had had its scandal-inducing premiere almost forty years earlier, that obsessive need to dance as scheduled despite the endless void of eternity staring at me from the streets below, that insane decision was one that stupefies me to this day. But somebody up there was watching over me, for I did not end up with a blood-splattered crushed body.

The unanswered question remains to this day. Was the lock on that aging bathroom door faulty, or did someone purposely lock me in in order to prevent my dancing that night?

Until writing this book, I have never told a living soul how I got out of that bathroom, nor have I ever accused anyone of locking me in. Vida, when displeased by errant spacing, or sloppy musicality, never hesitated to reprimand, for she took to her bossy role as a duck to water. Yet she never either asked me for an explanation as to my literally last second arrival, or reprimanded me for being as late as I was. Why? Could it be that she already knew the answer and therefore didn't need to go over already familiar territory?

Or to give her the benefit of the doubt, did the archaic door handle, having been yanked by the likes of Nijinsky and Sokolova, finally cave in? But if that had been the case, why hadn't the door handle become stuck earlier since the bathroom had been in use all day?

As for the troublesome missing costume, the reason for my insane invitation to death, I later heard that they overcame the emergency by some of the dancers running on and off stage at improvised key moments.

During the ballet, Mr. B was in his usual place in the wings watching and facially twitching even more than usual. There is no way that he could have missed my arriving at literally the last second and, familiar with my reliability, must have known I was held up for some valid reason. But he never, later, asked me a single question about why I flew onto that stage instead of being focused in the wings with my partner. He certainly saw that it was Vida Brown who was holding Bobby Barnett's hand in readiness, and not I as scheduled. But no, not a single query afterwards as to what emergency situation had prevented me from being as prompt and dependable as I always was.

As was Mr. Balanchine's immovable pattern, he had totally divorced himself from any dealings with people who had grave problems to resolve. This self-erected wall dismissed issues that even bordered on life and death, though he could not, for a moment, have foreseen the depressive Joseph Duell's suicide from his own fifth-story window.

CHAPTER FOURTEEN

THE HOUSE OF CHANEL

The next day, gratefully alive, I decided to take a morning ballet class at Mme Lubov Egorova's studio. She had been an illustrious Russian Imperial ballerina, coached personally by *Swan Lake* co-choreographer Marius Petipa. As her career progressed, she became the partner of Vaslav Nijinsky.

Some years later, she was to be one of the galaxy of ballerinas to dance Princess Aurora in the Diaghilev 1921 London *Sleeping Princess*. Then, upon her marriage, she was to become Princess Nikita Troubetzkoy. But that royal connection belonged to the distant past, long before I had met her. For the permanent exile, as governments are replaced, titles become meaningless and savings dwindle overnight.

Every dancer who visited Paris, even briefly, made it their business to attend her classes. She was then only 71, younger than I am today as these lines are written, yet the wear and tear of her transplanted life had aged her beyond her actual years. Despite time's imprint, Mme Egorova was still beautiful when she moved, her arms touchingly expressive. The aura of faded glory permeated the studio as she passed on her Czarist lineage to a new generation. She taught the class in Russian-accented French and it was a pleasant surprise to realize that I understood all her directions. After her explanations, she would then spring up on a chair to watch us dance.

When the class had ended, and I had curtseyed to her, I asked her how much the lesson cost. She looked at me and smiled. Thinking she didn't understand my question, I repeated it, "How much should I pay?" She then hugged me and said, "No pay." To take class from the luminous Lubov Egorova, once toast of the Maryinsky in St. Petersburg, was, in itself, an experience to cherish, but then to be told it was a gift, that helped no end to restore my flagging spirits. In the following days, I managed to take several more classes with her.

What a pleasure it was to be free to express every nuance of the emotive music her pianist offered. This, I understood, was the reason

I so needed to dance; over and above the sense of physical accomplishment, it was to be able to open the window to my soul.

When the lessons ended, as after the first class, she again vehemently insisted on waiving the fee, while I vehemently insisted that I pay. The thought of depriving this old woman, who had stepped out of the history books, of her food money, weighed heavily on my conscience. But Lubov Egorova's will prevailed; perhaps it was her way of proclaiming her belief in me.

We kissed each other goodbye. Training with Mme Egorova, the very fountainhead of Russian Imperial Ballet, was a highpoint of my time in Paris. Still resonating with her pedagogic artistry, I hurried back to the theatre after class to check the bulletin board for the latest rehearsal schedule. I was thrilled to see that there was an invitation for all of the members of the company to attend a reception at The House of Chanel, to be hosted by Coco Chanel herself! I was eager to go to the reception, what girl wouldn't be, for the legendary Chanel was the most influential name in all French fashion.

Happiness turned instantly to regret when I saw, contingent with the invitation, a *Jinx* rehearsal scheduled by Vida Brown for exactly the same time. Since I was dancing the lead in the ballet, alternating with Janet Reed, I needed all the rehearsal time that could be allotted. I had to put my best foot forward, literally and figuratively, to do justice to the role of the Wirewalker. And, as always, it was such a pleasure to be partnered by dear Herbie Bliss. Though it would have been wonderful to attend the House of Chanel reception, there was no question as to which event would take precedence. So I resigned myself to missing the reception.

Many years after the invitation was issued, I discovered that Coco Chanel's stupendous success was consolidated by the influence of her wartime lover, a high-ranking Nazi officer. When, later, she was interrogated about her Second World War associations, she flippantly retorted, "At my age, when a man wants to sleep with you, you don't ask to see his passport." However facile and glib her responses, she stopped at nothing to ensure her grip on power.

Taking advantage of the pro-Aryan Third Reich policies, in her perfumery branch she callously tried to siphon off the profits from her leading Jewish stockholders. Unlike the famous French actress,

Arletty, co-star of *Les Enfants du Paradis*, who also, throughout the Occupation, entertained a top SS officer in her boudoir, Chanel avoided the great star's punitive post-war aftermath.

My uncle Mainbocher shared with me some stories about Chanel's ruthlessness in trying to dethrone him when he had his Paris salon not far from hers. A back-stabber, she spared no effort in trying to commandeer the most newsworthy of his clientele. Closing his Paris salon for the war, he returned to New York to concentrate on his salon at Fifth Avenue and 57th Street. Coco, as Uncle Main referred to her, was now an ocean removed.

Mme Chanel, in actual fact, not only waylaid customers, but also husbands. She once had an intense fling with Igor Stravinsky, though not succeeding in breaking up his marriage. Somehow Coco and Igor remained linked because she attended the Paris Opera opening of the New York City Ballet, and was also there to watch the Maestro conduct his *Firebird*.

But back in 1952, oblivious to the moral squalor of her Wehrmacht affiliations, I identified her name and fame only with her silhouette-altering couture and the classic fragrance of her Chanel No. 5. So though deflated from not being able to attend the reception, I arrived at the so-called *Jinx* rehearsal, but not a soul was there and no one, then or in the next hour, showed up. In consequence, it was too late for me to get back to the hotel and change my clothes to something suitable. After all, you don't arrive at Coco Chanel's' salon wearing leg warmers and a leotard. I had to face the reality; I was too late.

Abysmally disappointed to miss such an occasion, I was deeply hurt that I had been the object of such an unscrupulous ruse. The trickery of that phony *Jinx* rehearsal, concocted by Vida so that I would miss the Chanel party, was the latest example of spiteful malice towards me. When I later pointedly asked Vida why she hadn't informed me about the cancellation, and why nothing was on the bulletin board stating the change, her take it or leave reply was that she thought I knew. No apology was forthcoming.

That evening before the warm-up on stage, I very hesitantly took a peek in the bathroom from which I had made my audacious escape the previous night. The window, I noticed immediately, had been replaced and the door was open. No questions were ever asked by the management on how the window came crashing to the sidewalk below. I felt that an assumption had been made that the decades of deterioration had inevitably taken their toll, and that the rusty window had just finally loosened and fallen from its hinges.

When all the dancers found out that I had been locked in the bathroom, a few were sympathetic, but when they asked me how in the world I got out, I simply said the main thing is that I did get out, and left it at that. No one was able to pry the answer from me, and I am giving the explanation in this book, now, for the very first time in sixty years. To write this chapter was to once again suffer palpitations and breathlessness.

My mother taught me to find something to be thankful for each and every day, so I was extraordinarily grateful to be alive after sliding my slippery pink satin *pointe* shoes along that ledge. What would have happened, I questioned myself, if the window that I had kicked open, had remained tightly shut, and in trying to return along the ledge to the bathroom, I had slipped, or even fainted? To this day, when I see workmen on the top of a building, secured by ropes around their waists, I feel queasy and have to avert my gaze.

We were now midway in our Paris season. As hard as I tried, I could not quite eliminate from my mind that living nightmare of my having goaded death. Images of the Roland Petit/Jean Cocteau ballet, *Le Jeune Homme et la Mort*, flitted across my mind, Nathalie Phillippart as grim Death, dancing across the rooftops of Paris until Jean Babilée obeys her order to hang himself.

As for my own brush with mortality, fate, Jesus, a guardian angel, an Indian eagle feather, steel will, call it what you will, saved me, for I survived. Now work and more work would serve as a palliative, I told myself. So one fresh morning, after stopping at a little bakery for a croissant and tea, I walked across the Pont Neuf, once home to medieval jugglers, acrobats, harlequins and itinerant musicians. How colorful and delightful they must have been! Soon I was at the theatre so that I could work on my technique. I wanted to increase my five pirouettes on *pointe* to more, and there were jumps that needed some additional elevation. I also wanted to develop a more scissor-like, sharper *batterie*.

With only the spirits of the venerable dancers of the past keeping me company on that darkened stage, it was a wonderful chance to be able to concentrate on getting technically stronger. Hearing the music in my head, I did the Princess Florine variation from the *Bluebird* pas de deux, and also some steps from Maria's solo in *Firebird*. No one was watching, so I had the privacy of seeing if I could do some of the very demanding Balanchine choreography without inquisitive and suspicious questions.

It was a surprise to discover that just from so often watching Maria dance *Firebird*, being in the ballet myself, I knew the entire variation. Like the kid who stays outside until after dark, shooting baskets over and over again just because he loves the game and wants to become a top basketball player, I danced every chance that came my way. For nothing made me happier than when I moved to music. As Maria was my idol, just to try and approximate her virtuosity inspired me.

Then, intruding upon what I thought was a private testing ground, for I had no idea anyone was watching, my nemesis, the girl from the Bizet corps de ballet, suddenly stepped out of the shadows and pointedly asked if I was learning *Firebird*. The look in her eye and the inquisitorial tone of her voice went beyond mere curiosity. I looked her back in the eye, shrugged, and said I was only trying out some of the steps, just for the fun of it. Then I terminated the conversation. Regretfully, I wasn't able to terminate its soon-to-be sequel.

CHAPTER FIFTEEN

IN THE SHADOW OF THE THIRD REICH

The May 15th closing performance at the Théâtre des Champs-Élysées was attended by President Vincent Auriol and his wife, Michelle. Igor Stravinsky conducted the Balanchine ballet, *Orpheus*, for a sold-out house after which there was tremendous applause for the composer. During the curtain calls, I saw Coco Chanel in the audience applauding her former lover, Igor.

It was a festive and apt farewell to Paris. Backstage, we emptied the dressing rooms of our belongings, readying ourselves to leave the following day. How lifeless seem stripped dressing rooms, only hours before such a hubbub of adrenaline-racing preparation.

Everything was packed and all the company were ready to board the bus to take us to the train station. The Paris Opera and Théâtre des Champs-Élysées engagements were behind us, with images of the world-famous Eiffel Tower, Notre-Dame, Montmartre, the Louvre and the River Seine all being decanted into the crystal and gold goblet of memory, memories both enchanting and, conversely, terrifying.

It was time to look ahead to the Teatro Comunale in Florence where we would be participating in the Maggio Musicale Fiorentino. We had proven ourselves as a major ballet company and Mr. Balanchine was lauded as a master choreographer. He had the success he most assuredly deserved and it was heartening to be part of that very real triumph. Once at the station, we waited for the train to pull in so we could board it. After getting settled, many of the dancers went to sleep, legs outstretched in the aisle. I used the time to darn the tips of my *pointe* slippers since I was wearing them out at a rapid rate and new slippers had to be prepared.

The train, puffing smoke, and rocking back and forth on the tracks, rode past country lane landscapes. Maria Tallchief was sitting in the seat just across the aisle from me. Out of respect for the vast artistic gulf that separated us, I had never engaged her in any kind of conversation. Despite her physical proximity to me now, I had no intention of changing the status quo.

The spy from the wings, that malicious troublemaker, sauntered down the aisle, accompanied by her always in tow accomplice. When they saw Maria, they realized that they were in luck. Stopping, they leaned over to her, saying rather loudly, "Did you know Bocher was learning your variation in *Firebird?*" I winced and Maria shot me a look I could have lived without! How could it be explained to her that I was not out to dethrone her, that I had just been trying out passages from the repertoire to see if I could master some of the daunting steps? Maria was my idol, our prima ballerina, and I held her in the highest esteem. She was at the very top of the royal pecking order and I was a lowly peasant, the youngest member of the company.

Now, my idol, Maria, had glared at me with a look of absolute contempt! To say someone "is learning" is a euphemism in the ballet world for, "She wants to dance your part!" In point of fact, Maria would have no understudy, her role of roles created for her exclusively by her then husband, Mr. B. I had absolutely no designs on the role, how could I have, I was only trying to see if I could manage some of the most difficult steps which, surprisingly, I could. I never did try to explain anything to Maria, as the damage had been done. I suffered, once again, a real blow. What could I do outside of putting a clamp on those two girls' mouths? Even that wouldn't have helped, for the hateful duo would have managed to pass out derogatory notes.

I was particularly hurt by this petty act of sabotage since I knew Maria perceived me as very promising. My former partner, Brendan, told me that after Maria had watched me dancing the *Swan Lake* white act pas de deux, as taught in an Oboukhov class, she said to Balanchine, also watching, that she would rather see me dance the role than Tanny, Maria's replacement wife and muse. Considering all the women in that company, to be so singled out by Maria Tallchief was a huge compliment.

As events were to transpire, Tanny was to be chosen by Balanchine to dance Odette. When dancing that role for the first time, the verdict of history breathes down one's neck, for all the ranking ballerinas of the past have danced it since the Italian Pierina Legnani in 1895. Poor Tanny was well aware of the pressure, for I am told when Balanchine did schedule her for her Swan Queen debut, she threw up in the wings before the curtain rose.

During the remainder of the train ride to Florence, now irrevocably ruined for me, I began to mull over the nature of female cruelty. For, on further thought, it does begin somewhere, albeit in trifling fashion. Evil is to be shunned no matter what its gender manifestation, but since women are identified with motherhood, we tend to be more shocked when the perpetrator belongs to the so-called gentler sex.

I thought of ancient Greek mythology and their harpies and viragos, names that today suggest offensive females. Since we were approaching Florence, I jumped ahead to Lucretia Borgia whose very name still resonates with secret poisonings and murderous intrigue. Then my mind zoomed ahead to the mid-twentieth century, to Ilse Koch, the Witch of Buchenwald, whose predilection for designing lampshades made of human skin has made her name synonymous with Nazi barbarism.

Despite my sullen and introspective mood, it was time to catch up on letter writing to my parents. Because my mother's travel and living expenses weren't covered by the company in Europe, and our family funds didn't permit her to travel independently to accompany me, I was without protective guidance. (Nor did I have Mrs. Wortham who had been such a warm companion during our Covent Garden engagement the previous year.)

I missed both my mom and dad terribly. As I wrote my letters, a wave of melancholia would engulf me. While recently reading letters written to my parents during that tour, I can still see faint remnants of tearstains on them.

How could I even begin to share the cyclonic events that had taken place in Paris? I shared only the good news and left out all of the negatives. They were proud of me and I didn't want to worry them about any of my difficulties. Most of all, I feared they would order me home if they knew the hateful stresses I was being subjected to. And as far as that Batwoman scaling the ledge escapade, that was a secret I was prepared to take to the grave, that is, until now.

Looking back, it was probably a mistake not to have confided in them, as I needed their loving support and advice on how to handle my life in the New York City Ballet. I was alone, still very young, and without the proper emotional tools yet developed to deal with so many factors unrelated to the dance. Ballet was my reason for being and despite the hard work, it was easy compared to dealing with the jealousies from known and unknown sources, the intrigues, the continued harassment by Jerome Robbins, and the unexpected absence of interest from my adored Mr. B. I had committed my life to him believing wholeheartedly that he would oversee my career with care and undiminished interest.

But that belief was a pipe dream. I was an instrument, nothing more. On top of this, I found, increasingly, that I was dancing in a sterile manner, expressionless, crisp and sharp, but devoid of any emotion. I had become, in point of fact, a Balanchine dancer. That, of course, had been my aim. Yet, I missed the beauty and romance of the traditional ballets learned from my Imperial Russian teachers. I made myself fit in to his neo-classical choreography, and after a lot of practice I acquired the clinical and well-drilled performances he wanted, especially for Paul Hindemith's *Four Temperaments* and J.S. Bach's *Concerto Barocco*. He was the master and I blindly followed, believing him to be the genius that he was.

Still, a hint of doubt as to his lack of concern for me began to infiltrate my mind. Did he have any future plans for me, or was I to be used up, then given the heave-ho when perhaps chronically injured or too old to dance?

When we arrived in Florence, our business manager, Betty Cage, gave us the address of our lodgings. My roommates were still the sabotage-addicted corps de ballet duo. What bad luck! It was like being squirted with superglue! When I asked them why in the world they had said what they said to Maria, though it was a rhetorical question since I already knew the answer, they protested that they hadn't meant any harm. Since they were to be my roommates for the rest of the European tour, I chose not to bear a grudge, though I was more aware than ever to keep my private thoughts contained. If you're going to get shot at, at least don't feed the gunners the ammunition.

The place we would call home for the two weeks we were to be in Florence was a charming little pension near the theatre with a sunny patio and a garden filled with a profusion of pink roses and lilac. After a night's sleep we arose to *buon giorno* and an appetite-inducing breakfast of wonderfully sweet Tuscan fruit, freshly baked rolls and something new to me, cappuccino.

We were now anxious to find the Teatro Comunale for we had to be on time for the company class, to be followed by rehearsals and the spacing of the evening ballets. When we arrived we found Nan Porcher, our stage manager, already hard at work laying down the law to the Italian stagehands. She didn't speak Italian, but she asserted her authority with several repeats of the French expletive, *merde*. Someway, they seemed to understand her orders, for a bossy woman is a bossy woman in any language! As Faye Dunaway, in the role of Joan Crawford in *Mommie Dearest*, says to the assembled Pepsi Cola executives intent on ousting her, "Don't fuck with me, fellas!" Nan Porcher employed the same no nonsense sub-text.

It was a perfect Tuscan sunny day so after rehearsal I decided to go for a walk to explore Florence, the cultural jewel of the Renaissance. The Piazza della Repubblica was my first stop, for that was where Julius Caesar had founded the city in the year 59 BC. As people have chills when they view the Parthenon or the Pyramids for the first time, so did I have chills when walking through the piazza, gathering place for centuries of Florentines. There was the Palazzo della Signoria with its imposing high crenellated tower. And there was the Uffizi Gallery with its generations of Medici art collections, but, frustratingly, my schedule didn't permit a visit then. Later I returned and lingered in the presence of the Botticelli, Titian, and Raphael paintings. Most days I managed to visit a gallery including the Galleria dell'Accademia which houses the original Michelangelo masterpiece, *David*. I was in love with Florence and I believe that visiting that city initiated my lifetime love of art.

There was some discussion about the wisdom of doing *Pied Piper* on opening night and it was suggested by Mr. B that something more appropriate for the elegant opera house be selected. The Teatro seated 4,500 and was completely sold out even to the benches in the gallery, as was even the standing room. Robbins almost always got his way and *Pied Piper* was scheduled as the second ballet of the opening night after *Serenade*. It was Robbins' intention that we come across as carefree and fancy-free Americans, a tall order after his customary and systematic tearing us down at every rehearsal.

Robbins' chosen whipping boy in Florence was Frank Moncion. Frank had been suffering back problems and he asked Robbins if, during the rehearsals, he could be exempt from dragging me all over the stage as designated in the choreography. Jerry refused outright and instead made Frank do the dragging over and over again, a punishment for daring to ask him to alter his sacrosanct choreography. I was powerless to oppose the sadistic Jerry Robbins, not watching over his ballet, but meting out his own brand of torture, masquerading under the name of a ballet rehearsal. As Frank was forced to exacerbate his back injury, I could feel, see and hear his excruciating pain as he pulled my dead weight around the studio, more times than I could count. Jerome Robbins, it was obvious, was using me as his instrument of retribution. Frank, though seething with rage towards Robbins, and in terrible pain, wore a deceptive mask of stoicism.

When curtain time arrived that night, Frank asked me to run with him instead of being dragged, for he feared that if he lugged my dead weight around just one more time, he would collapse on stage. Now it was my turn to reciprocate Frank's great kindness to me when, after a Robbins' *Cage* rehearsal, I was staring out of the studio window with a death wish. Not for a second did I hesitate to agree to let Frank's back pain take precedence over Robbins' choreography. So to reduce the acute pain Frank was suffering, I did run with him instead of being dragged.

Of course, when the curtain came down, all hell broke loose as Robbins had a near catatonic fit that we had dared alter his choreography. I tried in vain to explain, but he shut me up and threatened to take me out of the ballet altogether. There he drew the line, for I had a rather prominent part and no one else knew it. When it was clear that *Pied Piper* was well received, no more mention was made about our changing the choreography.

I still think if Frank and I had stuck to the literally backbreaking choreography, Frank would have collapsed in the middle of the performance and Robbins would not have had the success he had. The headline would have been, not about his joyous choreography, but the collapse of the principal male dancer, Francisco Moncion.

The reviews spoke of almost nothing but *Pied Piper* and the "energetic American happy hooligans"! I was even mentioned in several reviews since I was the first one to be possessed by and involuntarily moved by the sound of the clarinet.

But so what that the critics were happy! Frank and I weren't! All I could think of were the ballet world's despots and dictators. Frank had been subjected to a form of sophisticated torture. Where was Mr. Kirstein? Paddling in his private lake of doom? Where was Mr. Balanchine? Lost in the translation of his choreographic overflow?

Seven years earlier, Italy's most ignominious tyrant, Benito Mussolini, and his mistress, Clara Petacci, were shot then hung upside down at an Esso gas station in Milan. As vilified as Clara Petacci was, Catholic propriety prevailed, for as her bullet-riddled corpse was hung upside down next to Il Duce, someone tied a rope around her skirts to preserve her posthumous modesty.

Well, I thought, justice had at least caught up with political villains, if not artistic ones.

I tried to separate the monsters of the war newsreels, the strutting Himmler, Goebbels, Eichmann and Hess parading round with their Heil Hitler salutes, and the repellent behavior going on literally under my nose in the *Pied Piper* rehearsal. A despot is a despot whether wearing sneakers, *pointe* shoes or jackboots.

Before leaving Florence, to recoup my emotional resources, I did some shopping on the Ponte de Vecchio. The area was fascinating and full of individual shops of every kind, offering fine leather, stylish clothing, and individual jewelry. With my minimal salary, I indulged myself by buying a few small souvenirs.

As for the famous bridge itself, it had been built before Columbus sailed for America. With the close of the war still so recent, there was still evidence of damage throughout the city with some severely bombed buildings and homes in mounds of rubble. The horrors of war became a reality when viewing the damage right in front of me, only seven years after the close of hostilities.

Surveying the sunnier side of human nature, the Italian people were extremely friendly, always smiling and extending themselves to make us feel welcome. I felt very much at home there and thought I could live in Florence for the rest of my life. It was truly wonderful. Although my knowledge of the Italian language was restricted to a few key phrases, the kids from the ballet school in Florence, where we did additional practicing, were so sweet and patient. We always managed to communicate with each other, peals of laughter punctuating mispronounced words. As is often the case when traveling, it was difficult to say goodbye to them, the lovely friends we had made in the land of Leonardo.

Our European tour next covered the Théâtre Municipal in Lausanne, followed by the Stadtheater in Zurich. After we finished rehearsal for *Swan Lake*, my two hovering roommates, Bobby Barnett and Herbie Bliss all wanted to go to the beach. The Zürichsee was a deep blue lake, one of the most beautiful in Switzerland, and we had the whole afternoon off. I was happy to be asked to go and quickly found a store selling bathing suits where I bought a bright orange bikini then met the others at the beach. We marveled at the sight of the snow-covered mountains and their reflection in Lake Zurich.

Then someone said, "Hey! Let's swim out to that platform!" Everyone agreed and they started swimming to the large wooden platform maybe 40 yards off shore. There was only one problem and that was that I had never learned to swim!

When I was a child of the age when most children learn to swim, my mother was afraid to let me go to a public pool for the fear of polio was always a threat. There was no vaccine in those days, so the possibility of crippling or deadly polio was very real. Mom believed the dreaded virus was spread in swimming pools, so I never went swimming. Rather than be left out of the fun and stuck standing on the beach in my brand new bikini, all alone, I decided to just watch what they were doing, stroke by stroke and do that, and I, too, would be swimming as they were.

I reasoned that I, as a dancer, was used to watching moves and doing them after seeing them once, while learning a ballet. So why not learn to swim instantly by watching them swim? I watched each one very carefully and didn't want to think of how deep the glacial lake could be. However deep it was, it was deep enough to drown. I got up my nerve and splashed into the freezing cold lake, doing what they were doing, kicking and imitating the Australian crawl. So far, so good! I was buoyant and traveling toward the raft! I was swimming! I didn't confide to any of them until after we got back that I had never learned to swim. They chided me, but with a touch of incredulity for taking such a chance.

Actually, that day in the Zürichsee, I was taking more of a chance than met the eye, when one takes into consideration the presence of the two shadowing sharks in the guise of friendly dolphins. Being the non-swimmer that I was, If I had been "allowed" to drown, the alibi could have been that I had admitted my inability to swim, but went into the deep water regardless. From verbal sabotage to physical sabotage was merely a question of degree. To look back less than thirty years earlier, Mr. B's and Mme Danilova's schoolmate, Lidia Ivanova, was drowned in the River Neva. Many people attributed her death to her pillow talk proximity with top Soviet officials. In point of fact, there were other people, less charitable, who thought she was drowned by a rival ballerina determined to usurp her roles.

Why, then, aware of the company with whom I was swimming, did I agree to do so? Today, I understand the dynamics of serious gang culture, for the potential gang member will do anything in order to be accepted by the group. I experienced something of that feeling at least on that day, for I was going to risk drowning rather than be left alone and out of the group. Oh, the mentality of the young and desperate!

Back to dry land, my first cousin, Lawrence Bocher, a West Point graduate, was at that time affiliated with post-war Radio Free Europe and was living in Basel. He had heard from my parents that I would be in Zurich and drove specially to see me. We met at the theatre and I had him watch the performance from the wings. He was very handsome and caused a flurry among the corps, both male and female, wondering who that good-looking man was in the wings. I was so happy to see him! He had a real Oklahoma drawl, sounding like music to my ears. He offered to drive me back to Paris instead of my having to go back on the train with the company. I wasn't sure I would get permission, so I introduced him to Mr. B.

I told him Larry, my cousin, wanted to drive me back to Paris for our next engagement at the Théâtre des Champs-Élysées, and that I really wanted to go with him for we hadn't seen each other in years. Mr. B looked at me as if I were spinning a tall tale and said with more than a touch of suspicion, "Your cousin? No! I will not let you go with him."

I don't think Mr. B believed Larry and I were related. We were disappointed, but what could we do but accept it? When word got back to my family, they surprised me by saying, "Good for Mr. B; he is really looking out for you!" If they only knew the half of it! Mr. B certainly didn't think we were relatives, and therefore whatever he sensed was on our minds might delay my arrival at rehearsals. So did that unexpected family reunion take a back seat to the hectic touring schedule of the New York City Ballet.

After a further two weeks in Paris, we moved on to The Hague. Word had reached Holland that *The Cage* was "pornographic" and "shameless", so inevitably tickets were in demand, so much so, that scalpers were getting three times the regular price. Everyone wanted to get a look at Nora Kaye breaking a man's sturdy neck between her powerful thighs. There were concerted efforts to exclude the ballet from the repertoire, and pressure was brought to bear. But Robbins held firm and Nora threatened not to dance at all if *The Cage* was cut. A compromise was reached and *The Cage* was allowed a single performance at the prestigious Opera House in The Hague.

Did *The Cage* set the tone of Holland's future liberality? Half a century later, the locals of Amsterdam didn't blink an eyelash when they permitted the glass window displays of young panty and bra-clad prostitutes, most of them Eastern European. The monkeys in the local zoo were treated with more respect than those poor threatened prisoners of cash register orgasm.

Our hotel in Holland was on the beach in Scheveningen, a popular seaside resort. The weather was just barely warm enough to sit on the beach, but we braved it and, of all things, got sunburned. Who ever heard of sunburned swans? We were due to dance *Swan Lake* and we were red! No white swans, no black swans, only red swans. Gobs of white powder dusted over our chests, shoulders and arms covered most of the damage. We were reprimanded and told never to get sunburned again! The next day in class when I perspired, little blisters popped up all over my arms!

After The Hague, we crossed the English Channel by boat and it was a rather rough crossing. Many dancers turned yellow and sped below deck. Gratefully back on terra firma, we arrived in London just in time for the closing night of the Sadler's Wells Ballet. I was overjoyed to see Arnold Haskell. Giving me a big hug, he said, "I told you we would meet again!"

What a wonderful gentleman he was! There was a lavish party in the Crush bar at Covent Garden for all of the Sadler's Wells dancers and all of our company. Also in attendance were the mission-driven Dame Ninette de Valois and that great poet of the dance, Frederic Ashton.

I was glad to get back to Covent Garden for our seven-week engagement. It was familiar now. We had real devotees always waiting outside the stage door, the gallery fans! They knew the names of all of their favorite dancers, wrote them fan letters and were thrilled if you gave them a picture or an autograph. They all sacrificed to save the money for tickets, many of them there night after night. I could also relate to them, for it wasn't that long ago in the past when, virtually penniless, I used to sneak in to the Met to see my own favorite dancers.

In London, Ruth Sobotka joined our threesome. Her presence was like freshly cut grass in a patch of poison ivy. In later years, Ruth was to marry and divorce Hollywood film director Stanley Kubrick. But even then, she gravitated towards theatre people, finding them more stimulating than the ballet crowd.

One night, after a performance, Ruth hosted a gathering at our flat, most of the guests from the theatre rather than the dance world. This in itself was refreshing, for the fragments of conversation I heard were far removed from the usual ballet shop chitchat. One of the attendees I remember was a very young Peter Ustinov, later Sir Peter, the eminent playwright and director, among whose future hit plays were *Romanoff and Juliet* and *The Love of Four Colonels*. Peter had us in stitches with his irreverent impersonations of various actors in the coveted role of Hamlet, most notably Laurence Olivier and John Gielgud. One guffawed at his uncanny mimicry, while also guiltily enjoying such sacred cows given a playful slap on the rump.

Our London season was not quite as successful as the prior one in 1950. The London audience did not like *Firebird*, comparing it unfavorably with Fokine's original version. They also found *The Cage* vile and pollutive. Regarding Anthony Tudor's *Lilac Garden*, they dismissed it as boring. Critics attacked the Balanchine concept of the storyless ballet and called us cold and technically brilliant, but devoid of emotion. This assessment was somewhat sobering after all of the triumphs in France, Italy and Germany.

After the London engagement we were guests at the Edinburgh Festival from August 25th to August 30th, 1952, where we were well received. I was particularly happy there for it was the city of my 17th birthday, August 26th. That evening, I danced the lead in *Cakewalk* and my parents had wired flowers to be presented to me at the end of the performance. When we were taking our curtain calls, the bouquets started arriving in a steady procession, happy moments to be catalogued in the catacombs of memory.

We left Edinburgh for Berlin, sponsored by the United States State Department as goodwill ambassadors to Germany. Flown in on an old DC-3, this was a plane that had participated in the Berlin airlift, ending the city's isolation after the Second World War. We flew through a thunderstorm and it actually rained in on us, since there were still unrepaired holes in the plane. Upon landing, we were met by some ranking military personnel and taken to our hotel on the Kurfürstendamm in the Western sector of Berlin. We were told that under no circumstances were we to go to the Eastern sector of the city on our own, for we would likely be arrested or kidnapped.

After the opening performance, we were very hungry and found a little restaurant still open. An old heavy-set woman with straggly gray hair ambled over to us to take our orders. Confrontationally, she asked, "How do you like our Germany?" I said how nice the Kurfürstendamm looked and how we loved the theatre and that our hotel was very comfortable. She looked directly in my eyes and pounding her fist on the table so that the plates rattled, defiantly proclaimed, "Germany will rise again!"

I was almost afraid to order for fear we would be poisoned, but we stayed and had something, I cannot remember what. I was too shaken with the intensity with which she spoke. The war had been over for seven years and I felt like it was still going on. She struck me as one of those women who were guards in the concentration camps. Called kapos, to justify their appointments the women were often twice as sadistic as their male counterparts.

The Western sector of Berlin looked like any brightly lit European metropolis. Except for the bombed church in the middle of the street, the ravages of war were in scant evidence. The following day we were driven in a military bus to see the Eastern sector. What a tangible change of atmosphere once crossing over into East Berlin! Women and children were scooping up bricks from the bombed out rubble, to clear up the streets or to try and sell them, I didn't know. Street after street had been leveled. There were some corner grocery stores with only potatoes and cabbages for sale. It was bleak, dismal and depressing.

Some ragamuffin children ran down the street after our bus and threw rocks at us. I kept thinking, Hitler did this to his people, people who trusted him to lead their country. Instead, they fostered and foisted a maniac on all of Europe. How could they have let him get into power? Why didn't they stop him before it was too late?

As much as one steeps oneself in books detailing the suffering of Nazi victims, each successive publication still comes as a shock, a searing condemnation of the human race at its most detestable. The medical experiments, let alone the mass exterminations, are sickening beyond belief. I was also unsettled by the thought that any German I met, over the age of 24, could have herded Jews, homosexuals and political dissidents into the hissing gas chambers.

Getting on the train in Berlin to get to the airport for the flight back to New York, we noticed immediately that the shades on all the windows were securely drawn. Guards with holstered guns soon arrived, not only to collect our passports, but also to warn us not to raise the shades and look out. We took them at their word and were totally obedient. For those of us conversant with recent political history, we knew that the Eastern sector of Berlin had been awarded to the Russians at the Churchill, Roosevelt and Stalin Yalta Conference in 1945. Boxed in our claustrophobic compartment, we sped along with our cramped thoughts.

My mind shot back to the ceremonial book burning throughout Germany in 1933 by swastika-armbanded students and helmeted storm troopers, setting fire to thousands of books of many of the world's most eminent writers. The flaming funeral pyre of literature included the works of Heinrich Heine, the German Jewish poet of a century earlier, whose work had inspired the libretto of *Giselle*. What he had to say then was pinpointedly prophetic and no less applicable in 1952. "Wherever they burn books, they will soon burn men."

The sound of jackbooted guards tramping up and down the aisles made me think of a new book on my school reading list. Recently published in America, it was called *Anne Frank: the Diary of a Young Girl*. Over the years it was to become the most damning indictment ever written of the Second World War. Though my acute harassment within the company was in no way comparable to Anne Frank's enforced hiding, I couldn't help but identify with her, a girl my own age. There she was, brimming over with such a love of life, yet constrained within the attic's walls, always aware that discovery and death were but a few goosesteps away. And, tragically, that is what came to pass.

Though we had been assured of our safety, not until we were off that godforsaken train, passports in hand, did any of us relax. Flying back to New York after our three-month tour, we were met with rousing cheers by some of our ardent fans. Best of all, Mom was at the airport to welcome me home! Little did I know, nor could I foresee, that my idyllic relationship with my beloved mother would not go on indefinitely.

CHAPTER SIXTEEN

THE TRIALS OF OLIVIA TWIST

It was wonderful to be back in New York! Autumnal leaves of cinnamon, yellow and green were skimming across the gently swaying grass in Central Park. New York, whatever the changing season, was vital and exciting as always. Broadway shows were in readiness to open, the producers and casts keeping their communal fingers crossed before imminently facing the jury's verdict, namely the critics, loved when they praised and vilified when they damned.

The Rockefeller Center ice skating rink would within two months be pointillistically dotted with the colorful figures of gliding skaters. In this return to my adopted city, I felt grateful to have returned very much alive and ready, more than ever, to dance. If I hadn't been concerned about protecting my ankle tendons, I would have found the free time during the coming winter to join the skaters. As it happened, I was soon to teach ice-skating, my student, rich and famous, to be able one day to just about buy the rink himself. More of my so-called pedagogic skills later.

I was happy to be able to study again at the School of American Ballet. The tightly organized schedule of performances on our just completed tour took their toll on my technique, for the classes we had in transit were insufficient to keep us up to par, let alone improve. So to return to my superb teachers, Oboukhov, Vladimirov, Dubrovska, and dear Muriel Stuart, was a joy. Not one of them would allow me to slip into any sloppy habits, or unwanted mannerisms. Singly and collectively, they kept my dancing pure and classical. Brendan was there again for our adagio classes, with both of us delighted to be able to resume our studio partnership. I really did love living and working in New York!

One day after pas de deux class, Brendan surprised me by asking me to have dinner with him at the New York Athletic Club. His father was a member and Brendan wanted the evening to be special for us. I realized that it would be a date. All those times we had sneaked into the Met I didn't consider dates, for we were just pals determined to see ballets we otherwise couldn't have afforded to view. Even though we had been dancing together for two years at the School of American Ballet, this was going to be different; a date! I was slightly apprehensive about it. What would we talk about? What would I wear? Would he try to kiss me?

As it happened, we both had an exhilarating evening out, with seamless conversation, the dining room at the club providing a sweeping view of Central Park, and the food a gourmet treat. Brendan was every inch a gentleman and saw me home in a taxi. No kiss on that very first date! What did I expect? Well, expecting nothing, but still hoping, were poles apart. But Brendan had just scored a second bull's eye, for his mother, thinking I was her son's girlfriend, was secured in that perception, always smiling at me when she watched us doing pas de deux class together, As for Brendan's father, there for his colleagues and associates to see was his ballet dancing son escorting a very presentable young lady to the Athletic Club. So if any of their family friends were mentally casting aspersions on their son's sexuality, no, they were completely wrong, for there I was, proof positive that their Fordham University law student boy was as heterosexual as they come. Just look at that pretty little blonde who looks at him so adoringly!

Of course there was never any romance with Brendan – it does take two to tango – but I had deep affection for him and I knew he had the same for me. We were best friends. I was always disappointed that he wasn't invited to join the New York City Ballet, for I missed his presence. Not having many friends in the company, I feel he could have helped me keep my footing secure on the jagged terrain. I was a threat to most of the older girls, and particularly excluded from the teenage clique. Left to my own devices, I had no choice but to chart my own course. Under the circumstances, I remained pleasant to all, but with considerable reserve. It was dance and dance alone that kept my head above water.

As for Brendan, he was endlessly restless and frustrated in his pursuit of the perfect ballet company. So many years after our paths finally diverged, though he had become an influential ballet critic in Rome, at heart I think he remained as rootless as he was when we first met. He was still searching for the Italian counterpart of Balanchine (the choreographer Aurelio Milloss was no substitute), which of course he didn't find.

What had changed, I believe, was Brendan's need to project a false persona. For among his sexual partners was to be the most celebrated dancer of them all, Rudolf Nureyev, a lover whose proximity did not increase anyone's lifeline.

To get back to New York, Mom and I had a little apartment on 96th Street just above Central Park. When the theatre was dark, we took advantage of reconnecting with nature. On a clear day, you could see, if not forever, the flora and fauna that lined the path to the lake. Mom was an avid gardener and I know, though she never complained, that she missed her flowerbeds and the life she had enjoyed with my father in Oklahoma City. Her gardening efforts were reduced to potted geraniums on the windowsill of our third floor walk-up. Not exactly the Plaza Hotel, we shared a kitchen with some Hungarians who spoke no English, but who still managed to teach us how to make the most delectable chicken paprikash. This is a dish that I still make today with pungent herbs and spices. In return, Mom taught them how to make the most scrumptious southern fried chicken.

And while re-savoring exchanged recipes, the silent screen actress, the Polish Pola Negri, upon the death of her purported lover, the greatest silent screen idol, Rudolph Valentino, stated, "Never ever vill I share with anyone the secret recipe I fed him, my vunderful Hungarian goulash!" Well, considering the fact that two out of three of Valentino's wives were lesbian, with consummation in doubt as to the third, one wonders if Pola's special recipe had inadvertently reduced her Rudolph's testosterone!

Food treats aside, I had the immediate concerns of schoolwork. Classes at the Professional Children's School began again with academic assignments and tests given every Friday. I was so looking forward to my high school graduation that spring, that ceremony that would free me to have more time to devote to ballet. With that diploma in hand, there would be no more lugging books on buses and subways, trying to read and study in the wings and in the dressing room, or writing reports with looming deadlines. How I envied the lives of the pre-Bolshevik students in St. Petersburg, for they simultaneously balanced their academic schooling while pursuing their daily ballet training.

In her unforgettable book, *Theatre Street*, Tamara Karsavina described in detail her concurrent training in the 1890s, intense years leading to her graduation and then entrance into the Maryinsky. Such a schedule would have been heaven for me, but that kind of structure didn't exist in America in the 1940s and 50s.

It was time to begin rehearsals for the fall season and there were new ballets on the agenda. Jerome Robbins, having missed his indentured little servant girl, requested that I be on tap for him on an almost daily basis. Specifically, he wanted me to join him in the vacated studios after the daily classes and rehearsals had finished. When you're in the army, especially with an unpredictable general, you obey. Despite his request, much more an order, I was always willing to help, for I would certainly not have refused him. And, simultaneously, my passion to dance was being given another outlet. Of course, there was no extra payment for the additional after-hours spent there, but the absence of overtime salary didn't enter my mind.

He would then ask me to do all kinds of different steps. I couldn't tell if this was for a new ballet or just some ideas he was turning over. Naive creature that I was, I just did what I was told.

One evening he asked me to show him the entire monster portion of *Firebird*. I was happy to do that for it was a part I really enjoyed and had even received a rare compliment on it from Mr. B.

Some years later in 1955 I was sitting in the audience in Los Angeles at a performance of the Broadway musical, *Peter Pan*, choreographed by Robbins – so stated the program – and starring Mary Martin in the title role. Staring at the stage in near disbelief. I saw that Tiger Lily's entire dance sequence with the Indians and Pirates was made up of all of the *Firebird* monster steps he had asked me to teach him. I, unknowingly, had helped him directly steal the choreography from Mr. B's ballet, then take all the credit for himself!

In the world of books and bookmen, one often comes across the debate of where influence ends and downright plagiarism begins. In other words, illegal and litigious literary theft! Many academics, in their research on a specialized topic, takes notes from various sources, then forget about those sources as new information accrues. A year or two or three later, when collating their subconscious assemblage, they accidently use the original research, without crediting, attribution, acknowledgment or footnotes. The list of time-honored established authors who have become embroiled in these accusations includes some of the who's who of the publishing world, from yesterday's Jack London to today's Stephen King. The line between subliminal assimilation and pages of direct transplanting is sometimes a controversial one. At other times, however, deliberate theft is cut and dried, beyond the possibility of coincidence. All said and done, Jerome Robbins, using me as his fingerproof gloves, under the very nose of Mr. B, lifted, shanghaied and commandeered the entire monster section of *Firebird* for his much acclaimed Broadway production of *Peter Pan!* Had Robbins, as a present-day Fagin, succeeded in turning me into a girl thief accomplice? Would Dickens' *Oliver Twist* now more aptly be retitled *Olivia Twist?*

Robbins, ever-enterprising, had found in me not only the perfect scapegoat, but also the perfect helper to do his every bidding, even if suspect by the rules of law and order. With me at hand, or rather at foot, or both, he also worked out the choreography on me for the *Uncle Tom's Cabin* scene in *The King and I* before it opened on Broadway in 1951. It was a tremendous hit starring Gertrude Lawrence and Yul Brynner.

Night after night I stayed late to assist him with choreography I later found out had nothing to do with the New York City Ballet repertoire, or anything I was scheduled to dance. However you slice the cake, I was very helpful, managing to figure out how to give the illusion of gliding on ice in an *attitude*, while wearing ballet slippers, not, of course, ice skates. By rapidly moving from heel to toe travelling several feet to the right, then at once to the left, as if skating, I created the illusion of the return of Olympic champion Sonja Henie.

Those ice skating steps I had taught him were pivotal to the recounting of the *Uncle Tom's Cabin* scene in *The King and I.* Again, I had absolutely no idea this was not going to be a ballet for the company. No one today could take advantage like that, of using a dancer without pay after a full day of rehearsals. It would be unacceptable no matter how the choreographer tried to explain it. But I was young, eager, anxious to please, capable and naive to the point of stupidity. I had, unknowingly, augmented the huge gaps in Robbins' knowledge and creativity.

When Mom would ask why I was so late getting home, I would explain that Robbins asked me to stay and work with him and there the questioning ended. That was a good enough reason for Mom. It was also a good enough reason for me as I thought his selecting me to be his "helper" was a compliment to my potential, not, as was the case, waylaying the most obedient and helpless member of the company.

He asked neither vinegar-tongued Milly nor no-nonsense Nora, nor even the very sedate Patty Wilde. Why, in retrospect, didn't he ask Maria to stay late every night, the better to lift passages intact from her treasured great vehicle *Firebird*, choreographed for her as a gift of love from her adoring husband, George Balanchine? Why, indeed!

I had no idea I was being so unscrupulously tricked! In my ongoing gullibility, there was a price to pay. The long hours were taking their toll on me physically, due to the extended hours of rehearsal. As many of the young basketball players proudly boast that they play through the pain, I was willing to dance through the increasingly acute discomfort.

How ironic that I, with my paucity of dancing income, should be helping Jerome Robbins consolidate his considerable wealth! For among the soon-to-be king of Broadway's future hits was *Fiddler on the Roof* in 1964, with both direction and choreography by Robbins, a hit among hits that ran for more than 3,200 performances and has subsequently been made into a film and then revived several lucrative times.

Though Mom and I were living in a walk-up with a shared kitchen, I was paving the way for Robbins to live on Park Avenue! Since, as they say, ignorance is bliss, I was a very happy girl! For occasional diversion, and it had to be free, I would walk to the Museum of Modern Art and watch Charlie Chaplin films, all the more appreciated because the entrance was gratis.

Nothing in Robbins' behavior should have surprised me anymore, but such was not the case. Phil Bloom, our ever industrious and enterprising public relations man, continued to peddle me to the New

York press, for such exposure kept in the news our recent European triumph.

As such, I was interviewed on the Jinx Falkenburg Televison Show. A former tennis champion, and, by her own admission, a failed Hollywood actress, she was a top television personality, a charming and beautiful woman. She invited me for tea at the Oak Room in the elegant Plaza Hotel (no Automat this time), to warm me up, so to speak, though I didn't need it for by now I was an old hand at media communication. Since it was a national daytime program, viewed mostly by women, she asked me questions about my uncle Mainbocher and his dressing the Duchess of Windsor for her wedding to the King of England. As usual, I wasn't paid a cent, but I enjoyed the entire experience. Then back to the Automat for Cinderella!

But the coverage that really turned me into a communal punching bag was Walter Terry's review. Mr. Terry, the esteemed dance critic of the *New York Herald Tribune*, wrote on March 3rd, 1952:

"Barbara Bocher assumed the part of Queen of Hearts in *Card Game* and danced with fine style and humor." Coming as it did from one of America's two leading dance critics, the other being John Martin of *The Times*, his single encouraging sentence threw further fuel on the fire.

But the year was still young. By the time November rolled around, I had appeared on the cover of the *New York Post* on November 16th, 1952, and had been named Young Dancer of the Month, November, 1952 in *Dance Magazine*. Then, with further articles about me in *People Magazine* and the *Daily Mirror*, I had to fend off new and successive swats with the stinging broom.

Inevitably the day of reckoning, never far off, arrived. Jerome Robbins took me aside and told me in no uncertain terms not to give any more interviews, either to the newspapers, magazines or television! But here the line was drawn on my always-accommodating obedience to him. What could be wrong with my giving interviews if they publicized the company and helped increase attendance? So I continued to do Phil Bloom's bidding.

Now, in 2012, firmly into the next century, I can look back with unobstructed clarity and see that Robbins, unpopular with the media at that time due to his infamously naming names for Commiehunting Senator Joe McCarthy, had become resentful of the attention I was eliciting. Resenting the bevy of journalists responding to my youthful sincerity and enthusiasm, he wanted to devour the entire cake, crumbs and all. Once again, the green-eyed monster of jealousy had reared its ugly head. For an all-powerful man like Jerome Robbins to feel diminished by a 17-year-old girl in the company would have been ludicrous had it not given further impetus to the wrecking ball, swinging closer and closer to my head.

As there were new members joining the company. I found myself for the first time with a female friend. She was the lovely young dancer Allegra Kent, from California. Jewish, as were so many dancers of the New York City Ballet, she was enormously talented; very quiet and shy, her distinctive dancing her way of communicating. She had a natural turn-out, her extension was amazing and she was strong! In the near future, she was to dance a fantastic Odette in *Swan Lake*. Looking at her, one realized that swan queens are born, not made.

Allegra was dedicated, a girl of exceptional potential. No wonder Mr. B asked her to join the company almost as soon as she appeared at the school. Knowing what it felt like to be living in the exclusion zone, I extended myself in her direction so that she could acclimatize herself to her new surroundings as soon as possible. We became fast friends and organized it so that we could be roommates on the next European tour.

Allegra's mother, apparently relieved that her daughter had found a suitable friend, invited me to have a lovely dinner with them. At a certain point in the near future, Allegra's mother saw to it that her daughter married the eminent photographer Bert Stern. It was Bert who was to shoot one of the last portrait sessions of the greatest female film star of them all, Marilyn Monroe. Allegra's mother, sensing that George Balanchine would sink his possessive claws into her virginal daughter, engineered the marriage as a form of a legalized walkie-talkie bodyguard. My darling daughter belongs to her husband, no one else!

The day had arrived that I was no longer the youngest dancer in the company. After Allegra, there would be someone else to replace her, and so would the conveyor belt keep rotating. Where do child stars go once they have committed the unpardonable sin of growing up?

Why are they so perfunctorily discarded as last night's rancid vegetable peelings? One of the issues that terminates their careers and, often their lives, is the indelible image they have imprinted on producers who see them forever as children, forever young even when their own youthful flesh has sagged and wrinkled the way of everyone else's.

There is, to boot, another reason and that is often that the child star has coasted on his youthful precocity and intuitive charm, and when, in adolescence, self-consciousness begins to rear its uninvited head, there is no true technique with which to replace it. And the third factor is that people and audiences are fickle; this year's hottest ticket is tomorrow's bargain basement dishcloth. Idol toppling is a diversionary pastime.

For every soprano songbird such as Deanna Durbin, now a reclusive suburban housewife in France, there is her tragic counterpart. Susannah Foster, of *Phantom of the Opera* fame, was reduced to living and sleeping in her car on an isolated beach. For every Mickey Rooney, there is a Scotty Beckett, once screen son of Greta Garbo and Charles Boyer in *Conquest*, then Norma Shearer's ill-fated son in *Marie Antoinette*. Today, who except the occasional movie buff, even recalls the name of Scotty Beckett, who, after a young lifetime of clashes with officialdom including charges of violent assault, committed suicide at the age of 38? Sabu, young transplanted Indian star of *The Thief of Bagdad*, who passed his sell-by date when such action films went out of fashion, died of a heart attack one year older, at the age of 39.

None of these case histories presaged well for the wonderful Allegra Kent, nor, even more so, for me. It is true that unlike child actors, baby ballerinas can often survive into maturity, since their bedrock is a usually solidly grounded technique.

I was still, thankfully, riding the crest. An unexpected invitation came from Crandall Diehl who, in the future, was to choreograph the 1976 and 1981 revivals of *My Fair Lady*. The German choreographer Hanya Holm, student of Mary Wigman, had been the original choreographer in 1956 when that show, with Julie Andrews and Rex Harrison, became one of Broadway's most resounding hits.

Crandall, in the early 1950s, was then a young choreographer who invited me to be the leading dancer in his new ballet, *For Earth Too*

Quick. After the impresario Trudy Goth arranged for us to participate in the Bermuda Festival, we sailed to Hamilton, Bermuda. As Mom wasn't able to accompany me, I found that I had been given my own stateroom.

After we left the New York harbor, the sea became very choppy. Many of the passengers on board became seasick, shades of the English Channel. I was among the fortunate and still felt fine. I went up on deck to see what was happening and saw to my amazement that the grand piano was rolling back and forth across the dining room floor and, resultantly, was slamming against one wall then into the other! No one appeared in the dining room that night during the storm and I then realized why the tables each had a low ridge built around them, the better to keep the dishes from sliding off! The dining room was closed, since nearly all of the people on board were indisposed. Unaware of the procedure for having food delivered to the stateroom, I just went to bed hungry. But what were a few hunger pangs compared to the retching other passengers were suffering?

The New York seasons were brief and intermittent, thereby enabling me to accept invitations to dance for others. When we weren't working, of course, our income stopped, so the administration was relieved that their dancers could earn from other sources, that is, when a salary was being offered.

The ruling staff of the New York City Ballet, so as not to lose their experienced dancers to permanent outside work, helped us with television opportunities. There was no shortage of money there! To my delight, I found myself on *The Show of Shows*, Sid Caesar's popular weekly comedy slot. Mr. Caesar was a true aficionado of opera and ballet and always included a loving spoof on both in his hour-long live show. I appeared several times and was paid the huge sum of $400 per week! While with the New York City Ballet, for performances I was earning $60 a week, so the meteoric rise in income was an amazing boost. At least Mom and I were to be spared the possibility of sleeping on the park benches of adjacent Central Park!

Rehearsing with Sid Caesar, I didn't have an inkling that I was rubbing elbows with his golden stable of comedy writers including none other than the future film star and director Woody Allen, Broadway's record-breaking to be playwright Neil Simon, and, moreover, popular favorites Carl Reiner and Morey Amsterdam! What a sidesplitting collection and comedic hall of fame!

As comical as their results were, the men themselves were the very antithesis during the act of creation. Acute anxiety was high on the set, with the director of the show a complete basket case the day before the transmission. The veins would stand out in his temples and he would screech out a string of expletives to everyone near and far, from the cameramen to Sid Caesar himself, who would yell back, an equal sparring partner in filthy language. Imogene Coca, such a truly funny and fey woman, was not one to be left out, so she too contributed her share of swear words.

I was careful to stay out of sight when I could, lest I provoke a further verbal attack. I didn't need any more, having enough with the associate director of the New York City Ballet. So caution ruling the roost; I switched to invisible until it was time to dance!

Unlike Mr. Robbins, the popular television comedian didn't waylay me after hours to join Woody Allen and the rest of the team to write his shows for him. Had Mr. Caesar taken a leaf out of Robbins' manipulative book, I would have been asked to join their very public, foul-mouthed, cigar-chomping slanging matches. Who knows what new laurels *The Show of Shows* might have garnered with me as their latest comedy writer – possibly *The Harvard Lampoon* award as the unfunniest show of the year?

To close the door on plagiarism, stealing is no laughing matter. It is, and one cannot deny it, a form of theft, though, generally speaking, not in the category of an armed bank robbery. Within a short while, many of us were to find ourselves at the tail end of a felony that would be described by the police as a major crime. Somehow, in one's equation of art with lofty motives, one doesn't anticipate criminals so blatantly breaking the law in the magisterial corridors of Carnegie Hall. Where and how, one may well ask?

I was so pleased to be invited by impresario Trudy Goth to dance in a Renaissance program of music and dance to be choreographed by Valentina Oumansky. It was indeed a thrill to appear in that historic auditorium. However, the thrill quickly dissipated when everyone was dismayed by the audacious theft that had occurred only the day before. Apparently two men dressed in white uniforms had announced matter-of-factly to the stage doorman that they were there to collect the two grand pianos. Given a nod of access to the two moving men, so-called, the pair went about shifting the two pianos that had, in the past, resonated to the likes of Vladimir Horowitz and Arthur Rubinstein. The pianos carefully loaded onto the waiting truck, they drove away, the grand pianos and the thieves never to be seen again! Without any authorization or credentials whatsoever, the daring duo had rolled the grand pianos out of the stage door as easily as one shifts a sofa. I would go as far to say that the hapless stage doorman did not, under the circumstances, hold on to his job much longer!

Fortunately, our program featured a noted harpsichordist and antique instruments of the Renaissance period, so we could proceed with the evening's performance. I recall wearing a floor-length costume embroidered with medieval-styled tapestry, topped by a very high pointed conical hat with a silk scarf attached that reached to the floor. Evoking the style of Botticelli's Italy – my recent trip to Florence gave me the connection to the period – we did a lot of weaving in and out of each other's arm-shaped arches. All the while, I feared stabbing someone in the eye with the pointed tip of my hat, or possibly have it knocked off of my head or, heaven forbid, tripping on the diaphanous scarf. After maneuvering myself through the pitfalls of that apparel, I was thankful I didn't have to deal with this type of costume hazard while dancing for the New York City Ballet.

Most of what we wore was minimal, though with exceptions for Mme Karinska, Marc Chagall and Cecil Beaton. Our funds were limited, so we settled for tights and leotards. On further thought, I think perhaps that Mr B used the paucity of funds as an excuse, because he liked to reveal the beauty of the body, especially the female body. Besides which, our technical skills and lines were more evident with body-hugging outfits.

Mr. B, loving sleek, lithe lines, wanted his dancers, ideally, to be whippet-thin, like Tanny. Though it no doubt existed then, I personally never saw a case of either anorexia or bulimia. Insofar as drugs were concerned, either recreational or prescription, I saw only one example of that, surprisingly from one of our principals, Melissa Hayden. A very late starter, she was possessed of a ferocious will power. Before performances, she took little green pills, Benzedrine, that must have shot extra energy through her body. Her resultant performances were powerful, but the price to pay for the chemical infusion was that her normally caustic tongue turned into double-edged Gillette blades. Her fits of temper never lagged far behind.

In this hotbed of elbow-jabbing ambition, backstabbing determination and warped psyches, I did my best to function, and always with obedience and enthusiasm. My saving grace in the midst of this sea of desperate straw-clutching was that dancing brought me joy.

One night, as I was about to enter the stage for the leading role in Ruthanna Boris's *Cakewalk*, I sat down in the swing, getting ready to be released onto the stage by the stagehands. As this was a humorous entrance, invariably eliciting giggles and laughter from the audience, I was getting myself into a lighthearted mood.

Just then, right beside me, out of the shadows, but with a perfectly timed subtle act of sabotage, Jillana's mother, Mrs. Zimmerman, said pseudo-sympathetically, "B-a-rbara, don't you miss your f-a-ther? Jilly couldn't stand to be away from *her* f-a-ther at a-ll!" Her stretching of the vowels accentuated her thrusting a guilt trip on me just seconds before I was to swing over the stage. Now, Mrs. Zimmerman, on the surface, looked just like the ordinary New Jersey housewife that she was, that is, until the poisonous strychnine of ballet mama-dom coursed through her veins.

Then and there, goodbye to my lighthearted preparation. All I could think of was that I hardly ever saw my father anymore, and that he had never even seen me dance with the company in New York due to financial constraints, and that if he were to die, I'd never see him again. As I was pushed on to the stage, tears welled up in my eyes, causing double vision in rainbow patterns due to the piercing stage lights. Somehow I was able to draw upon an acting technique I didn't even realize I had, for I managed, I was told, to be funny.

Jill, only a year older than I, was a lovely dancer, and though not strong, had a generous breadth of movement. She was to become one of the company's principals. A pleasant enough girl, we should have been friends, but after this episode, in order to protect myself from her mother, I remained remote from Jill for the remainder of my time with the company.

And while on the subject of ruthless ballet mamas, I will elaborate on this topic that I only glossed over in an earlier chapter. Within my own experience, I have seen the damaging influence of not only ballet mamas, but also mamas and, as well, papas, within the enclosed but intense world of athletics. In their ambition for their children, an ambition triggered by their own unfulfilled egos for achievement, they do irreparable harm to their offspring. The world of soccer, baseball, basketball, gymnastics, swim and tennis teams draw parents onto an unstoppable treadmill of blinkered drive. To the list of child star actors, baby ballerinas, precocious athletes, add child virtuoso musicians.

I know of a woman, Amelia Young, once a most gifted child prodigy cellist, who appeared on every British talent show under the sun; *Junior Showtime, Opportunity Knocks, New Faces, Multicoloured Swop Shop, Magpie* and other popular television programs. She also won international cello awards while still a mere slip of a child. But the cello is a heavy instrument to lug around and by practicing hours every day, her young body went into rebellion. With tendinitis in her lower left forearm, joint wear and tear, and a neck vertebra that kept slipping out of place, so ended prematurely the most promising of musical careers.

Today, as a wife and mother in France, she is also a teacher who passes on her hard-earned wisdom to not only her young and eager students, but also to their parents, giving them cautionary counsel as to the pitfalls of excessive push.

"I do feel some anger towards the grownups surrounding me as a very determined small child," she has stated. "It was up to them to hold me back, not indulge my need to do more and more concerts and shows. But my mother was doing what she thought best, making her child happy. She didn't know that I was slowly and permanently damaging my body."

To skip back to my own early days, on June 19th, 1953, the New York City Ballet was in New York preparing to board the cross-country train across the continent. Screeching out at us from the headlines of every newspaper was the shock announcement of the double execution of the convicted spies, Ethel and Julius Rosenberg.

I am ashamed to say that I was totally apolitical in those far off years, my only thoughts on world-altering events being the parroted opinions of others. Obedient and unquestioning teenager that I was, I registered the double death sentences, then tried to think little more about it, instead watching through the train window the distracting and zooming landscapes of middle America.

CHAPTER SEVENTEEN

The Hills of Hollywood

Yet as the train raced across state borders, the pitiful *Daily News* photograph of Ethel Rosenberg's hysterical mother, the grandmother, cradling her two sobbing just-orphaned grandsons, my mother's cautionary words sprang to mind. For every dubious action pursued in life, there are consequences, often with the gravest repercussions.

The only American civilians ever executed for espionage during peacetime, the Rosenbergs were charged with passing on atomic secrets to the Soviets, although it was information already known by the Kremlin. Long after the event, it was revealed that though Julius Rosenberg was culpable, his wife, Ethel, despite being aware of his activities, and herself a Communist, was not even a minor player.

Why, then, did she meet such a fate? Ethel Rosenberg had the misfortune to have her brother, David Greenglass, give false testimony in court against her. The ignominious perjury, later confessed, was made so as to protect from prosecution his own wife, Ethel's sister-in-law. So did the younger brother catapult his older sister into the electric chair, an act of infamous sibling betrayal.

The train sped along, faster than my optical nerves could register the fleeting scenery. Out came another pair of *pointe* shoes to be ribboned, darned, thumped then pummeled into the desired flexibility, a ritual that had always served as a bulwark against confusing and intrusive thoughts.

After appearing in Chicago, we next arrived in Red Rock, Denver, Colorado. A mile high above sea level, the stage was a natural circular bowl carved into the earth by Mother Nature, overseen by cliffs that were really the color red, hence the name. Due to the altitude, during the *Sylvia Pas de Deux*, Maria came off stage gasping, grasping her usual half lemon and then being administered oxygen, all of this during André's short solo. Then, the emergency aid completed, she rushed back on the stage for the coda of the pas de deux, yet another example of ballet's private pain underlying the public poetry.

Hollywood was next, the legendary metropolis of impassioned runaway dreams, and, simultaneously, the living graveyard of would-be stars and stars that had been, but were no more. This, then, was the dangerously alluring Mecca of the world's most beautiful young men and women, the orange-blossomed patch of land where pimping, prostitution, drug addiction, alcohol, suicide and even murder became the last resort of the desperate and discarded. In this milieu of celluloid gods and cigar-chomping gargoyles, we were scheduled to appear at the open-air Greek Theatre.

For the month-long duration of our season, we shared apartments at the Hollywood Court Hotel. In the basement of the hotel, the choreographer Eugene Loring conducted his thriving school. Taking regular class was top MGM film star Cyd Charisse who, in the 1930s, had been in one of the several Ballet Russe companies then touring Europe. A glamorous woman, an all-around and outstanding dancer, despite her world-wide fame for such films as *Meet Me In Las Vegas* and *Silk Stockings*, she was completely outgoing and approachable. Recently deceased, it is hard to reconcile Cyd Charisse's gorgeous long legs no longer extending over the heads of her ever-attentive partners, most notably Gene Kelly and Fred Astaire.

There were always a few movie stars sprinkled throughout the audience, but on this particular night, just before starting time, it was rumored that Danny Kaye was in attendance. He was then the most popular comic film star in the world, observing our repertoire in preparation for his forthcoming film, *Knock On Wood*, in which he would partner Diana Adams in a hilarious ballet sequence.

When Tanaquil LeClerq heard he was present, she wrote a note to him inviting him to come backstage after the performance was over, sending the message with one of the ushers. Sure enough, after the final curtain he appeared. There he was, Hans Christian Andersen himself, or his screen reincarnation. I happened to be standing in the hallway adjacent to Tanny's dressing room when the unrivalled comic star appeared. He gave me a warm smile, asking which dressing room was Tanny's.

In response to his polite knock, she opened the door and immediately started gushing in a very squeaky, high-pitched voice, "Oh, Mr. Kaye, I have always wanted to meet you! I just l-u-u-u-ve you! You are s-s-o-o-o funny!" her idolatrous response punctuated by her animatedly waving arms while her bobbing head tilted this way and that way.

Danny Kaye, with his instant and uncontainable compulsion to mimic, repeated exactly, verbatim, yes, word for word, what she was saying, including her flailing gestures. His timing was as simultaneous as a UN translation. If Mr. Kaye was aware that his echoing parody was trespassing on the future Mrs. Balanchine's sensibilities, it didn't deter him.

Watching this brief encounter, I found it hysterically funny, though Tanny certainly did not. Instead of appreciating a private performance by the one and only virtuoso comedian, she took extreme umbrage, crossing her arms and pouting, not uttering another word. As I saw it, there had been nothing malicious in his imitation of her, but Tanny wasn't able to appreciate being the catalyst of her once favorite comedian's improvised humor. Danny and Tanny, a pas de deux not made in heaven!

Then Nora Kaye, with impeccable timing, appeared and swept the bewildered Danny Kaye into her dressing room, closing the door behind them. And so they disappeared, the two Kayes, Nora, ballet's queen of tragedy, and Danny, Hollywood's king of comedy.

While still on the subject of diction, enunciation, and voice placement, Nora had just danced *Swan Lake*, clearly a major challenge for her, since she was more at home with the likes of Tudor and Robbins than Petipa and Ivanov. Though the critics were to be rather frugal in their response to her performance, nevertheless, in that same Greek Theatre season, she had unequivocally captivated a young man in the audience. Mesmerized by the thrill of seeing his first *Swan Lake*, he managed to get to the dressing room area since the stage doorman was very lax regarding post-performance visitors.

And there she was, still in her white-feathered tutu, meeting her young fan, standing there bewitched by the blue-lit vision directly in front of him! Nora was pleased to receive his ardent note, and still exuding her pearly-white Swan Queen aura, graciously smiled at him in welcome. Transfixed as he gazed upon her, he managed to find his tongue to compliment her. Responding to his praise, Nora, in her abrasive and nasal New York accent, answered:

"Je-sus Chri-ist! My feet are killin' me and I'm pooped!" Expecting the dulcet tones of a modern day Lorelei, the fan's expression dissolved from adoration to one of disbelief! With his eardrums clogged and his illusions shattered, the young man backed off in silence.

Again I was in the hallway, alongside dancer Shaun O'Brien, when this besotted young man had met his idol. For a long time afterwards, at select gatherings, Shaun would do a spot-on imitation of Nora, and with each re-telling, embroider it to sidesplitting accuracy.

During that same long, hot summer, top movie star Shelley Winters hosted an afternoon party at her Malibu beach house. The actress, once Marilyn Monroe's roommate, and later to win two Oscars for her roles in the films *The Diary of Anne Frank* and *A Patch of Blue,* had emblazoned her white-hot career out of sheer chutzpah spiced with an unstoppable drive. Completely dedicated to acting as an art form, it was not for her to exhibit herself merely as an excuse to demand and command attention.

In later life, Shelley Winters became very heavy, unable to restrict her appetite for fattening food. And according to her autobiography, she was equally unable to restrict her appetite for sexually charged leading men. As ravenous as a child let loose in a candy shop, she gorged herself on such peppermint stick studs as Errol Flynn, Marlon Brando, Sean Connery and Clark Gable.

Anyway, there was Shelley, the former Shirley Schrift, originally from St. Louis, Missouri, more latterly of Brooklyn, New York, getting more boisterous by the minute. Soon she would struggle just to stand upright. Fearful of alcohol-swollen brains, for I had had more than enough with Hugh Laing in Paris, I went out to the beach where the ominous and pounding waves were about four feet high. Having braved the waters of that tranquil Zürichsee, I didn't want to push my luck with this angry stretch of the Pacific Ocean. So I didn't even dip my toes into the water. I just stood there, re-invigorating myself with the tangy and mist-sprayed fresh air.

Why was such a mega-successful actress as Shelley Winters, to become a renowned dramatic coach as well, drowning her insecurities with alcohol? Puzzled, I posed the question to myself. The answer, in retrospect, is that success, six mink coats, and even more medals are not necessarily prescriptions for happiness.

Like Nora Kaye, Melissa Hayden, Ruthanna Boris and my best friend Allegra Kent, let alone Anna Pavlova, Alicia Markova and Maya Plissetskaya, Shelley's Jewish roots were deeply embedded. And those ethnic roots could not easily be yanked up from the earth. Why, I was curious to know? Perhaps because blood memories of pogroms and persecution never quite disappear, even after children of immigrants are brought up on distant and safe shores.

Standing nearby me on that stretch of pebble-stoned beach was the instantly recognizable Hollywood film idol, Farley Granger, star of Alfred Hitchcock's now classic films *Rope* and *Strangers on a Train*. He was reputedly Shelley Winters' current flame, but since this was Tinseltown, one took such information with a generous pinch of salt. For it was a well-established fact that Farley Granger, among his countless romantic imbroglios, had had a fiery relationship with Leonard Bernstein. Horny Lenny, it was apparent, was not one to let grass grow under his feet. When, one may well ask, did he find the time to compose and conduct?

Mr. Granger's long-time, live-in lover, Robert Calhoun, must have repeatedly turned a blind eye to the panting hordes of both sexes that followed his Farley everywhere. When the once screen idol recently died at the age of 85, the roar of the crowd had long since subsided into the muted echo chamber of forgetfulness. Farley who?

I went back inside the house and said my goodbyes, for it was not my kind of party. Probably the youngest female there, some of the male guests were looking at me with what my father would have described as dishonorable intentions. Their lecherous thoughts notwithstanding, I had more important things to accomplish than be nibbled into as some succulent after dinner chocolates. Was this little afternoon get-together, I asked myself uncomfortably, going to turn into a mini-Babylon by the sea? I will never know, for I didn't stay there long enough to find out.

During that Greek Theatre season, after dancing the lead in *Cakewalk*, my parents had arranged for me to receive a large bouquet of flowers. As I was acknowledging the applause of the audience, I noticed a handsome young man walking over to me to present the bouquet. The reigning teen idol then was the strawberry-blond movie star Van Johnson, and the young man handing me the flowers looked enough like him to have been his stand-in.

As I was going down the stairs to the dressing room, he politely stopped me and asked that, if instead of going to the lavish party to take place at the Hollywood Hills mansion of the impresario, James Doolittle, I would join him instead to listen to Red Nichols and his Five Pennies playing Dixieland music. I hesitated for a moment and then, throwing caution to the winds, for I didn't even know the young man's name, I said yes.

Almost completely enveloped by the brotherly love of gay boys, it was a tonic to receive the attentions of a young man who apparently responded to me as Adam to Eve, rather than Adam to Steve. And so I succumbed to his invitation. While being driven there, far away, and in the darkness of the Pacific night, I found out that he was a UCLA graduate and in his last year of studying to be an Episcopal priest.

On the long European tour that followed, a love letter from him awaited me in the mailboxes of every opera house on the itinerary. So was my impetuous acceptance of his drive-by-night invitation to alter the next few decades of my life.

At the age of still seventeen, I wasn't too young to dance the leading role in a ballet at the huge Greek Theatre, but I was definitely too unworldly to have been left on my own across the span of two continents. This Van Johnson lookalike, for all I knew, could have been one of those California serial killers who preys on young girls, then dumps their bodies to decompose in the desert.

Fortunately, several hours later, he returned me in one piece to my hotel, my frantic roommates rightfully and forcefully berating me for disappearing into the night with an absolute stranger. Yes, old enough to be the recipient of thousands of hands applauding me, but far too young and trusting to protect myself from who knows what devious thoughts of strange men on the prowl?

It was during that Greek Theatre engagement that I turned eighteen. The retired founder of the Balanchine Foundation, Barbara Horgan, sharing the same birthday with me, suggested that we celebrate together at the fashionable Romanov's in Beverly Hills, the favorite eating place of Hollywood stars in the 1940s and 50s.

The restaurant's owner, Michael Romanov, was a colorful character who dwarfed even airport fiction, for he was born Hershel Geguzin in Lithuania, immigrated to America at the age of ten and became a Brooklyn pants presser. Having recuperated from an earlier imprisonment for fraud in France, his need to pull the wool over people's eyes escalated until he had become an imposter, second to none, though innocuous, in the style of a Sigmund Romberg operetta. Pretending to be the Russian Prince Michael Dimitri Obolensky-Romanov, nephew of Czar Nicholas II, everyone in the movie colony who frequented his popular restaurant well knew he wasn't, but since he wasn't actually doing anything injurious to anyone, they all went along with his preposterous pretence.

When I was introduced to the so-called Prince Michael, I was totally unaware of his bogus curriculum vitae. Somehow I hesitated in curtsying to him, nipping the fleeting thought in the bud, and with hindsight, just as well, for Lord Mountbatten and Princess Margaret he was not. But I have to concede that the man was exceedingly charming, having fully assimilated his role, so that no doubt he long believed it himself. Is this duplicity or great acting, where the boundary between fact and fantasy disappears? Like Anna Anderson, the German mental inmate who vociferously and falsely claimed that she was Anastasia, the Czar's bayoneted and bludgeoned daughter.

Following the most elegant gourmet lunch, with tuxedoed waiters discreetly in vigilant attendance, our every serving was supervised by the prince himself. There in the warmth of the California summer, we had been transported to the fabled Winter Palace, or so did we harmlessly imagine.

Then, our appetites appeased, we went shopping. With a handful of crumpled then flattened-out five-dollar bills, scrimped, saved and put aside for a luxury item, I couldn't resist buying a stylish cashmere dress that I wore until it was threadbare. Only when it literally fell apart some ten years later did I discard it and even then reluctantly. How attached we can get to mere pieces of fabric, for they whisper to us of memorable and special occasions.

The company next danced at the War Memorial Opera House in San Francisco for a short run. One special evening my ballet teacher from Oklahoma City, Fronie Asher, who had encouraged me to continue to study ballet, traveled a few thousand miles to attend one of the performances in which I danced the leading role of the Queen of Hearts in *Card Game*. After the performance, she took me to the famed Top of the Mark restaurant where the windows overlooked the most sweeping view of that hilly city.

Froni was effusive with her compliments and I tried to imagine the pride she felt as she watched her once little student assume a ranking role in a Balanchine and Stravinsky ballet under the directions of the masters themselves. I, in turn, thanked her for the major contribution she had made in shaping the unimagined events of my very young life.

Joy, I was to discover, is not a constant, but an occasional exclamation point on the yet-to-be written pages of our existence. Before the Thai tsunami, tourists were lolling on the champagne sands with the sea looking invitingly calm. Before a middle-of-the-night earthquake, such as San Francisco itself had undergone almost half a century earlier, people's sleep was largely undisturbed, that is, until the sudden and swift rumble of death and destruction. And so it was with me. Within the calendar year of my eighteenth birthday, I was to become the architect of my own artistic demise, the engineer of my own permanent exit. Shortly, I was to savor the final jubilation of my last European tour with the New York City Ballet.

CHAPTER EIGHTEEN

CROSSROADS AT LA SCALA

My graduation from the School for Young Professionals in New York took place with both my parents present for the event, one of life's several rites of passage. It was a palpable relief for now I had more time to devote to dance and my parents were simultaneously relieved of the financial pressure of the monthly tuition. After the Headmaster gave the commencement address, we sang the school song for the last time, *There's No Business Like Show Business*, Irving Berlin's national anthem for the desperate gypsies of the entertainment world. If the title of the song were to be changed to *Les Misérables*, it might be more accurate.

And why must the show go on? People in other professions take time off in the wake of family deaths and public disasters. Be that as it may, always obedient, both my virtue and defect, I sang along with everyone else and absorbing the fervor of the moment, acted my role full out.

The diplomas awarded, the teary congratulations having subsided, now I was on my own at the age of 17. Mom had gone back to Oklahoma to resume her life there with my father and I rented my own apartment on 71st Street. It was empowering to be in my own place and just able to support myself, but it was also somewhat offsetting, for I was soon to discover that it could be, at times, very isolating and lonely.

With a few weeks off before the tour began, I went to visit my parents in Oklahoma City for a rest and some quiet time with them. It turned out to be a different kind of visit! My teacher Fronie Asher was not the only one bursting with pride at my accomplishments. When I arrived at the airport I was very surprised to find reporters there to interview me. My proud father had alerted the press of my visit and though he was not experienced in public relations, he did a very good job with his daughter!

I was asked for photo shoots and interviews for the *Daily Oklahoman*, the local newspaper. Dad had also arranged for me to appear on the very first color television show broadcast in Oklahoma City. Facing the color cameras, I was interviewed about my life in the New York City Ballet and also about my famous uncle, the couturier to the stars, Mainbocher. My image of small- town girl making good in the big city was what people expected, so, of course, my every response fulfilled that expectation. No reports of backstage bullying were to be vented on color television.

My father was unstoppable, having mastered his on-the-job training apprenticeship, for he had also made arrangements with the Gene Ingram Ballet School for me to teach some advanced ballet classes for them. I had never taught before and was happy to find that I was treated respectfully by all of the students and faculty. In point of fact, I was related to as a celebrity, the baby ballerina returning, albeit temporarily, to her roots. I gave the students sample classes of how I had been taught at the School of American Ballet, modifying the more complex combinations.

I was also very pleased to teach some ballet exercises to young athletes of the Oklahoma University Men's Basketball Team. Those exercises were designed to strengthen their legs and improve their speed and ability to jump. Their coach wisely knew what an advantage it would be to have the benefit of ballet training. At that time there was a strict rule that no college basketball team could hold practice sessions between seasons. What better way to acquire strength for players in the off-season than a ballet class, and as an added bonus remain within the cautionary rules? None of the young athletes turned out to be a threat to Jacques d'Amboise, but I found it enjoyable to teach them. The young basketball players, were, I must add, amused by my presence at first, but then blown away by the difficulty of the exercises. "But they look so easy," they commented.

The intended quiet interlude with my parents turned out to be a chockerblock full schedule of teaching, giving interviews and attending luncheons with some of my mother's golfing girlfriends. Then, as the gongs of midnight reminded Cinderella that she must leave the ball, a telegram from Betty Cage, the company's business manager, notified me to get back to New York as soon as possible for the departure to Milan, our first stop on the second and more extensive European tour.

I said my reluctant goodbyes, flew to New York and checked in at the Wellington Hotel right around the corner from the theatre. The next morning I saw Betty Cage and was given the practical information I needed for the tour. Instead of looking forward to what promised to be a new and exciting experience, I was filled with misgivings, for I didn't know how I'd cope with the inevitable and renewed presence of Mr. Robbins. But a momentary reprieve seemed to arrive from some unknown source since I was given the very welcome news that he would not be accompanying the company to Milan! This was, as I saw it, nothing less than a deliverance!

Our flight was, again, on the newest British Overseas Airways four-engine propeller-driven Boeing Stratocruiser. I do not remember much about it, for when I wasn't darning *pointe* slippers, I slept for most of the fourteen-hour flight.

After landing, we were speedily escorted through customs. Allegra was assigned to be my roommate for the tour. I could not have been more pleased and relieved, for we were good friends and had mutual respect for each other's undiluted dedication to the dance. I could empathize with her as she was now the youngest member of the company. Fortunately, she did not have to go through the acute discomfort of brazen hostility from the other girls as I had, for there was no private dressing room involved and our overzealous publicity director did not seek her out for publicity purposes. She just melted in to the company framework learning all of the corps de ballet parts in the repertoire, unhampered by foul four-lettered word attacks.

When we were delivered to the hotel, we found the staff very warm and inviting, with a musical way of greeting us in Italian. Our room was very small and I had to step over Allegra's legs each night if I wanted to get across, for she always spent at least half an hour sitting on the floor with her legs outstretched completely in second while writing letters to her mother, or reading.

Allegra, a very fine dancer, was a rather withdrawn, sweet and sensitive girl. I often had the feeling that she was sometimes skirting another world, oblivious as she was of the people around her. I, on the other hand, was practical and liked to plan for any contingency that might arise. Despite our differences in temperament, we got along very well. As long as I've known her, I cannot recall any disagreements between us, not in the dimly lit alcoves of Europe's backstages, or the more prosaic hotel bathrooms when one of the roommates takes too long in the shower!

Allegra's mother couldn't go on the tour and neither could mine. In that pre-internet age of innocence, the two of us, 16 and 17 years old respectively, were left to fend for ourselves in Milan and all the other cities of the tour. Despite the dangers that have always threatened young unattended girls, we, thankfully, survived intact.

Once settled in, we followed the instructions we were given and headed for Teatro alla Scala. The opera house had been inaugurated in 1778, just two years after America had become a nation! George Washington was still the First Commander in Chief of the United States Continental Army, though not yet the First American President.

During those very first years of La Scala, my mother's ancestor, Mary Moore, seized as a hostage, was being raised by the women of the Shawnee Indian tribe. Eventually her deliverance came at the hands of her rescuing brother.

And there it was, Teatro alla Scala itself! I was overcome with awe, for that historic building had hosted the world premieres of operas by Bellini, Donizetti, Ponchielli, Meyerbeer, Rossini and, of course, Verdi and Puccini. There is no comparable opera house that has given birth to such a galaxy of musical genius.

And as for ballet, there was a period when Italian dancers ruled the firmaments, dancers such as Carlo Blasis, Enrico Cecchetti (the first Bluebird), Carlotta Grisi (the first Giselle), Fanny Cerrito (one of the original *Pas de Quatre*),Virginia Zucchi (whose dancing inspired Bakst and Benois), Pierina Legnani (the first Odette/Odile), Carlotta Brianza (the first Aurora), all of them made incandescent by the holy fire of La Scala.

We found the stage door and made it clear to the doormen that we were from the expected New York City Ballet. Allegra and I were the first people from the company to arrive, always the impatient eager beavers! We checked the dressing room and found little smiling middle-aged ladies dressed in uniforms of black dresses with starched white aprons who motioned that they were there to help us with whatever we might need. They were there at our beck and call all day and every night until the performances ended, faithful sweet little ladies whose lack of English was no impediment to our communication.

I wanted to lose some weight and decided to eat only hard-boiled eggs and fruit until I felt I was, if not as elongated as a Modigliani painting, at least visibly more slender. Somehow, by hook or by crook, we made our diet intentions clear to the ladies so desirous of assisting us. The Mayo Clinic diet plan was now in action.

There was a fruit stand on the corner of La Scala where I bought farm fresh raw eggs and fruit every day from a handsome young farmer named Mario. Despite the language obstacle, he managed to communicate with us and several days later invited us to attend his grandmother's birthday party at their farm some distance from Milan. So one free Sunday, Allegra and I hopped into his truck and rode past vineyards and fields that looked very much like California, but didn't, of course, resound with the echoes of Renaissance art and royalty.

Were we not afraid of riding in a truck with a swarthy young Italian we knew so casually? No, call it trusting or naive, but in those more innocent days and in that very Catholic land, our virtue was in no way threatened. As the pastoral green and russet scenery blurred by, I was at peace with the world and thought that I could live in that part of the world forever.

When we arrived at the farm for Mario's grandmother's birthday party, all the members of his extended family were there, anticipating our arrival. All of them were speaking Italian at once and though I didn't know what any of them were saying, they were all so vibrant that it was clear we were being offered a heartfelt welcome.

Then they asked us to dance for his grandmother. Allegra declined with the excuse that she had no shoes and wasn't prepared. That shyness again. Not to disappoint the matriarch of Mario's relatives, I danced an improvisation in bare feet to some melodic air they put on the phonograph. You could have heard a pin drop. When the music ended there was much applause and there were many hugs and tears of appreciation from his aged grandmother. I also shed a few tears of happiness to have been able to dance, not only as I soon would for Milanese society and the titled wealthy, but for the salt of the earth as was Mario's closely knit family.

The party over, Mario delivered us back safely to our hotel in his rumbling farm truck and I continued to buy loquats, fresh figs and eggs from the handsome farmer. "Mario, Mario," Tosca sings in the famous opera. That day, I had my own Mario and hope that he lived a more fortunate life than his Puccini counterpart.

Did my vegetable vendor live happily ever after? I hope so, but will never know, for in the travelling life of dancers, brief encounters are the norm, all taking place within mere speeding hours or days.

On the gala opening night, September 8, 1953, I danced in all four of the ballets: *La Valse, Il Lago dei Cigni (Swan Lake), La Gabbia (The Cage)* and *Bourrée Fantasque*. La Scala has the largest stage in all of Italy and it also has a very prominent rake. Despite the stage being full of trap doors, splinters and holes, it held for me the iridescent aura of the artists who had appeared there through the ages. Thoughts of the inimitable maestro Arturo Toscanini conducting the world premiere of Puccini's *Madama Butterfly* and the sublime singers and dancers of the last 175 years inundated me, eliciting a succession of chills.

The morning after the premiere, we were back at the barre, for we had to maintain our techniques. Expectations of the public were running high and the Milanese public were not known for sitting on their feelings if disappointed. Mr. B., ever mindful of his image in a major metropolis, taught classes every day at 10:00 a.m. in an upstairs studio within the opera house. They were not his usual compressed barre excerpts, but full one and a half hour lessons. Though he corrrected many, his main attention, clear to one and all, was directed towards the tall and angular Tanaquil LeClercq. He did not hide his attraction and special attention was poured upon her during those classes.

Maria Tallchief was in every class, as well, and she was still Mr. B's wife. So we had to watch our beloved prima ballerina, Maria, fade painfully away from Mr.B's focus, humiliatingly in full view of the company. And every day the same degrading procedure. There was Maria, fast becoming a rubbed-out chalk pavement drawing while Tanny, nowhere even approaching her elevated category, being publicly chiselled to become her replacement. Mr. B's fountain of creative youth depended on new blood and that blood transfusion was to be supplied by Tanny.

Although Maria continued to dance the works created for her, Mr. B's fascination and obsession with Tanny escalated as it did with every new muse. The peculiar plus side of Maria's demotion was the fact that Mr. B was giving very demanding classes in order to give Tanny the speed and strength she did not have yet. Her individuality was apparent, her ballerina status, not by a long shot. Applying every correction he constantly gave Tanny, all of us became much stronger technically than we would have been otherwise. Soon, with the marathon classes given on a daily basis by Mr. B, I was back to my preferred dancing weight of 105 pounds. My costumes were loose within the first week of the best teaching I had ever experienced from him. How ironic that Mr. B's public shredding of his ballerina wife should provide such artistic benefit for the rest of us.

Some days after our classes began in Milan, Jacques asked if I would meet him and take the 8 a.m. class with Mme Esmée Bulnes. She was the director and principal teacher of Scuola di Ballo del Teatro alla Scala, the academy that nurtured their ballet company. Mme Bulnes, originally from Argentina, had danced with Anna Pavlova's company.

Jacques brimmed over with enthusiasm when he asked me, saying that she was a fantastic teacher, so I agreed to get up at the crack of dawn and meet him every morning to take the class. We did not want Mr. B to find out for fear he might become jealous or resentful by our detour at just past sunrise. We thought that he wouldn't find out about Mme Bulnes if we also took his class and that is what we did. Oh, the runaway energy of youth! We went from 8 a.m. to 10 with Mme Bulnes, and then 10 to 11:30 with Mr. B, running from class to class without a break. Both lessons were as difficult as the most strenuous Oboukhov class.

We practically killed ourselves taking both classes every morning after a grueling four-ballet performance every night. Allegra wanted to know why I was getting up so early. So I told her about Mme Bulnes and she began to take the class as well. Only three of us from the company took those remarkable lessons.

Mme Bulnes taught very flowing and traditional classes with both Vaganova and Cecchetti influences. She inspired you to reach for just what was beyond your grasp. As I leaped over each technical hurdle placed before me, La Scala was becoming a home away from home and within its hallowed walls, I was sublimely happy.

Madame was strict but kind, a productive balance for a teacher. Retaining the slenderness of youth, she wore her chestnut brown hair in classical style, as one would arrange for *Les Sylphides, Swan Lake* or *Giselle*. Her carriage was grand and elegant, and as she glided across the studio floor in her ballet slippers, her prominent arches were impressively noticeable. She demonstrated with ease, dancing the entire *adage* section herself, then using only her hands to demonstrate the complicated jumping and turning combinations.

When I see dancers today twisting in contortionist-styled beyond six-o'clock extensions, I inwardly wince for I know they are risking hip replacement surgery at a later date. When a dancer is properly trained, there is awareness of the body's physical limits. To continually go beyond those limits is to invite crippling injuries with more time doing physiotherapy than performances.

Among the members of the class were some very promising dancers and I was especially impressed by one teenaged girl, exactly one year younger than myself, as I was to find out. With her gentle expression, she already revealed a penchant for the 19th century Romantic period. Italian, as was everone else in the class, she spoke no English but it was not at all a barrier to the almost instant bonding between us. The love of dance fostered our friendship and compensated for the lack of a mutual language. After I completed a difficult combination in class, she would gesture silent applause, and I would do the same for her. We stood next to each other at the barre and it was a pleasure and a relief not to be regarded as a threat to be dealt with by some new Machiavellan intrigue.

My new friend's name was Carla Fracci.

Before one of our performances, I was on the La Scala stage practicing pirouettes. I could always count on five turns but, at that moment, I did ten unsupported pirouettes on *pointe*. Jacques witnesssed it it as did Carla, her partner Mario Pistoni, himself to become a leading ballet star of La Scala, and some of the New York City Ballet dancers. Such a feat was a once in a lifetime event for me! Never did I manage that again, though not for want of trying! Like my *Black Swan pas de deux* at Ballet Arts in Carnegie Hall, my technical feat was seen only by my fellow dancers, not the general public!

As for Carla, she grew up to become the prima ballerina assoluta of Italy, as parallel in magnitude as Renata Tebaldi to opera and Anna Magnani to the cinema, a triptych of three supreme Italian artists. Carla also developed into an actress, having done the role of Tamara Karsavina in Herbert Ross and Nora Kaye's film, *Nijinsky*. And a very polished performance it was, rare for a dancer to be so at home verbally. Among her other straight acting achievements, in a popular Italian television series she acted the role of the tragedy-struck Giuseppe Verdi's second wife, the opera singer, Giuseppina Strepponi.

Moving ahead through the invisibility of hurtling time, to this day Carla's star remains undimmed, for in a recent revival of *Nutcracker* at the Rome Opera Ballet, her appearance as the mother was given star billing, a surefire way to sell out every performance. Carla married the director Beppe Menegatti to whom she is still married and who has devoted himself to the furthering of her career. She is the mother of Francesco and grandmother to his children Giovanni and Ariele. Not for her the fate of Maria Tallchief who went down the conveyor belt of Balanchine's discarded muses.

Internationally, Carla has been guest ballerina at the world's leading opera houses, her Giselle as spectral and wraith-like as any mid-19th century lithograph. Looking at photographs of the young Carla, I see an uncanny resemblance to the young Marie Taglioni, herself half Italian.

Along the route of career ascension, Carla had to learn how to cope with opposition, for the principal dancers of the American Ballet Theatre vehemently protested when informed that for one of their New York seasons, Natalia Makarova and Carla Fracci would dance the leading roles, not the resident principals. The management was interested, not in equality of role distribution, but box office receipts that such luminaries as Makarova and Fracci would ensure.

Somewhere along the rocky route, Carla must have learned how to speak up when necessary, because recently there was a story of her publicly castigating the Mayor of Rome for his financial cuts to the ballet while she was still director.

"Shame on you, shame on you, you scoundrel!" she tongue-lashed him.

Good for you, Carla! If only I had remained in the gladiatorial arena a while longer, I may well have cultivated the weaponry needed to stand up for myself. But it is, I well know, pointless to cry over spilled milk, or blood, as the case may be. As for dear Carla, I am truly happy for her good and fruitful life. For besides being an incomparable Giselle, she remains, in my treasure trove of memories, my loving La Scala friend.

At the close of our engagement in Milan, Mme Bulnes approached me and asked if, after our tour, I would be intereasted in returning and staying in Milan to become a part of La Scala Ballet! She showered me with compliments regarding my being so absorbent to every nuance of her teaching and then added that I was possessor of an exceptional technique, not only rare for someone as young as I, but rare for any age. I was overwhelmed by her response to me, but without hesitation I told her that I needed to stay with Mr. Balanchine as I felt obligated to him for providing me with my ballet education.

Though she continued to smile at me, there was disappointment in her eyes. Then she nodded with a tinge of regret, wishing me the very best in my decision, adding that she expected me to achieve great things in the future. Was she thinking that I would have been Snow White to Carla Fracci's Rose Red? I hugged her, thanked her profusely, and hurried off to cry all the way through the next Balanchine lesson. No one in class asked why I was crying, not that I would have told anyone.

I instinctively knew I belonged with La Scala, yet something in me, from this point on, led me to make wrong decisions at every cross-roads I was to encounter. There are, I discovered too late, decisions we make when very young that determine the frustration or fulfillment of the rest of our lives.

At the peak of Jerome Robbins' abuse, Arnold Haskell, as director of the Sadler's Wells Ballet School, could have managed my entrance into what was to become the Royal Ballet. Having worked with Frederic Ashton in *Illuminations*, I recall how he responded to me, another man of impacting influence in the United Kingdom. Perhaps such a move in the mid-1950s would have necessitated my acquiring an English husband, but that was a formality countless people have subscribed to in order to remain in a foreign land.

But I stayed rooted and, in the name of brainless loyalty, remained with the New York City ballet. Now I was repeating the same major mistake with La Scala, an opera house that made me feel not just respect, but a profound reverence for the citadel of glory that it was.

At that time of refusing Mme Bulnes, I mistakenly believed that George Balanchine was interested in nurturing my career. What an unseeing fool I was, for all one had to do was observe what he was publicly doing to his wife, Maria Tallchief.

Though Maria, in Mr. B's eyes, could be replaced in his swirling whirlpool of inspiration, to find a substitute in her roles was something of a pipe dream. In later revivals of *Firebird*, he was forced so simplify her steps since no subsequent inheritor of that role could duplicate her virtuosity, let alone her uniquely individual dazzle.

CHAPTER NINETEEN

ON THE BRINK OF WAR IN TRIESTE

No wife takes kindly to being discarded, to being demoted from first place to being thrust out into the cold, from being the light of one's husband's life to the little match girl in the shadows. As Camilla was to misshape the final years of Her Royal Highness, Princess Diana, so was such a parallel event happening to our Indian princess, Maria Tallchief, the unwitting trespasser being, of course, the hapless Tanny.

Maria, always one to fiercely honor her commitments, turned a blind eye to events, at least optically, if not emotionally. The Italian public was going to see her at her best. Nevertheless, it was a trial by fire for the firebird herself. Her wings would be singed, but she would stay aloft. And the New York City Ballet would emerge victorious.

Which we did, for the Milanese ballet audience and press enthused over what they perceived as our very American and athletic style. Our speed and attack were quite new to them. We were considered avant-garde and innovative, providing provocative discussions for ballet lovers throughout all the intermissions.

Though the many tiers of the resplendent opera house were well-heated, not so the stage. As I found my place on stage in preparation for *Serenade*. I felt the cold evening wind of autumn. I knew where the draft was coming from, for La Scala had been damaged by bombs during World War II with repairs being slow and costly. Only eight years after the war had ended, gaping holes in the building remained as eyesores. During the day I could look straight up from the stage and see glimpses of very blue skies.

Ready for the curtain to open, as *Serenade* began, my right arm was raised as if to shield my eyes from the sun. This was in the choreography because while Mr. B was choreographing the ballet in 1934, the company rehearsed on an outdoor stage where the sun was piercing in its afternoon intensity. This extreme brightness caused some of the girls to cover their eyes from its blinding rays. It was so like Mr. B to sprinkle even his serious works with little private allusions to remembrances of things past, like Proust, but without words.

Holding up my raised arm for the required measures of music, to my surprise I felt water starting to drip directly on to the back of my hand just as the La Scala orchestra began to play the opening strains of the sonorous Tchaikovsky score. I watched the drop of water roll down my arm with fascination as more drops came, growing to a trickle, then a stream. Seconds afterwards, I felt and saw the stream running faster down my arm past my shoulder and down my costume before even the first steps were taken. I was getting drenched by rainwater falling from the bombed-out roof! Everyone danced as if oblivious to the downpour. Very surprisingly, not one person slipped, fell or was injured, a reaffirmation of our ability to adjust. Dunya, our wardrobe mistress, was fit to be tied when all of us returned to the wardrobe room to dress for the next ballet, our costumes clinging to us and dripping wet.

It was a wrench to leave Milan, a farewell punctuated by tears for all those who had enriched our passing lives, tears for the inner awareness that none of us would ever meet again.

Lago di Como was next on our schedule. Since we were not due there until just before the performance, we had the luxury of some free time beforehand. I had agreed to meet some of the other girls in a nearby piazza to do some sightseeing before taking the train there with the company. I urged Allegra to join me, but when 9 a.m. came, her bags weren't packed and we had been instructed to leave them outside the hotel for collection. I tried to get her to hurry and waited a while for her but she urged me to go on as I was already late to meet the other girls.

With my tardy arrival at the meeting place, the girls, thinking I had changed my mind, had left on their sightseeing adventure without me. This left me alone in the middle of the piazza with no idea how to get to Lago di Como and no way to contact anyone in the company. I went to La Scala and found it empty and by the time I got back to the hotel to look for Allegra, she had gone! I found my way to the railway station and, with some trusty American Express Travelers' Checks, bought my own ticket.

Lago di Como was a popular European resort, a playground for millionaires and royalty. I spoke so little Italian that it was a mini-miracle that I managed to find my way to the right train and actually get there by myself. It was raining when the train pulled in at about 2 p.m. yet I decided to walk to the theatre from the train station, rather than cope with the hassle of trying to flag a cab down. I stopped in a shop and bought a stylish black silk umbrella with sterling silver tips, which I still carry today. With my very few words in Italian, I asked and received instructions on how to get to the theatre, the instructions given by strangers in the streets with warmth and helpfulness.

And there was the opera house, a little jewel, built in 1813. It was a mini-Paris Opera decorated with gilt and gold around the horseshoe-shaped tiers with lush red velvet everywhere. Once at the theatre, I sought out the dressing quarters assigned to us, picking out a dressing table in a room that smelled of mildew.

After checking the stage, I worried about Allegra the rest of the day. I was so relieved to find she had also been resourceful enough to get there on her own. As it turned out, many people were worried about both of us since the two of us had seemingly disappeared. Poor Betty Cage was frantic! If only cell phones had been invented then, such anxiety as Betty experienced would have been avoided.

Among the many opera houses we appeared in, one of the most unforgettable was Venice's La Fenice. In its long and remarkable history of triumph and tragedy, it had burned to the ground three times, but always rose from its ashes. Verdi's association with La Fenice began in 1844, with a number of his masterpieces having first been seen and heard there, perennial favorites to this day such as *Ernani, Attila, Rigoletto, La Traviata* and *Simon Boccanegra.* Just as at La Scala, I felt humbled by dancing in La Fenice, hearing the living echo of Verdi's sublime genius.

Less sacrosanct were our dressing room conditions. All of us had heard that Venice was steadily sinking, a fact we were made aware at every performance. For with almost all of the magnificent opera houses of Europe, no matter how elegant and luxurious the area for the audience, the dressing rooms were invariably dimly lit, cramped and a long way from the stage. But that was the least of the discomforts.

We made up and changed into costumes in a basement room beneath the stage with three inches of water on the floor all through the day and night. This was not a temporary flood, but the normal state of the dressing rooms. I had to stand on a chair to put on my tights and when we finally managed to get into our costumes, our next hurdle was to walk the narrow planks placed along the flooded floor so that we could tightrope our way to the stairs and get to the stage without ruining our pink satin *pointe* slippers! As if that wasn't enough to contend with, the smells from the dank water were reminiscent of decaying mold, dead fish and fresh garbage!

Upstairs, with the powdered bosoms of society women weighted down by family heirloom jewels, the splendiferous opera house with its perfect acoustics didn't reveal even a hint of what the artists endured backstage.

Jacques took me on a lovely gondola ride, for how can one be in Venice without experiencing its most famous form of transportation? I had grown very attached to him and when he had to leave for California to make the mega-successful film *Seven Brides for Seven Brothers,* I felt a wrench. So there I was, watching over Allegra, with Jacques too far away to watch over me.

As the tour progressed, we appeared at the ornately beautiful Rome Opera House, where in the four-tiered auditorium hung a six-meter crystal chandelier with 27,000 droplets. At the end of the premiere, every dancer was given a silver medal inscribed with an engraving of the interior of the Opera House. The American Ambasssador to Italy, Clare Boothe Luce, along with her husband, Henry Luce, the publisher of *Time, Fortune* and *Life* magazines, gave an afternoon reception for the company in the gardens of their luxurious villa outside of Rome.

Mrs. Luce, then 50, had an extraordinary background. At the age of ten she had understudied on Broadway a young girl who, when she grew up, was to become the reigning silent screen star, Mary Pickford. As an adult, Ambassador Luce wrote the Broadway smash hit, *The Women,* in 1936, later made into a 1939 Hollywood film. With Norma Shearer, Rosalind Russell, Paulette Goddard, Joan Crawford and Joan Fontaine, this was a constellation of cinematic stars with their sharpened talons at the ready both in the script and actual life.

In the course of her multi-faceted career, Mrs. Luce had been a far-reaching investigative journalist, interviewing such world leaders of millions as Chiang Kai-Shek and Jawaharial Nehru. Of such courageous ilk was she, that in 1941, while in Trinidad and Tobago, she faced but managed to avoid house arrest by Britain due to the militarily critical contents of a draft article she had written for *Life* magazine.

Her steely political mettle didn't protect her, unfortunately, from the unforeseen tragedies of life, for when her 20-year-old daughter was killed in a car crash, inconsolable, she desperately embraced psychotherapy and Roman Catholicism.

As for myself, meeting Clare Boothe Luce in her President Dwight D. Eisenhower appointed role, I found her to be the epitome of what a gracious hostess should be. So lustrous was her example that in future years she became my own role model when presiding over summer garden parties. Greeting everone with a warm handshake and smiling words of welcome, Mrs. Luce then moved about the terrace in a flowing yellow silk dress. Everyone, it was apparent, was the recipient of her one-to-one attention.

In the midst of the bubbly French champagne being poured, there were striking ice sculptures containing carved watermelons and canteloupes, a half-century before it became de rigeur for designer chefs to sculpt flowers made out of tropical fruit. For those with more substantial appetites, there were seafood platters on solid silver antique trays. I noticed particularly the Roquefort cheese containers carved out of bark-covered slices of trees. This was a drinks party fit for a Roman empress of which, in the mid-twentieth century, Clare Boothe Luce was the contemporary equivalent.

It is, however, as Madam Ambassador that she was to make her mark in that contested region. During her tenure, she was to resolve the conflict between Italy and Yugoslavia over the UN territorial division of Trieste.

As usual, only about half the company had answered the Ambassador's engraved invitations, even with the procession of chauffeured cars at their beck and call. How, I again asked myself, could so many of the company dismiss the rare opportunity of extending their life experience? For the former Congresswoman Mrs. Luce was indisputably one of the world's most influential women.

In 1959 Mrs. Luce was nominated as Ambassador to Brazil, but she resigned before leaving for her post following a public quarrel with a Democratic senator. Why, couldn't I take a page out of her book and learn to, when necessary, cross swords?

Next dancing in Naples and Bologna, we appeared also in the German cities of Stuttgart (to be made famous by John Cranko's Stuttgart Ballet) and Munich (already made infamous by Adolf Hitler), then in the Swiss cities of Lausanne and Zurich.

At every opera house there would always be a letter waiting for me from the young minister to be, then returned to Yale for his final year. Flattered by all the attention from him, I answered his every communication. He was persistent and I, in my emotional apartness, and hanging from the bough of a swaying tree, was ready to be caught. Had I not been so strictly brought up, I would have been involved by then in a relationship and therefore, resultantly, spoken for and off bounds. Such was not the case.

The New York City Ballet ended its tour in Trieste, arriving just as rival political factions were staking their claims to its leadership, namely the Allied Forces, the Italians and the Yugoslavs. People were told to stay off the streets, a nine o'clock curfew going into immediate force. With tanks lined up on both sides of the city, Italian versus Yugoslav, it was a frightening sight, for war between the rival divisions seemed imminent. Ambassador Clare Boothe Luce was, during this tense period, still at the conference table, using her every considerable skill to avert bloodshed.

It was in this militarily fraught atmosphere that I had the considerable honor to be partnered by André Eglevsky, one of the world's greatest premiers danseurs, dancing the leading role in *A la Françaix,* with choreography by Balanchine and music by the prolific French composer Jean Françaix, who had previously written several ballets, among them Roland Petit's *Les Demoiselles de la Nuit.* Even with the curfew, the house was over half full with the audience at the end generously applauding us.

If Allegra didn't dance in the last ballet, as she didn't in *A la Françaix,* she usually then left the theatre. That left me to get back to the hotel alone. In acute trepidation, I began walking in the direction of the hotel. Did I hear stalking footsteps as I once did when coming home alone in New York? No, I was imagining it, I told myself without any conviction. Then I accelerated my walk into a run, for at 10:30 p.m. the curfew deadline had long been passed, leaving me the only one on the darkened streets. Every massive, shadowy shape struck me as a tank ready to go into action. Is that what they were and, if so, were there soldiers manning them, I asked myself in muted panic?

Any second I expected the police to stop me for defying the curfew. By now I was in mortal fear, but my race back to the hotel, thankfully, ended without incident. Once in the brightly lit warmth of the lobby, I fell back on the sofa in sheer relief, waiting until I had caught my breath and my heartbeat could resume its normal rhythm. Then I took the elevator to the safety of my room. And there was Allegra, stretched out on the floor as usual, writing her dutiful letters home. It was a welcome sight.

This was one incident that I would not relay to my parents. That I ran through war-shadowed Trieste at night in tank-filled streets would have severely disturbed both my mother and father.

On the happy side, to commemorate that Trieste Opera House performance, Herbie Bliss and Bobby Barnett gave me a very special present, a shimmering gold pendant of a music treble clef with a vivid turquoise set in the center. On a monetary scale, I assumed the pendant would not have found favor on the Duchess of Windsor's bony bosom, or on Elizabeth Taylor's ample one. But for me, each time I have worn that gift, and it has adorned my throat for fifty-eight years on almost every major social occasion, I feel the vibrations of Herbie and Bobby's long ago love. As such, their gift to me remains untarnished and as shimmering as ever.

The tour ended and when we arrived back in Paris, we found out that the flight home had been delayed by a thick fog. Though we were checked in to the exclusive Hotel George V for two days, we had strict orders not to leave the hotel because as soon as the fog lifted we would depart for the airport. As in Cole Porter's lyrics from *Can-Can,* "I love Paris in the springtime, I love Paris in the fall", I too loved Paris even in a heavy fog, but adhering to Betty Cage's orders, the fog could only be experienced through the velvet-curtained hotel room windows.

After we returned to New York, the fog I then experienced was emotional, for after all those history-steeped cities, to return to the empty solitude of my apartment was a very big letdown. Jacques was filming in Hollywood and there were no rehearsals or performances to occupy my mind or test my body. I found the enveloping silence noisy and my own company unwanted, for it was accompanied by all my imagined and possibly justified fears.

Prodding me without respite was the nagging prospect of Jerome Robbins. Was he going to be working with the company again, or would he be occupied with his latest Broadway show? Jumping ahead to the far future, when my life in ballet had by then been long over, one of my adult sons gave me a book for my birthday. It was *Dance with Demons,* the life of Jerome Robbins by Greg Lawrence.

"Did you know him?" he asked.

Calling upon my atrophied acting aptitude, I nodded vaguely, for if I had kept my secret nemesis away from my family for some fifty years, I had no intention then of rattling such a skeleton.

There was no way that my doctor son or any of his siblings could know that they owed their very lives to the man on the book cover, for without his demolishing influence on my career, I would have continued to dance, to become possibly a major ballerina like Carla Fracci. I was, as it happened, still a teenager, sometimes dancing ballerina roles in magnficent European opera houses, and being partnered by the ranking star that was André Eglevsky.

If I had confronted and contested Robbins, the king of Broadway, as Carla did the Mayor of Rome, and, in consequence, continued with my dancing career so auspiciously begun and so early in my adolescence, then none of my children, grandchildren and great-grandchildren would ever have been born.

Unknown to me, the beginning of the end was creeping up like a sniper on a war-torn rooftop. My final harassment by Jerome Robbins would lead me to seek out hitherto unimagined emergency measures.

CHAPTER TWENTY

At the Cathedral of Saint John the Divine

Instead of the biblically alloted time span of three score and ten, if only we could live to be 150, the first 75 years the learning process in which we mumble and stumble our way across the pitfalls placed before us. Then, from 75 years old to 150, we could implement the wisdom accrued during the first half. Alas, such is not the case with the rationed almanac.

Soon I was to leave not only the New York City Ballet, but the ballet world in which I had grown up, in which all my joys and sorrows had been nurtured, blossomed, then withered.

I had adored, no, worshipped George Balanchine, though my idolatry was to defuse into mammoth disappointment with him as a human being and, moreover, as my Pygmalion who would sculpt me into the ballerina I yearned to become. As for Jerome Robbins, he had hounded me since I was 14 years old. Was there no escape route in which I could find a kinder life?

Unfortunately for me, George Balanchine was ballet; there were no other choreographers. So was I shackled with my atrophied definition of the choreographic art. Without a mature guide to steer me, I was like a rudderless ship and, as such, made irrevocable decisions accordingly. I was to ignore the likes of Maurice Béjart, Birgit Cullberg, Tatiana Gsovsky, Roland Petit, Janine Charrat, Serge Lifar, the list is long and winding like the Great Wall of China. If I couldn't tolerate Jerome Robbins, then I didn't deserve to dance for the world's only choreographer, Balanchine, for Robbins came along with the turf. So did I inanely think.

The Episcopalian minister in the making had cast his net in my direction, for I, in my youthful naiveté and obedience, would suit his every purpose. In my abject confusion and aloneness, his persistent pursuit of me was beginnng to take root. I was very young, totally inexperienced with sex, well-mannered, presentable looking and could not discern a face behind a mask. The minister-to-be would provide a lifeline, an escape route away from the subjugation and intrigue that dancing in the New York City Ballet had become.

There were other possible avenues I could have explored. But no, old enough to be entrusted with principal roles, but too young to make crossroad decisions that would become irreversible, I had an unerring facility to make counterproductive choices.

Unable to see the forest for the trees, I decided that I would leave the company, but when and how and what would I say? Was I being hasty or victim of misjudgement, I hounded myself for a Solomonian solution? None was forthcoming. But the handwriting on the wall made clear that I was not to elicit new roles or ballets from George Balanchine. I felt that I was no more than just another odalisque in his competitive dancing harem.

While contemplating my imminent farewell to Balanchine, I felt that I would be saying goodbye to, if not God, then an almighty deity. Though Balanchine was worshipped as a choreographer, as a man his limitations and shortcomings now stood out more glaringly than ever. Even as an artist, I began to become aware of what was missing in his cascade of ballets – soul. Though there was always an abundance of steps, there was a paucity of communication.

I, along with just about everyone else, found it painful to be forced to witness his public subjugation of Maria. Even though she re-married, the second time unhappily, but the third time successfully, her dancing career went into a slow and irreversible decline. Though Maria continued to dance in the company for a while, the situation was very different after Balanchine completely lost his interest in her. No new ballets were being created for her, so she eventually left and made guest appearances in other companies. But her dramatic potential had barely been tapped, since Balanchine was interested in her dazzle, not her expressive potential. He was a choreographer of speed demon musical steps and kaleidoscopic patterns, not a dramatist in any sense of the word. So, Maria, swimming in alien and murky waters, could not replicate her earlier triumphs.

In later years, I visited her in Chicago, where she took me on a tour of her ballet school. She seemed genuinely pleased to see me, for I was part of the tapestry of her earlier successes. She had become the director of the Chicago City Ballet. I believed that she should have danced longer, but fate and circumstances have a way of stage-managing our lives.

The tragedy of Tanaquil LeClerq hadn't occurred yet. After the onset of her life-threatening and crippling disease of polio, she was left an invalid for the rest of her life. How ironic that a man such as Balanchine who adored and was artistically inflamed by young female bodies that conquered space, should be saddled with pushing his immobilized wife around in a wheelchair for some 15 years. That is, until he fell irrationally in love with Suzanne Farrell whose strict Catholicism prevented her from consummating the relationship with her creative master. Even Balanchine's divorce from Tanny didn't alter her made up mind, and when she married Paul Mejia as an escape tunnel, it released the vindictive furies within the usually gentle Mr. B. No less a woman than Mme Danilova said that when crossed, Balanchine took on the characteristics of a male Medea. And she knew whereof she spoke, since in the early years, she was his mistress, if not his wife.

Allegra Kent, Balanchine's forgotten muse, was another who was discarded as yesterday's newspaper. It was she who assumed most of Tanny's roles following the polio tragedy in Copenhagen. Learning quickly and dancing effortlessly, she became Mr. B's next inspiration. *Swan Lake* was added to her repertoire, a ballet she danced all over Australia. Her Odette, which I saw her do in California, was danced with a detached and otherworldly beauty.

Allegra was to defy Mr. B by having three children, even after her dancing master had expressly forbidden her to take the time out to give birth again. And so the flame he felt for her extinguished, even after she returned dancing better than ever. Balanchine's women gave birth only to his creations. Husbands, lovers and children were perceived as rivals for the sole focus he demanded.

Some part of his psyche must have felt some sense of obligation to her, for he provided her with the opportunity of dancing once a year, so as to keep her on his payroll, as did Charlie Chaplin with his early co-star Edna Purviance until her death.

Allegra was grateful for the ongoing salary though she was shattered by being so publicly demoted. Never again did she elicit Mr. B's earlier attention. For the stimuli that was Mr. B's artistic fix, there was an endless waiting line of eager and ambitious potential muses. For as long as Mr. B was alive, Allegra had no other income, so was grateful for being kept on salary, though it yanked at her lifeline that she had been reduced to not much more than a glorified extra. Then, when Mr. B died, the blade of the guillotine dropped with a sudden and heavy thud. During the week that followed Mr. B's death, the multi-millionaire Lincoln Kirstein cut off all of her financial support. Why should he fork out good money to pay Allegra Kent when that money would be better used for the cleaning woman who mopped up the toilets?

Suzanne Farrell, in her own words, contemplating suicide, danced with Maurice Béjart for some five years before the prodigal daughter was received again by Mr. B, though the inflammatory spark had stabilized. As for Suzanne's husband, Paul Mejia, Mr. B did not allow his return to the company.

I had nagging thoughts that if I should incur an injury, inevitably and frequently taking place in a ballet company, would I be given my marching orders? The answer was as clear as the nose on Ida Rubinstein's face.

And while on the subject of debilitating injuries, in Jacques d'Amboise's recently published and admirable autobiography, *I Was A Dancer*, he referred to the 50th year reunion of New York City Ballet dancers, with signs designating each decade from the 1940s to the 1980s. Jacques then pointed out that in the first three decades, a quarter of the now retired dancers had undergone joint substitutions, with hip replacements taking precedence. Jacques, himself, reveals that he has two artificial knees, adding that what he and all others did was always done in the name of love. But what kind of love is this that leaves in its wake such a collection of invasive operations and pain?

None of those remarkable dancers such as Felia Dubrovska, Alexandra Danilova, Pierre Vladimirov and Anatole Oboukhov had suffered a hardware shop of bolts, screws and artificial sockets cut into their bodies, for they had all been trained in the careful and sequential method of the Imperial Ballet School in St. Petersburg. No ten-minute barres for them leading directly into joint-twisting choreographic experiments without even an adage preceding, such as Mr. B continuously did with his hospital fodder.

On the plus side of my early departure from the company, today, even at my age, my hips, knees and ankles are all my own, without even a trace of arthritis. Love is blind, so it is said, and I will add never more so than when the object of adoration is George Balanchine.

With these unsettling thoughts in mind, so did I begin to contemplate a life outside the world of dance. What it would be like to live like others, far away from the only life I had ever known, far removed from the inner compulsions that forced me to dance?

If I heard music, I began to move and, if not physically, then mentally. If I felt elation or depression, then I needed to communicate those extreme emotions in movement. Just about every response I had would be translated into dance. It was never a separate mode of communication to be put aside, like a violin, and picked up again when I began to work. My violin was me; I was the instrument and could not be put aside. I lived to dance and, one could say, danced to live.

With such a definition of what dance meant to me, could I bear to leave? I was firmly bound to Mr. B, yet he was always remote and silent when I needed his approval and encouragement. And it would have been so simple for him to remove me from Jerome Robbins' cast lists. But he didn't raise a finger of intervention, despite it being common knowledge among the administration what I was undergoing. Perhaps they thought, like acne, the problem would eventually disappear. But I didn't have acne, though I did have Mr. Robbins.

It was November 25, 1953 when rehearsals began for a three-month season at the City Center of Music and Drama. This was the longest season ever, and for a ballet company to perform in New York for that length of time was unprecedented. We would dance Mr. B's version of the famed *Nutcracker* as well as offering our usual repertoire during the course of that extended season. It was good to be dancing again, back in our home theatre. My doubts, for the time being, were put aside.

I was pleased that Mr. B had chosen me to dance the Spanish Dance in the second act with three other dancers. I was also to be a whirling snowflake, the music enriched by the voices of Saint John the Divine boys' choir. It was a truly moving and elevating experience to move in such a sublime milieu. During this rehearsal period of Tchaikovsky's

Nutcracker, I was conscious that the clock was ticktocking faster than ever, reminding me that my days of dancing Balanchine ballets were numbered.

Added to my recurring sadness of imminent farewell, there was the necessity to cope with nightly conference sessions with Jerome Robbins following nearly every performance before *Nutcracker* to be premiered in February. He was, without respite, wearing me down, for he would summon me from the dressing room even when I was still perspiring. With my endorphins released after what I considered increasingly good performances, I would hastily put on a robe and sometimes didn't finish taking off my make up, or finish getting into my street clothes so as not to keep him waiting.

The only semi-private place to talk was at the bottom of the drafty stairs next to the dressing room. There we would sit on the cold steps, his arm around me, while I shivered with his lecture going on until just about everyone had left the theatre. Was it to keep me warm, or to symbolically protect me, or was it a gesture of affection from an older brother or younger father? I could decipher neither his body talk nor his oppositional advice. His comments and counsel were always contradictory, confusing me with each further statement.

"Always look at the audience and smile", followed by "Never look directly out to the audience and smile". Each of his statements negated the previous one. To add to my confusion, he would tell me I was working too hard and taking too many classes. Yet if I missed a class, he would call me out to ask why I was not in class.

Shifting topics, he was pleased to hear that I "had gotten got rid of my mother" which couldn't have been further from the truth. In point of fact, it was a financial necessity for her to go back to Oklahoma and I missed her terribly. In no way did I "get rid" of her, her absence exacerbating my aloneness.

From chipping away at my mother, he moved on to my non-existent love life, telling me that I should be dating, then asking if I had any boyfriends. "No," I answered in all frankness, for I could not call my letter-writing minister a boyfriend. We had only had a few dates and he was in New Haven while I lived in New York. Later in the season when Robbins found my minister in the making waiting to take me out for a late night supper, he told me in no uncertain terms not to go out after performances! No matter what I did, it seemed to him that it was wrong. What I was unaware of, too young then to realize it, was that by wearing me down as he was, he exerted a stronger and stronger power grip on me, thereby consolidating our relationship of lion tamer and caged animal. I was in a quandary, our staircase communications, not without a peculiar touch of tenderness, adding to my fear of his erosive tactics in rehearsals.

Jerome Robbins was inexorably crushing me and the hopes I had for a fulfilling future in ballet. I didn't know how much longer I could withstand his weird and perverse attachment to me and his unreasonable attempt to control every aspect of my life.

In 2010, while this book was being written, I re-opened Greg Lawrence's biography of Robbins, *Dance With Demons,* and saw the photo of Robbins' erstwhile fiancée, Rose Tobias. Their live-in engagement was only frantic window dressing, shattered when the bona fide fixation of his life, movie star Montgomery Clift, came literally and hysterically knocking on his late-night door. Robbins was desperate for the semblance of appearing heterosexual, but never reached first base with the women of his choice. One's libido, unlike a shirt, cannot be casually exchanged over a shopping mall counter.

When Mr. B had had said that I reminded Robbins of a former girlfriend, he was right in that regard, for I looked enough like the blonde Rose Tobias to be taken for her sister. Staring at the photo, I found it disconcerting to see how much I resembled her. In Rose Tobias's own words, quoted on the back cover of the Lawrence biography, Robbins' psychiatrist advised him "to find the most femine woman/girl and start a relationship, and I was it." So recalled the hapless Rose whose announced engagement turned out to be a complete non-starter.

Had Jerome Robbins, clutching at straws, seen in me some of the qualities he had responded to in Rose? Was I, I asked myself without answer, Rose's younger, more defenceless substitute? As is the case with many men of unbridled power, Robbins had an impatient sense of entitlement. What he wanted, he was used to getting, that is, except a reciprocal and enduring love relationship.

To return to that chilly staircase in 1954 where I sat huddled, Robbins had cast me in almost every ballet he choreographed, continuing to call me out to "talk" after each performance. He had given me a principal part in *The Pied Piper*, where I had received some excellent reviews. There was also Benjamin Britten's *Fanfare, The Young Person's Guide to The Orchestra* that Sir Benjamin conducted for us in England and New York. I was a dancing violin but, as usual, I had to understudy everyone in the ballet. Then there was *The Cage*, where in every rehearsal I tried to immediately and fully obey his demands, thereby dousing the fire of his simmering temper.

As for *Interplay*, Robbins gave me a part and then kept taking it away from me, giving it to Carolyn George, Jacques' future wife. Was he, with his bewildering game of role juggling, trying to create enmity between us? If so, he failed in that regard, but he more than succeeded in creating absolute hell for both of us. I danced it about ten times that last season and Carolyn about the same. Each time we did it he would mockingly criticize and switch us, throwing me out and putting her in, then reinstating me again.

Jerome Robbins always ruled with fear, never with love, a world of difference between the two. His every dictum towards me was dictatorial, blocking any attempts at friendships I could have had with the other dancers in the studio. He systematically isolated me from everyone except Jacques and Allegra, for since they weren't in his ballets, he had no power over them.

Jacques was street-smart and so favored by Mr. B and also by Lincoln Kirstein, that he could call his own shots. He didn't care to make a habit of working with Robbins, so he limited himself to dancing in the choreographer's version of *Afternoon of a Faun*. Since Balanchine looked down his nose at Robbins' work, an attitude echoed by Kirstein, Jacques was able to keep himself at a safe distance from a man who caused even strong hearts to panic. As for Allegra, for whom Balanchine had high regard for a time, perhaps Robbins thought it prudent to let her remain in her own fairy tale turret. She was fortunate, for she would have quickly snapped under the welt-inducing crack of his whip.

As for *Age of Anxiety*, as related in an earlier chapter, and as with Caroline George in *Interplay*, Robbins pitted Patricia Wilde against me; she was in, I was out, then vice-verse, until both of us were in dizzying confusion.

One evening after the performance, I somehow managed to muster up my nerve and ask Robbins if he thought I would ever become a ballerina. His answer was, "Yes, in a different company!"

That puzzled me for I didn't know at the time, in fact, no one knew that soon, Jerome Robbins was to form his own company, Ballets USA, and in doing so, poach dancers from the New York City Ballet. I later learned this and found it to be an act of treason, for stealing from the very people who enabled him to achieve such artistic success, was, to my mind, a serious and unethical breach of trust.

I understood in the recesses of my mind that it was not Balanchine's neglect or disinterest, but Robbins' version of waterboarding that was the determining factor in my making the fateful decision. I wanted to be released from what had long been his knotted bondage.

I was still receiving fervid love letters from the seminarian from California. Although I didn't consider him a boyfriend, the letters were beginning to make a positive impact on me. I found myself running to the stage door to see if he had written, beginning to speculate what life might be like from the audience side of the curtain.

And so, melting under the heat of his pursuit, I accepted an invitation to have dinner with him following a performance. Ater that, we saw each other more frequently in New York or New Haven. He would take the train down from Yale, see the performance, take me out afterwards and catch the last train from Grand Central Station back to New Haven at 2 a.m.

I would go up to the seminary to see him on days when the theatre was dark and stay at the family home of his Old Testament professor. I always enjoyed my suitor's company and we laughed a lot and spoke of things not related to the ballet world. Was I falling in love or just grateful for being perceived as a person rather than an instrument?

In a quandary, I needed help urgently. On an impulse, I decided to attend a service at The Cathedral of Saint John the Divine, and pray. The home of the *Nutcracker's* boy choir, perhaps the heavenly blend of their angelic voices could help me! The Very Reverend James A. Pike was the Dean of the Cathedral then, and at the close of the service I gathered all my resources and introduced myself to him.

A fearless and iconoclastic theological pioneer, he boldly questioned the Virgin Birth, Original Sin and The Trinity. Featured on the cover of *Time Magazine,* his turbulent private life was to climax with the suicide of his oldest son in 1966, and with his own death in 1968 in the Judean Desert in Israel. After his car got stuck, he and his third wife, Diane, became lost in the endless stretches of sand, wandering in the unbearable heat without any sustenance. Slipping in a canyon, he died in a cave, his body not found for some days afterwards by off-duty Israeli military, selfless volunteers and Bedouin Arabs.

Going back 14 years to 1954, Dean Pike sympathetically invited me to have a series of appointments with him in his private office to discuss some of my deep concerns. A most insightful counselor, he drew out some of my innermost thoughts and feelings. It was his advice that made me examine and resolve the quandary I was in. He determined that the nightly sessions with Jerome Robbins were not only counter-productive, they were, in fact, ultimately harmful.

I told Dean Pike about the young seminarian who seemed to truly love me for myself and not for my dancing ability, and he encouraged me to see him and sort out my feelings for him. Dean Pike then loaned me relevant books from his personal library and even brought his family to see a performance.

I thought the world of him and how could it have been otherwise? Always at the forefront of fighting to right social injustices, he owed me absolutely no allegiance, yet found the time for my personal issues. What a contrast to Mr. B who, as long as he knew me, never gave me even two seconds on a personal level.

CHAPTER TWENTY-ONE

THE ANNOUNCEMENT

Christmas was approaching and I was asked to appear in another Sid Caesar Show, a live holiday special aired on national television on Christmas Eve. I was thrilled to do the show, for the extra income was a welcome addition to my rapidly depleting bank account. The show went well and as everyone was leaving they all said, "Merry Christmas!" and left. It was not until then that I realized that I had not made any plans to spend Christmas with anyone. I stood there on the street and thought I had better pick up a sandwich before all the delis closed, for I had no food in the apartment. When did I have time to go shopping? It was the loneliest of moments that has stayed with me ever since. No tree, no presents and no loving family members around me for the first time in my life on Christmas, a day whose emotional significance superseded its religious connotations.

My parents were in Oklahoma City and everyone else I knew had plans with their families. My admirer, the seminarian, was in California with his mother. I vowed after pulling myself together that I would never spend Christmas alone again for the rest of my life, and so far, I never have! In my soul searching that Christmas, I decided that if the seminarian asked me to marry him, I would accept and give up dancing once and for all, forever, turning my back on a career that had begun so auspiciously and so young.

The husband to be returned from California with a diamond ring and a proposal of marriage and I, just 18 years old, accepted. We called my parents in Oklahoma City and told them the news. My mother did not take kindly to the announcement, stating emphatically, "You are not getting married! You have worked too hard to give up your ballet to become a housewife and besides, you come from a long line of Presbyterian ministers and you have no business in the Episcopal Church."

All through the preparation for the wedding and the laborious addressing of 700 engraved invitations she would say, "Barbara, if there is a marriage" hoping that it would all fall through. I finally told her that she was invited to the wedding and that I truly hoped she would come, that she was free to accept or decline, but that my mind was set on getting married. Then and there, she stopped complaining and came to the wedding with my father who proudly walked me down the aisle and gave me away.

Mother never approved of my getting married at 18, nor of my choice of a husband and, most of all, to my relinquishing a career that, literally, was built on coagulated blood, jabs of recurring pain and a measureless degree of passion. To my everlasting regret, my decision caused a permanent rupture in our relationship that lasted for the rest of her lifetime.

Does one ever fully recuperate from the diminished love of a mother, the very first person we have loved and needed even when still a fetus, the being who provided us with unconditional love? Birth, though not recalled, is the first environmental insult, for then and there we have been extracted from the indivisable oneness we have known since conception. To have later circumstances warp that unique bond is a scar that neither plastic surgery nor psychiatry can fully cure. For a state of separateness has begun its inexhaustible existence and must be dealt with by each individual.

My mother would acknowledge my birthday and send me a small check at Christmas for the grandchildren, but otherwise took no interest in them. I had traded in my rhinestone tiaras for cotton aprons, substituted the bravos of American and European balletomanes for the whining of toddlers in their playpens. I had relinquished the golden curtain calls of the Royal Opera House in London, the Paris Opera House, the Teatro del Liceo in Barcelona, and La Scala in Italy. For what?

For indulging in meaningless chitchat with the dull wives of church ministers? Her daughter, Barbara, who had chatted with Lord Mountbatten, the last Viceroy of India, had conversed with Dame Alicia Markova, Dame Margot Fonteyn, Ambassador Clare Boothe Luce, had her face painted personally by Sir Cecil Beaton, and danced under the baton of the legendary Igor Stravinsky, her daughter had swapped such proximity with the boring faceless tea-sipping wives of brimstone and fire pulpit preachers! How could I do this to myself?

How could I do this to *her?* What about my father's years of financial sacrifice to enable the two of us to live in New York?

My father, unlike my mother, not dragging out a shopping list of complaints, just said, "What about your ballet?" though his subtext was," Do you know what you're doing?" I told him that I loved ballet but it did not return my love, that I had found someone who truly loved me for myself! His words were, "I understand. When can we meet this Romeo?"

I assumed my father would talk to Mom and that she would come to terms with welcoming a son-in-law. I gave them the date for the closing night of the season, April 4, 1954, so they could plan their trip to New York to meet my husband-to-be and then take me back to Oklahoma to plan for the July wedding that would be in Los Angeles.

I kept my ring hidden and the decision I had made to marry a complete secret from the company until just the week before the closing night. Strangely, the only person I told right away was Lester Chace, the artist who had painted my portrait. He called me the day after I had accepted the ring and the proposal and wanted to take me to dinner. I had not heard from him in a long time. Though I declined dinner, I did agree to meet him for coffee at a nearby place. When I showed him the ring and told him of my plans, he suddenly began to cry, a reaction I was not at all prepared for. Then he got up from the table and, without a word, abruptly left. I never heard from him again.

He had sent my parents the portrait he had painted of me which had gained him admittance to the prestigious Portraits Incorporated in New York City. I had no idea that my marrying would upset him so, for he had never indicated that he had any romantic interest in me. I was to later find out that he had an oppressive religious father, a factor that may have contributed to what I sensed was an asexual temperament. Why then, did he cry and leave? Perhaps he cried in empathy because he knew how much dancing meant in my life, and resultantly couldn't reconcile such a casual disclosure with the passion he had always identified with me. Or had the painter become spiritually enamored of his subject, as Mr. B with his long line of muses? I could find no answer and still, occasionally, when fragments of memories keep me company at the kitchen dishwasher, do wonder about this.

In the vanishing years that followed, I completely lost track of him. Yet it was Lester who indirectly was responsible for the writing of this book, for it is through his death that I was put once again in touch with Adam Darius, my dear and wonderful co-author, who prompted, persuaded and relentlessly prodded me to tell my story, then encouraged me when the weight of the past threatened to call a halt to my narrative. And, I who had never written more than aerogrammes home, had the assurance of being guided by not only such an experienced author, but also a dancer and mime artist who shared so many of the same memories.

I went to New Haven to meet my seminarian and we announced our engagement on Valentine's Day at an impromptu party for students at Berkeley Divinity School, located on the Yale campus. It seemed that because I hadn't told anyone in New York about my engagement, I didn't have to deal with the thought of soon leaving the company.

What was I doing? I had agreed to marry, move to Pasadena, California and give up dancing, forever, for the love of a young, soon-to-be ordained, Episcopal priest. Was I crazy? I dared not let myself doubt my decision for it was final. I had agreed to marry and that was that.

I must add that in 1954 it was not permissible for clergy wives to work in any secular position, let alone be a ballet dancer wearing leotards and tights and dancing with half-naked young men. If any of them were ever to come across a photo of me in *The Cage*, I would have been instant persona non grata! How the gossip would have spiked the air while the group nibbled their blueberry cupcakes and sipped their tea, two sugars please!

Most parishes expected the minister's wife to volunteer for the Church helping her husband in every way possible to minister to his flock. I was also advised by the Dean of the seminary, The Very Reverend Percy Urban, not to make any friends in the parish, for it might adversely affect the parishioner's relationship with the Church! I was also told I would be giving a great number of teas. So I bought a copy of Amy Vanderbilt's *Complete Book of Etiquette* and studied it as if I were going to take a test, which in fact, I was, the test of being a minister's wife.

Dancing the repertoire, even the Robbins ballets, knowing that each ballet I danced would be the last time I danced it, was heart-rending. Seeing my name in the costume as I removed it and hung it up, then imagining another name being applied, was a painful thought. As was leaving Dunya, our high-strung dresser, who was truly a friend. And my dressing table, who would be sitting there, transforming her face from the mundane to the magical?

No more traditional opera houses or invigorating tours, no School of American Ballet classes that I loved dearly, and all of the teachers, how I would miss them! Would they ever wonder what happened to me?

I made a mental list of what I was discarding, but still the prospect of having to continue with Robbins hammering away at me in rehearsal and after almost every performance his unremitting interrogations, that reality made me certain that if I didn't leave, and soon, he was going to permanently de-stabilize me.

I finally announced to the girls in the dressing room that I was engaged and started to sport my diamond ring about a week before our closing performance. Everyone expressed their genuine wish for great happiness and I had never had so many of the girls seem so delighted for me. Newly betrothed, I was looking at the world through rose-coloured glasses, not pausing to think that possibly their apparent elation was due to other reasons. Now, there would be no more Barbara Bocher to be given choice leading roles, usurp media attention on two sides of the Atlantic, and be partner to the male star André Eglevsky. Yes, they were happy, but not for the reason that it seemed. There are, of course, exceptions. Not all the corps de ballet girls were cut from the same bolt of spiteful cloth as the few who had been vindictive.

It had been a very difficult thing to tell Jacques, for he had grave misgivings about my decision. I believe he cared about me and didn't want to see me make a mistake that couldn't be amended. He had met my soon-to-be husband and had some very real reservations about his psychological makeup and character in general. He advised me not to leave the company. I cared deeply for Jacques and I thought I would miss him most of all, but still I ignored his advice as I did my mother's words of lurking danger.

Jacques, wise to the ways of the world, realized that Jerome Robbins was the real reason I was leaving the company, the other reasons just contributing factors, with the marriage the escape clause excuse that laid no blame on anyone.

I had not yet spoken with Mr. B, which I dreaded. How could I tell him? I put it off until my parents arrived and they were standing there with me on stage before a performance when I was on the verge of uttering the fateful words. I felt frozen to the spot, my tongue rigid in its inarticulacy.

"Speak, speak,"I commanded myself. "Get out, get out!" What had been a bucolic Garden of Eden had dry-rotted into a kafkaesque confinement.

But how would I announce my departure, my final farewell to George Balanchine who had been my artistic progenitor? How do you sever your artist's umbilical cord with a man who was nothing less than messianic in everyone's estimation? My jaw was locked with the daunting task merely seconds before me.

CHAPTER TWENTY-TWO

Death of a Baby Ballerina

"Mr. B," I managed to eject these three terminal syllables, and then with a supreme effort, poured out the plans for my impending departure and marriage. He listened to me almost in disbelief, then he answered with marked emphasis, "Do not leave!"

I told him I was in love and would be living in California and that I would be marrying a priest of the church. He said, "I always wanted to be priest" – as stream of consciousness as ever.

"Barbara, do not leave! Do not leave," he firmly reiterated, his twitching and blinking accelerating in tempo. I just stood there, my stomach churning, visualizing the revered Igor Stravinsky, the electrifying Leonard Bernstein, the poetic Sir Benjamin Britten and the dynamic Aaron Copland, all conducting as I danced my heart out in front of them.

"Do not leave," he repeated.

..."Barbara," I heard his once thrilling words again, "would you like to dance for me?"...

I stared at him with a vacancy born of shock. Seeing my mummified stance, he continued, "Anyone can have children, but not everyone can dance like you, stay, stay!"

My peripheral vision took in my immobilized parents, standing rigidly on the sidelines, just a few feet away as I was reversing the steady artistic ascent of my life.

Then my mind, locked in some kind of emotional spasm, darted back to the most terrifying minutes I had ever experienced as I smashed the locked Théâtre des Champs-Élysees bathroom window, then placed a pink-satined *pointe* shoe firmly on the granite ledge, seeing the pedestrians and traffic five deadly stories below.

And there I was, facing George Balanchine, the man for whom I was more than ready to sacrifice my young life. Defeated in his effort to make me change my mind, Mr. B reluctantly gave me a big hug and said, "If you must go, be a missionary for ballet!" And I agreed, for the next 17 years teaching children's ballet classes even while attending to my manifold duties as a minister's wife. With each class, I had to emotionally fortify myself so that I wouldn't succumb to tears as I listened to music from the great ballets; Chopin, Drigo, Minkus, Glazunov, Tchaikovsky and Prokofiev.

I could not bring myself to tell Mr. B, or anyone else, except Dean Pike, though Jacques guessed it, that I was leaving for one reason only – and that was because I had reached the saturation point with my personal jailer, Mr. Robbins.

..."Barbara, you're a fantastic dancer; don't let Jerry crush your spirit"...

So spoke Frank Moncion, but I was too young and non-combative to fend for myself with a man so skilled in being ringmaster to caged humans.

All my adult life I have had a fear, no, a phobia, of saying goodbye. It may well have begun at that moment as I knew that I would never work with any of my respected and admired colleagues again.

I switched mental gears to my marriage plans, to the large wedding to take place at Trinity Church in Los Angeles during the company's Greek Theatre appearance in July. I had already penny-pinched to purchase my white satin and lace wedding dress with a full cathedral train and a floor-length veil topped with a tiara. I sent out 700 invitations to four completely separate groups of people; all of the members of the company, all of my parents' friends in Oklahoma City, and all of my husband-to-be's friends from the seminary in New Haven as well as his mother's friends in California. This was a big production involving complex coordination.

Most of the company attended the wedding including Mr. B himself. I even invited Jerome Robbins – was I a glutton for punishment? That rhetorical question needs no answer. Robbins didn't respond to the invitation, nor did he attend the wedding, for he must have been chewing at the bit, since his little captive fox had freed herself from the stifling trap of his carefully constructed setting. It's just as well that he ignored the invitation though, in retrospect, I think he may have issued, in absentia, his *maledizione* as the Carabosse that he was albeit in jeans and squeaky sneakers.

The day before the wedding, Jacques asked me, "Hey, is this guy straight?" I was taken aback by the bluntness of the question but replied, "Of course!"

"Have you slept with him?"

"Oh no, " I answered even more vehemently. Since I was raised a Christian, I was to remain a virgin, saving myself for my husband. It was considered in those mid-1950s that any girl who slept with a man before marriage was immoral and never the kind of girl a man would marry! I played by the rules, a concept nowadays as antiquated as fragmented fossil bones.

On my last day of performing as a member of the New York City Ballet, after the matinee my parents and I stepped outside of the stage door to see a swelling crowd gathering in the street. The City Center's stage door was diagonally across the street from the stage door of Carnegie Hall. When I inquired as to what was happening, a little Italian lady shouted, "Maestro Toscanini!" The crowd waited in anticipation and my parents and I waited with them, for it isn't commonplace to see one of the most idolized musicians of the late 19th and early 20th centuries right before one's eyes.

This was the man, born in 1867, who conducted the world premieres of Leoncavallo's *Pagliacci* in 1892, and Puccini's *La Bohème* in 1896, *La Fanciulla del West* in 1910 and *Turandot* in 1926.

The street was blocked with adoring fans chanting, "Maestro, Maestro, Maestro!" for it was the close of Arturo Toscanini's final concert given at Carnegie Hall. A black limousine pulled up close to the stage door maneuvering cautiously through the throng of waiting people. Then, at last, the friend and colleague of such musical geniuses as Verdi, Mascagni, Cilea, Giordano, Leoncavallo and Puccini, appeared at the stage door, his snow-white hair standing up in every direction, smiling and triumphantly waving both arms in the air. He stood there basking in the adoration and *fortissimo* roar of the crowd. The maestro was visibly moved.

The chanting of "Maestro" continued as he stepped into the limousine, which, by now, was bedecked with flowers that had been tossed by the adoring crowd. The limousine slowly drove away with people running after it, tossing flowers on to the roof and still calling after him. Men and women everywhere were moved to tears, as was I.

It was April 4, 1954, an unforgettable historic event, for it was the 87-year-old Arturo Toscanini's final farewell to the podium and, as events transpired, soon to life itself.

Watching the maestro's departure, I felt a bitter poignancy and irony in that later that evening I was to dance on a stage for the very last time in my life, *Swan Lake,* aged a mere 18. There would be no hysterical crowds and the tears that would be shed would be all my own.

Mme Esmé Bulnes's invitation to remain with La Scala returned to me, for within the golden and hallowed walls of La Scala Opera House, Maestro Toscanini in the latter part of the 19th and early 20th centuries had conducted what were to be the staples of today's operatic repertoire. Decisions! Where was my divine guidance and, above all, my own intelligence to refuse the highly influential Mme Bulnes? And for what reason – to be faithful to a great choreographer for whom I was merely a well-oiled and useful cog in the wheel? To subject myself to Jerome Robbins' next round of "fat pig" humiliation – now only 105 pounds – the pig awaiting its turn to be publicly skewered?

Almost in a trance, I went to the dressing room and mechanically put on my pasty white make up.

"...Dear Miss Bocher,
I feel inspired to write this letter as I have just returned from the ballet after seeing you in Cakewalk. ...I was so thrilled tonight when I saw in my program that you were to be the Wallflower – such a delightful role and you certainly surpassed all my optimistic expectations. I've seen many others dance this part but never before have I laughed and loved watching it as I did tonight. I'm so happy that you were such a success!...
Nancy Reinhardt, Rockville Centre, New York,
May 15th, 1953"

While my mind swished about in a whirlpool of memories, I automatically warmed up as usual, but the imminence of my retirement began to throttle me. As I put on my *pointe* shoes for the very last time in this life span, I was weighted with a profound sorrow. Tears were welling up and my every effort to control them was to no avail. I quickly put on my costume, knowing I would never wear a tutu again, and went downstairs to be ready for my entrance. The subdued chitchat around me faded away as I could only hear my muted last goodbyes.

...a heartfelt and tearful au revoir to Maria, the phosphorescent firebird of mystical Russian folklore, to Herbie, the celestial Apollo of ancient Greek mythology, to Bobby, my virtuoso partner in so many Balanchine classics, to Frank Moncion, my savior and luminous dark angel, to André, the epitome of the fairy tale prince who honored me by being my partner in war-threatened Trieste, to superstar Jacques, my ever-protective friend and champion, and to Allegra, the fey white swan of the blue-mooned lake, to all of you, a soulful farewell.

And to all my superlative pedagogues, I will be indebted to you for as long as there is breath in my lungs, for what you have instilled in me immeasurably increased my self-discipline throughout my future life.

...Goodbye my beloved Muriel Stuart, and farewell to Mme Dubrovska, Mme Egorova, Mme Bulnes, Pierre Vladimirov, Anatole Oboukhov, Yurek Lazovski, Nana Gollner and Paul Petroff, all artists who have knelt at the altar of absolute devotion.

The strains of the emotive Tchaikovsky score began and this was it, the unvarnished truth and realization of what I was doing hit me like a fierce blast of hot air from a suddenly opened furnace door. The heat was scalding my very spirit.

I was thankful for kinetic memory, for I was in shock and my mind went vacant. I responded only to the music and my muscles remembered what my brain had forgotten. As I stood in my place waiting for my next move, I could see the reflection of the tears glistening on my cheeks and felt them flowing down the front of my costume. I had no way to stop them and no way to wipe my eyes! I cried through the whole of *Swan Lake* not only until it was over, but in the deadening and extended silence that followed.

The guilt of leaving unfufilfilled the firm belief in my future held by the stellar figures of the dance world, that guilt lashed at me without respite. The autobiography *Dance to the Piper* encircled my immobilized head as those panoramic X-rays do in a dental office.

"...To Barbara Bocher
With high hopes!
Agnes de Mille..."

The X-ray ends, but not so quickly the dark and hooded face of guilt, the guilt of having let down and disappointed Miss de Mille.

Three months after I was married, I had a recurring and inexplicable dream of disturbing proportions. My newly married husband was dispassionately shovelling muddied earth onto my face as I lay, without a coffin, in an open and freshly dug grave. With no mourners as witnesses, I begin spitting out the grit, gravel and tiny pebbles of the hastily dug-up ground. My mouth cleared of the dirt of the burial plot, I begin to levitate horizontally before floating vertically over the grave in a long white tulle tutu. I recognized myself as the deceased and spirit-released Giselle.

How did I interpret that dream upon awakening? I didn't; it just severely sullied my consciousness throughout the day, even though I knew it was a dream. That haunting dream, closer to a nightmare, was to re-occur two more times, each time trailing me through each succeeding waking hour.

As for seeing myself as Giselle, that is the ultimate role regarding blind trust and stolen innocence; the village maiden who, despite her premature death, protects the very life of the prince who has betrayed her. Her graveside forgiveness of the repentent Albrecht was the ultimate absolution that I, too, in reality, wanted to bestow on Jerry Robbins. It would not be simple, for with his jumbled psyche, he had exerted such a choking soul control over my life. But as I sensed then and later life confirmed, it is best to rid oneself of all past grievances, to seek permanent closure, for then, and only then, can one be sprayed by the fountain of happiness.

And so ended my life in ballet. Was it really a death? Yes, it most certainly was. It was the death of my nocturnal hopes and daytime dreams as a dancer with the New York City Ballet, or with any other ballet company in the world. That former life was a sealed and claustrophobic vault never to be opened again until the most unexpected circumstances reversed so many decades of denial.

Was it chance, accident or some kind of cosmic destiny when I reconnected with my dear Adam Darius who, with his formidable willpower, never stopped convincing, persuading and encouraging me that it was my moral duty to preserve a period of history, of which I had been an integral part, that would otherwise be as buried as the crumbled walls of Pompeii? And regarding his role as co-author of this book, I see him as a true poet of the pen.

I have a feeling that my own children, all four of them, my grand-children, all six of them, and my great grandchildren, all three of them, will be very surprised, even amazed, to read *The Cage.* As the mother in the Elizabeth Taylor movie, *National Velvet,* kept her Olympic medal hidden from prying eyes in the back of a drawer, I have kept my years with the New York City Ballet entirely concealed from them all their lives, encased in a steel vault of deeds and documents with the key protectively misplaced.

Yes, it was the end of a life, though if not in an actual cemetery, the end of my dancing existence. Though not entombed in a metropolis of the dead, I surveyed from the land of the living, the implausible and premature end of my career, for I was grieving for my own passing, the death of a baby ballerina.

When I left the stage door hours after Maestro Toscanini, it was a joint farewell, but there was a colossal difference. He had the courage to publicly defy the likes of Il Duce Benito Mussolini, I had neither the experience nor the bravado to contest the likes of my own in-house tyrant. The maestro was 87, having scaled every Everest in the musical heavens; I was just 18, only in the foothills of the glory peaks.

But I was to discover that there is life after fifth position, a lesson learned with pain and sorrow: life does go on. I was to adapt the song *The Best of Times is Now* from the Jerry Herman musical *La Cage aux Folles* as my own personal anthem, and be thankful for the gift of enthusiasm with which I've been blessed that has never abated.

I am forever grateful for the extraordinary life I once led, albeit for a relatively short period. As for my dear parents, in whichever sphere their good souls now reside, I send through the ether my abiding love and gratitude for their unrationed sacrifices.

With these final pages, having sifted through the memories of two centuries, I have now succeeded in dispersing those gnawing ghosts. And the principal ghost was the ever-present Jerry Robbins. Yes, it cannot be denied, he did feel some kind of irregular bond for me, though unfortunately, conveyed negatively. After either his fear-filled rehearsals, tension-felt performances or inescapable lectures, I felt no malice towards him, only that I had been crushed and flattened.

However, with the passage of the decades, I no longer harbor any ill feelings towards him, for I see his own gaping neuroses as the root of his diabolical actions. How, it may be asked, have I remained so immune to the cruelty he caused me, then barely 14 years old? It is, in point of fact, not in my nature to be fueled by hate. Even when the wounds he inflicted were deepest, there was only one occasion, on the edge of a stage on which he was standing, when I fantasized about pushing him into the orchestra pit. At all other times, I just wanted to distance myself from his destructive forces.

Transporting myself back to those post-performance, brainwashing chats, it later crossed my mind that perhaps he was trying to wean me away from Mr. B, so that I would transfer my great love of Balanchine to him, and to become totally dependent on him in the process. But with all the fallout from the previous years, his reaching out to me fell on arid soil. Too little, too late.

What Jerry taught me, albeit unintended, were intensive courses in psychological survival, training that would keep me afloat in the unforeseen downpours of the future. If only, I used to think, his personal compassion could have approached his creative passion, but the chasm was unbridgeable.

Then, again, had he been possessed of a more aligned temperament, perhaps he would not have risen to dominate the neon-lit worlds of both Broadway and ballet. The singular alchemy that is at the base of a spectacular career is made up of intangible and mysterious ingredients. Had Jerome Robbins been favored with an infinite capacity to love, he may not have become the Colossus of the Great White Way as he unquestionably did. All said and done, I hope that somewhere in the unvisited void that is the afterlife, he has finally found his peace.

My years with the New York City Ballet are now, for better or for worse, history, and in this transient present, I face each hour with vigorous renewal, grateful for each further day of the unique and precious gift that is life.

Free, unfettered and aloft, I awake each day to the early morning rays of a new and sapphirine dawn, ready and eager to love with my entire being; to help other people with whatever power that resides within me, somewhat alleviating the burden of those unfortunates who cry out, either silently, or with a primal scream, for help.

Epilogue

In the many years that have followed my farewell performance, long after the yellowed press clippings were placed in the attic alongside my vacant-staring but still bright-eyed Shirley Temple doll, life moved inexorably on.

Subsequently, it became clear to me that my time with the New York City Ballet was the most fruitful preparation I could have had for the extended decades before me. For all those grand opera house stages instilled in me the ability to cope with and deal with the unforseeable. As I grew older, I found ongoing joy as the mother of four children.

But after 36 years of a fulfilling marriage, during which time I was always a loving and helpful wife, unexpected events took place that necessitated my filing for divorce. So unhappily ended that peaceful existence, leading into the next phase of this unpredictable life.

As for my work in healing, once my motherhood responsibilities allowed, I became the medical office manager for Santa Barbara Cottage Hospital where I assisted Reproductive Surgeon Mark W. Surrey, MD, FACOG, FACS and Gynecologic Oncologist W. Michael Hogan, MD. For five years I managed the medical practice for celebrity television chef and *New York Times* best-selling author John La Puma, MD, FACP. Presently, I'm in charge of the medical office for the noted Korean-born American acupuncturist and rheumatologist, Wonuk Lee, MD, FACR.

My later years were further enhanced by my 30-year friendship with Dr. Max Zeller and his wife, Laura, the brilliant founders of the Carl Jung Society in Los Angeles.

Dr. Zeller, a German Jew, had been condemned to death during the nightmare of Hitler's final solution. Lined up to be shot in a row of victims alongside his parents and brother, their bodies fell on top of him as they were dumped onto a waiting disposal truck. En route to the freshly dug mass grave, still alive, he toppled off the mound of corpses, landing in a ditch.

Discovered by childen playing in the countryside, they carried him to a farmhouse where the resident Christian family risked their very lives to lovingly nurse him back to health. After the war ended in

1945, he rose, literally from the ashes, to become one of the most influential psychiatrists of his time.

I reminded myself that the loss of what I had loved most, my life in ballet, was insignificant compared to the massive tragedies inflicted upon humankind by the Nazis, Fascists and Soviets.

But like a magnet, I was always suctioned back to the nagging personal issue of why I could never fully escape the ballet obsession, the commune mentality that often devours its self-chained followers.

In all of my repeated efforts to find the answer as to why I nourished this desperate desire to dance, I had never encountered an explanation that truly satisfied me.

Then I chanced upon one of Adam Darius's books, *A Nomadic Life*. In his very first chapter, In the Land of the River Neva, he probed the question for which I had never found a suitable answer.

When I asked Adam if I could quote his revelatory passage for my autobiography, he hesitated, explaining that *The Cage* is *my* autobiography and that, as such, he preferred to guide me from the adjacent shadows. I countered his reluctance by explaining that his thoughts ran parallel to my own. But the following day, to my relief, he emailed his consent.

Here, then, from Adam's book, *A Nomadic Life,* is what I see as the ultimate answer to my long elusive query.

"Why, one may well ask, does an artist pursue a life certain to cause himself both mental and physical pain; a steady diet of disregard, rejection and, on occasion, the critics' ridicule? Is there a reason for this blinkered obsession?

"Perhaps it is because the artist will do anything to reaffirm the fact that once he lived, however brief his tenure. To freeze existence, to be glory's slave he will stop at nothing; to imprint his soul upon the sea-swept sands of time he will suffer all indignities. But if and when his efforts have been honoured by his fellow men, his joy is boundless, his past suffering a mere chimera.

"At the end of Pierrot in Exile in St. Petersburg, entering from the wings were beaming young girls placing bouquets in my arms and Kazimir's. Then I felt a short, sharp scratch from the stem of a fragrant rose. Why, one could ask, for the fleeting duration of that rose's red-velvet perfection, do

we suffer its prickly thorns? Why do we put up with poverty-pocked stage surfaces, splintered feet, a plethora of injuries and a paucity of income?

"Are we martyrs, masochists, or both, battling, though injured, to fulfil visions that only we can see? Punctured in both palms and soles, the artist pays no heed to his incurable stigmata. Dropping to his scraped knees, he laughs triumphantly at his gaping wounds. Grazed, he willingly bleeds to death so that he can desperately bleed to life.

"So, once more, goodbye to the land of the magical firebird, soaring in the wind to the exotic strains of Stravinsky and Rimsky-Korsakov. And finally, a farewell to the religious mystics of gold-domed Russia, and the hunched women beggars on the bustling Nevsky Prospekt, crossing themselves repeatedly in the hope that they will be saved from the freezing wrath of the Russian winter until the Easter sun and the son of God reappear to melt their wretched lives into the bliss of imminent eternity."

The generations come and go, with new ballet dancers, both male and female, pounding on the doors of today's mirrored communes, replacing their long-gone forebears. These similarly addicted dancers, self-flagellating as any secluded order of novitiates, still dare to scale the icy slopes of ballet's white-death mountain. And so they climb, though clearly below them is snow turned crimson from the dried blood of the many fallen.

To dance is a joyous experience and should invariably be encouraged, for it is one of the loftier forms of expression known to humankind. It is, I most fervently believe, a jubilant celebration of the gift of life. But to dance within the confines of a cage, that is a structure that impedes the soul in its evolving journey.

Yet, all said and done, if I, the Barbara Bocher of old, that once baby ballerina of the mid-20th century, could somehow, by some cosmic miracle, turn back the chimes of time, would I, if offered a second chance at life, choose to dance again? Would I?

Dear reader, bear with me, for I fear, I fear, in all truthfulness, the answer has to be, and is, an echoing yes.

PHOTOGRAPHS

As The Little Inside Out Girl, dance recital, Oklahoma City, 1939
Photo: personal collection of Barbara Bocher

On my bicycle
in Oklahoma
City, aged 13,
just before going
to New York
to audition for
the School of
American Ballet,
May 1949
*Photo: personal
collection of
Barbara Bocher*

With Dick Beard and Tomi Wortham in Todd Bolender's *Mother Goose Suite,*
New York, November, 1949
Photo. personal collection of Barbara Bocher

My parents, Virginia and
Leonard S. Bocher, 1981
*Photo: personal collection
of Barbara Bocher*

Herbert Bliss in the
role of Apollo in the
Balanchine-Stravinsky
ballet *Orpheus*,
New York, 1949
*Photo: personal collection
of Barbara Bocher*

Pierre Vladimirov and Anna Pavlova
in *Harlequinade,* Montevideo, Uruguay,
late 1920s
Photo: Yarovoff / Pierre Vladimirov collection

Anatole Oboukhov and Vera Nemchinova
in *Swan Lake,* Paris, middle 1930s
Photo: Iris / Anatole Oboukhov collection

Last photo of Anna Pavlova with
Felia Dubrovska, Monte Carlo,
Jan. 1931
*Photo: Victor Dandré / Felia Dubrovska
collection*

The young Muriel Stuart, in center, at Ivy
House, London, where she
trained with Anna Pavlova, c. 1913
Photo: Muriel Stuart collection

Adam Darius as Christ, with Kazimir Kolesnik in
Resurrection: The Nazi and the Nazarene, Havana, Cuba, 1982
Photo: Prensa Latina

George Balanchine in discussion with Igor Stravinsky
at the time of *Agon*, New York, 1958
Photo: Martha Swope

Maria Tallchief as Eurydice from the
Balanchine-Stravinsky ballet *Orpheus*,
New York 1950
*Photo: George Platt Lynes, personal
collection of Barbara Bocher*

As the Wirewalker in the Lew
Christiansen ballet *Jinx*,
New York, 1950
*Photo: Walter E. Owen, personal
collection of Barbara Bocher*

BALLERINA AT 14

Barbara Bocher is fourteen years old, and very soon she will be dancing on the great stage at Covent Garden. She is the youngest ballerina in the New York City Ballet Company, which shortly opens its London season. At the prospect of that exciting event Barbara goes up in the air at Roehampton.

But there will always be some people who snore through symphonies and such things, or, like the man in the picture, turn their backs on ballet.

And she really IS only 14

Above: In a publicity shot for the Balanchine/Robbins *Jones Beach*, Roehampton, England, July 1950
Photo: Daily Mail, London

Right: Flight arrival in London of the New York City Ballet for first appearance at the Royal Opera House, July 5th, 1950
Photo: Courtesy of the London Daily Mirror

With Nicholas Magallanes and Frank Hobi at Windsor Castle, England
Photo courtesy of Dance News, 1950

Painting of me by Lester Chace,
New York City, 1951
*Photo: personal collection of
Barbara Bocher*

*La Scala billboard,
Milan, 1953
Photo: personal collection
of Barbara Bocher*

Jerome Robbins rehearsing his *Quiet City,* New York, 1986;
Left to right mirrored are Damian Woetzel, Robert La Fosse and Peter Boal
Photo: Martha Swope

In the Karinska costume
for *Bourrée Fantasque,*
choreography by George
Balanchine. 1952
*Photo: Walter E. Owen,
personal collection of
Barbara Bocher*

Practicing with Brendan Fitzgerald for the Grand Pas de Deux in *Sleeping Beauty*,
New York, 1952
Photo: Walter E. Owen, personal collection of Barbara Bocher

Symphony in C tutus hanging in the wardrobe room at the Théâtre des Champs-Élysées, Paris, May 1952
Photo: personal collection of Barbara Bocher

With Jacques d'Amboise in front of the Gran Teatro del Liceo, Barcelona, Spain, 1952
Photo: personal collection of Barbara Bocher

During a performance of *Bourrée Fantasque* at the
Paris Opera House, 1952
Photo: personal collection of Barbara Bocher

Allegra Kent and Jacques d'Amboise in *Afternoon of a Faun*
by Jerome Robbins, New York, 1953
Photo: personal collection of Barbara Bocher

Flanked by my bridesmaids, on wedding day, July 11, 1954; left to right;
Gloria Vauge, Pauline Morrison, Allegra Kent and Dido Sayers,
Trinity Church, Los Angeles, July 11, 1954
Photo: personal collection of Barbara Bocher

BALLETS DANCED BY BARBARA BOCHER

A list of ballets I danced , between 1949 and 1954, in the United States, Great Britain, France, Germany, Switzerland, Italy, Spain, Belgium, Holland and Bermuda. The names of the choreographers and composers are listed with the ballets.

Antigone, Adam Darius, Russell Smith
For Earth Too Quick, Crandall Diehl
Serenade, George Balanchine, Tchaikovsky
Orpheus, George Balanchine, Stravinsky
The Card Party (originally called *Jeu de Cartes*, later called *Card Game)*, George Balanchine, Stravinsky
Le Baiser de La Fée, (later called *The Fairy's Kiss*),
George Balanchine, Stravinsky
Concerto Barocco, George Balanchine, Bach
The Four Temperaments, George Balanchine, Paul Hindemith
Symphonie Concertante, George Balanchine, Mozart
Symphony in C, George Balanchine, Bizet
Mother Goose Suite, Todd Bolender, Ravel
The Guests, Jerome Robbins, Marc Blitzstein
Jinx, Lew Christensen, Sir Benjamin Britten
Firebird, George Balanchine, Stravinsky
Bourrée Fantasque, George Balanchine, Chabrier
Ondine, William Dollar, Vivaldi
Age of Anxiety, Jerome Robbins, Leonard Bernstein
Illuminations, Frederick Ashton, Benjamin Britten
Jones Beach, George Balanchine and Jerome Robbins,
Jurriaan Andriessen
La Valse, George Balanchine, Ravel
Capriccio Brilliante, George Balanchine, Mendelssohn
Cakewalk, Ruthanna Boris, Louis Gottschalk
The Cage, Jerome Robbins, Stravinsky
A La Françaix, George Balanchine, Jean Françaix
Tyl Eulenspiegel, George Balanchine, Richard Strauss
Swan Lake, George Balanchine (after Lev Ivanov), Tchaikovsky

The Pied Piper, Jerome Robbins, Aaron Copland
Fanfare: The Young Person's Guide to the Orchestra,
Jerome Robbins, Benjamin Britten
Interplay, Jerome Robbins. Morton Gould
Metamorphoses, George Balanchine, Paul Hindemith
The Nutcracker, George Balanchine, Tchaikovsky
The Witches, John Cranko, Ravel

Not included in this list are the dance sequences I performed on the Sid Caesar television programs and the concert program which I danced in Carnegie Hall, choreographed by Valentina Oumansky.

About the Authors

Barbara Bocher, born in Oklahoma in 1935, joined the New York City Ballet in 1949 at the age of 14. The youngest dancer in the company, she appeared under the batons of Igor Stravinsky, Leonard Bernstein, Aaron Copland and Sir Benjamin Britten. In the course of her shooting star career, she worked with choreographers George Balanchine, Sir Frederic Ashton and Jerome Robbins in whose ballet, *Pied Piper,* she danced to the clarinet of Benny Goodman. Still in her middle teens, she graced the stages of such major venues as the Royal Opera House in London, the Paris Opera House, La Scala Opera in Milan and the Trieste Opera House where she was partnered by premier danseur André Eglevsky.

Barbara Bocher lives by the sea in Santa Barbara, California.

Adam Darius, born in New York City in 1930, has appeared as a dancer and mime artist in over 85 countries. From the Himalayas in Nepal to Sugar Loaf Mountain in Brazil, and from Surabaya in Java to the island of Madagascar, he continues to influence the generations with his own approach to physical theatre and expressive mime. As a choreographer, his most acclaimed work was *The Anne Frank Ballet,* the Italian Television production now seen on YouTube, concluding with an interview with Otto Frank, Anne's father. Additionally, Adam Darius is the dance world's most prolific author, having written a score of plays and 15 published books on a diversity of subjects. Among the many honors accorded him have been, on two occasions, the Noor Al-Hussein Award in Jordan.

Adam Darius lives on a hill in Espoo, Finland.

Index

Page numbers in bold refer to the photographs

Collins, Janet 44
Columbus, Christopher 177
Concerto Barocco 122, 174
Connery, Sean 203
Cook, Bart 160
Copland, Aaron 134, 135, 137, 243
Coppélia 155
Cranko, John 224
Crawford, Joan 175
Cullberg, Birgit 227
Cunningham, Merce 43, 44

D

d'Amboise, Jacques 49, **266, 268**
Danilova, Alexandra 32, 33, 39, 76, 77, 90, 96, 179, 229, 230
Darius, Adam 91–97, 205, 240, 249, 253, **260**
Darsonval, Lysette 145
de Mille, Agnes 48, 248
de Mille, Cecil B. 48
Demoiselles de la Nuit, Les 224
de Valois, Ninette 111, 181
Diaghilev, Serge 43, 45, 46, 53, 66, 76, 84, 109, 111, 112, 129, 166
Diana, Princess of Wales 53, 219
Dickens, Charles 189
Diehl, Crandall 193
DiMaggio, Joe 83
Dolin, Anton 111, 112
Dollar, William 58
Donizetti, Gaetano 211
Don Quixote 45
Dorsey, Jimmy 134
Dorsey, Tommy 134
Dostoevsky, Fyodor 23
Douglas, Alfred 89
Drigo, Riccardo 244
Dubrovska, Felia 45, 77, 84, 185, 230, 247, **259**
Duchin, Peter 134
Duell, Joseph 154, 165
Duel, The 72, 84
Dumilâtre, Adèle 156
Dunaway, Faye 175
Duncan, Isadora 64
Dunn, James C. 148
Durbin, Deanna 193

H

M

N

O

P

T

U

V

W

Y

Z

Made in the USA
San Bernardino, CA
15 February 2013